BUSES OF BRISTOL AND SOMERSET

Richard Stubbings

AMBERLEY

First published 2023

Amberley Publishing
The Hill, Stroud
Gloucestershire, GL5 4EP

www.amberley-books.com

ISBN 978 1 3981 0596 6 (print)
ISBN 978 1 3981 0597 3 (ebook)

British Library Cataloguing in Publication Data.
A catalogue record for this book is available from the British Library.

Origination by Amberley Publishing.
Printed in the UK.

Introduction

One of the things I have found most interesting as a bus enthusiast is seeing the ways buses and coaches have evolved over the years, as well as seeing how they are an essential part of the environment as they go about their everyday work. It is not often realised just how much buses and coaches are part of social history, aiding the mass movement of the public, both locally and nationally, leading to the development of villages, towns, and the concept of commuting as well as helping to lead the growth of leisure travel – from holiday tours to day-trips. They have also helped with education, enabling school trips and overseas tours by youth organisations, such as the youth orchestra trips I used to be a part of.

This volume is the first of a series of six books covering the south of England, three each for the south-west, which was originally firmly Tilling territory, and the south-east, which was more heavily BET-land. They will cover a period of nearly fifty years, from the early years of the National Bus Company and independents to the big groups of the twenty-first century. The vehicles used have changed dramatically over this period of time. This first book covers my home area of Bristol and Somerset. Being former Tilling territory, Bristol buses with ECW bodywork abounded, as the earlier photos of elderly examples show. These are the vehicles I grew up with and rode on to and from school. The advances in design and technology from these to the modern low-floor vehicles with low-emission engines, sometimes gas-powered, is quite breathtaking.

Somerset has never had any municipal operators; the services in the two main centres of population, Bristol and Bath, plus the seaside resort of Weston super-Mare and the cathedral city of Wells, the smallest city in England, were provided by the Bristol Omnibus Company. Services in Bristol were a joint undertaking between the company and the local council, formed in 1937 as Bristol Joint Services, which existed until 1978. Vehicles used on these services carried a C-prefix to their fleet number and the Bristol city coat of arms. When the National Bus Company came into being they continued to carry this coat of arms and also continued with the famous Bristol scroll as a fleet name rather than the NBC standard style. The other major towns that I have covered in this book were served principally by either the Western National Omnibus Company or the associated Southern National Omnibus Company. As far as my memory serves me, the only real concentration of independent operation was around Yeovil, with firms such as Wakes of Sparkford and Safeway of South Petherton, plus a number of other operators such as Hutchings & Cornelius, who I sadly never got to photograph. Independent operation in Yeovil is now largely the domain of the successor to Wake's, South West Coaches. The south-west of England as a whole is now almost entirely the province of First Group. In the specific area covered in this book, the former Bristol Omnibus/Badgerline operations in Bristol, Bath, Weston-super-Mare and Wells now come under First West of England, based in Bristol. Services in Bridgwater, Taunton, Minehead and Yeovil, in what was the Western National, or in Yeovil's case Southern National, working areas now come under First South West, working as The Buses of Somerset, but based in Camborne in Cornwall. There are small inroads by Stagecoach in Weston-super-Mare, as well as in Bath and Bristol.

The nature of the operators has changed as well. When I started taking bus photographs in the early seventies, the National Bus Company was still in its infancy, probably about four years old, with the red and green corporate liveries just being introduced. The green livery prevailed in this part of the world, ousting the very smart green and cream OMO (as it was called then) livery of Bristol Omnibus, the company I probably saw the most. There were still quite a large number of vehicles in their pre-NBC liveries. With privatisation in 1986 came the break with the corporate identity, the introduction of more varied and colourful liveries, and also the increased use of minibuses. In the 1990s came the rise of groups such as Stagecoach and First, bringing with them a return to the corporate identity, followed by a move away from this unified image to the more localised liveries of recent years, which has again injected a host of more colourful schemes, notably in Bristol. The only livery that has basically stayed the same is that of National Express, fifty years old this year and still mainly white with red and blue lettering.

In many respects the actual towns pictured in this book haven't changed that much. Despite redevelopment, in some instances quite major, they do maintain their essential character. Bristol, Bath and Bridgwater have new bus stations on or near to the sites of the originals. Yeovil's bus station hasn't moved, or indeed changed much, since it was built in the seventies. The bus station in Wells has moved round the corner from Priory Road to Princes Street, but the depot, where the bus station was originally situated, is still on the same site as when it was first opened a hundred years ago in 1922. Minehead's bus station is gone, the site now occupied by a Co-Op store. Weston-super-Mare's well-known Art Deco seafront bus station and depot, opened in 1936, was sadly demolished in 1988 and now has a large block of flats on the site. The town does however have a new bus interchange that is more central to the town and shopping areas, opened in 2022. Taunton's bus station closed a couple of years ago, and has not been replaced, leaving the county town without a central bus terminus, buses terminating in the roads adjacent to the town centre.

The south-west of England is primarily rural, having no great industrial manufacturing centres. While Bristol has a long history of work in the aero-space sector and is well-known as the home of Concorde, and Yeovil has long connections with the manufacturing of helicopters, the main sources of revenue in the south-west as a whole are agriculture and tourism. The latter is seasonal by its very nature, and was heavily impacted by the awful COVID pandemic. This event hit bus and coach operators everywhere hard, especially with the government advice to avoid public transport, and was responsible for the demise of a number of firms over the whole country. Somerset, unfortunately, has the lowest approval rating for bus services in England, and the second lowest number of bus journeys per resident. However, the work going on at the Hinckley Point nuclear power station near Bridgwater, Europe's largest construction site, has seen a large increase in bus provision across Somerset to provide services for the construction workers and staff, with services provided by Somerset Passenger Solutions. Bus usage across the whole of Somerset has, however, fallen by 40 per cent compared with pre-Covid levels. I recall avidly studying bus timetables as a child, and the timetables today are a shadow of what I recall as a youngster. Let us all hope that bus services in rural areas will be funded properly, both locally and nationally, rather than be the 'Cinderella' of transport, so that their levels of patronage can be increased and rural communities can again have the decent bus service they so badly need.

I must apologise for the quality of some of the older photographs. My first camera was an instamatic that cost about £5, plus a number of tops from cereal packets, back in the early seventies, and was not therefore exactly the height of photographic technology. However, I felt that the pictures were historically important enough to be included in this volume. The information contained on 'Bus View', produced by Busdata Computing Services, has proved invaluable as a reference for checking service dates and histories of a large number of vehicles. I must also acknowledge the information on Wikipedia that also serves as an extremely useful reference point. At this point I must acknowledge and thank my partner Debs for allowing me to use some of her photographs in this book, as well as her constant support and encouragement in writing this book and accompanying me on many photographic trips.

Sadly, my mother passed away while I was preparing this book. She and my late father never stopped encouraging me in my chosen hobby and I would therefore like to dedicate this volume about buses in a part of the country they loved and were both proud to call home.

BRISTOL

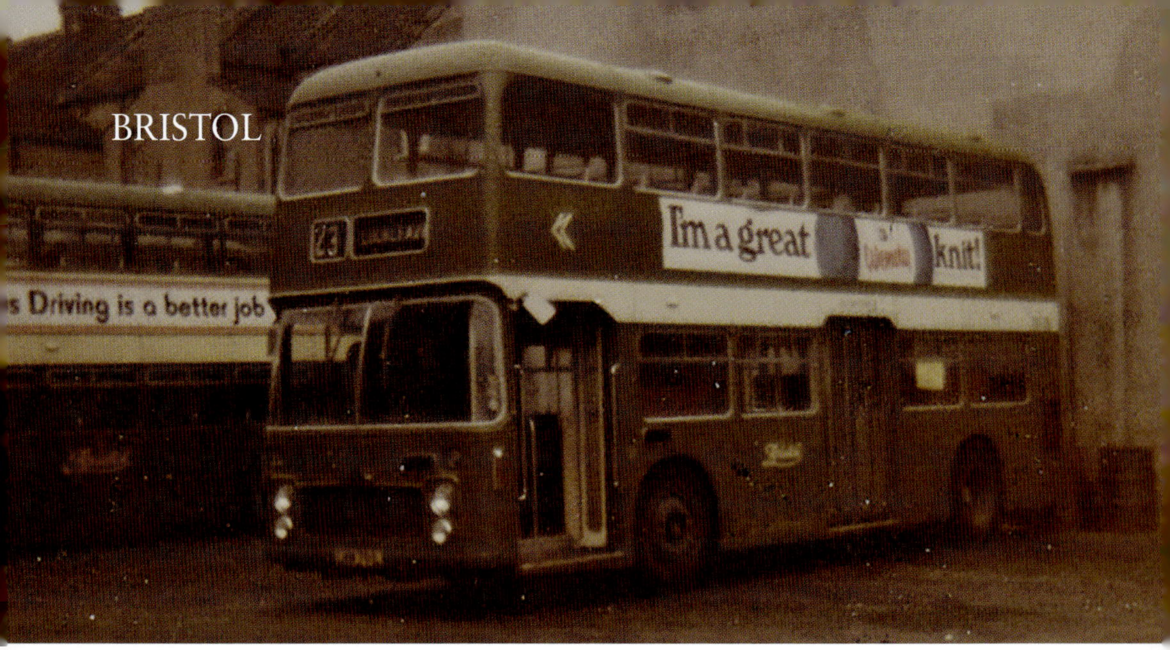

Bristol Omnibus Company was an operator with a large fleet and operating area. It was responsible for Bristol's city services jointly with the local council. This admittedly poor quality shot is of then new Bristol VRT C5010, LHW 791L, at an open day at Lawrence Hill depot in 1973. However, it does show how the old-style scroll fleetname continued to be used in NBC days on vehicles allocated to the city fleet, with the NBC logo moved to between decks. I well remember trying to persuade my mother to have a go at driving on one of the Bristol K-type driver trainers at this event! She was resolute in her refusal!

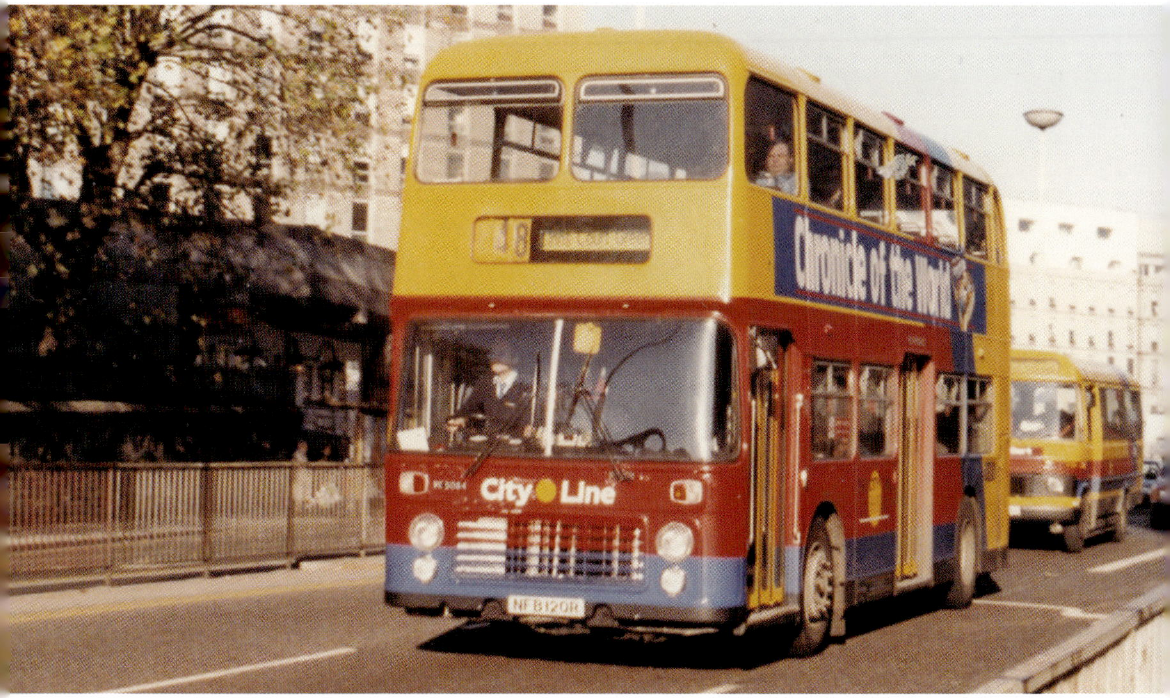

After privatisation, the city services were marketed as City Line, with a new bright livery. Bristol VRT 5084, NFB 120R, is seen in Haymarket on 23 November 1989. I wasn't always totally convinced the livery suited the lines of the ECW body.

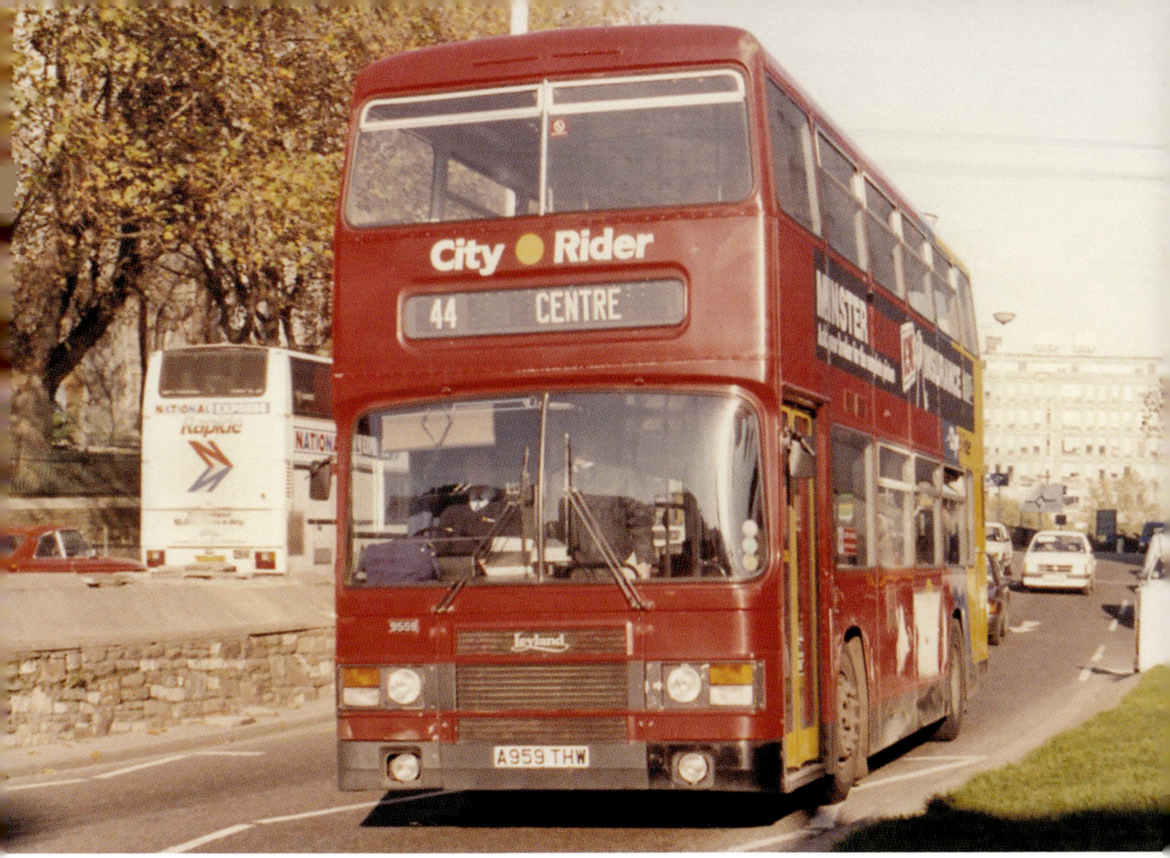

Seen on the same day in the same place, on city service 44 is 9559, A959 THW, a Roe-bodied Leyland Olympian. On the other side of the road is a Van Hool Astrobel-bodied Volvo of Western National on a National Express Rapide service, probably heading for London from Penzance.

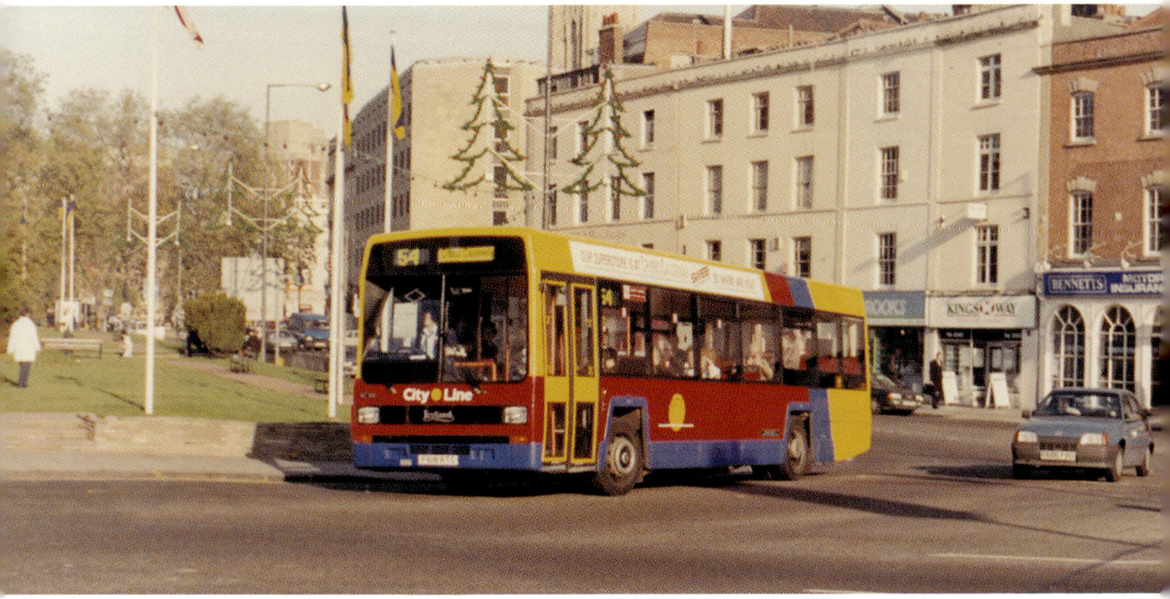

Also seen on 23 November 1989 at Broad Quay is four-month old 1618, F618 RTC, a Leyland Lynx, heading for Cribbs Causeway. Bristol City Line only took delivery of two batches of Leyland Lynxes, in 1989 and 1990.

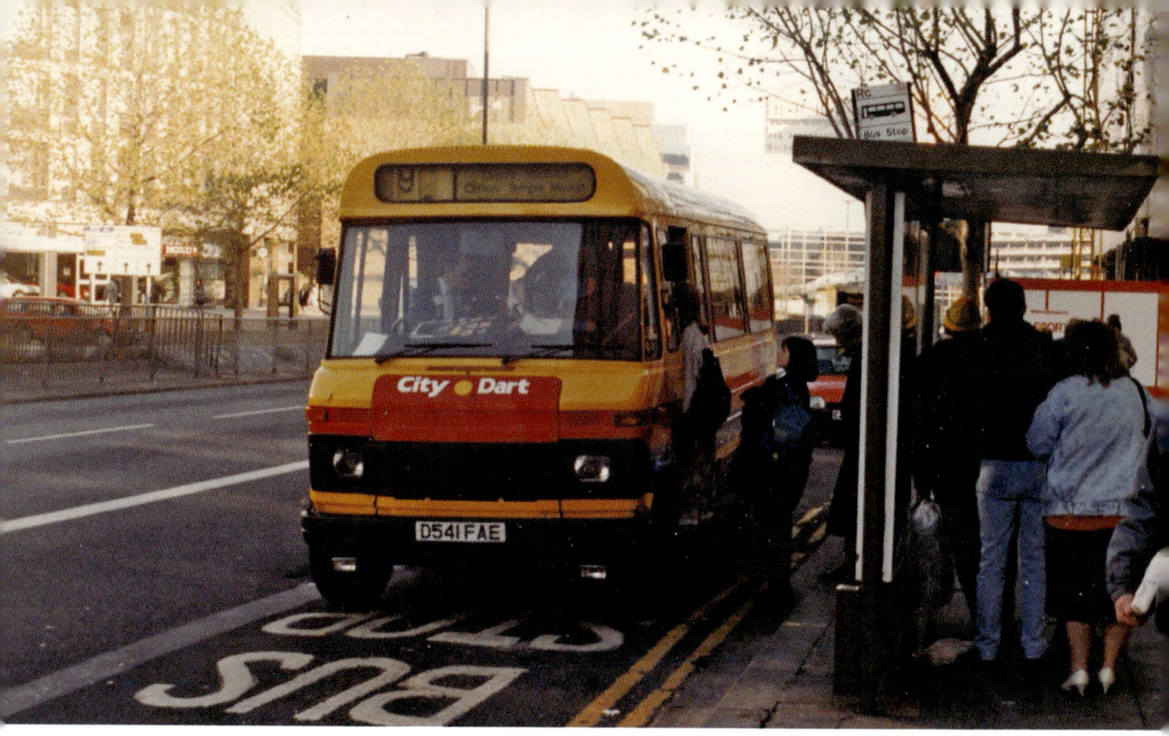

Caught in Bond Street, Bristol, on 23 November 1989, is Reeve-Burgess-bodied Mercedes-Benz L608D 7541, D541 FAE. City Line was effectively the area of the old Bristol Joint Services operation, the minibus services being marketed as City Dart.

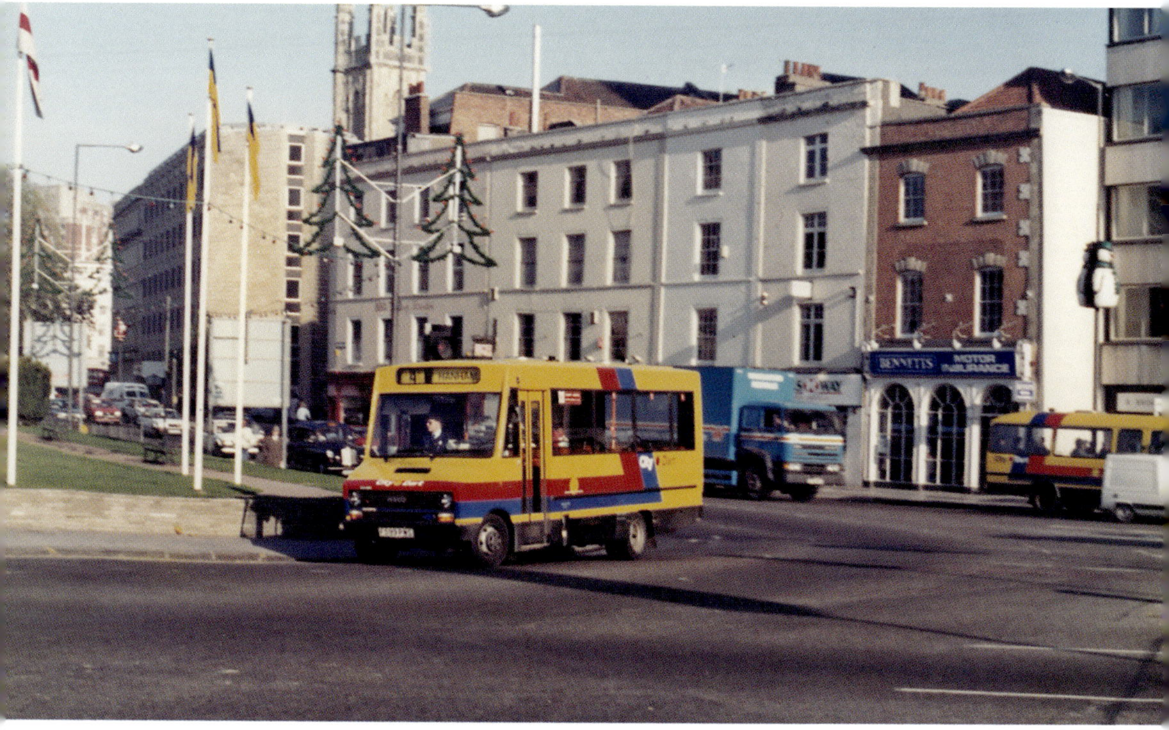

Seen at Broad Quay, again on 23 November 1989, is another City Dart, this time 7599, F599 PWS, an Iveco Daily 49.10 with a somewhat box-like Dormobile body heading for Hanham on service 4.

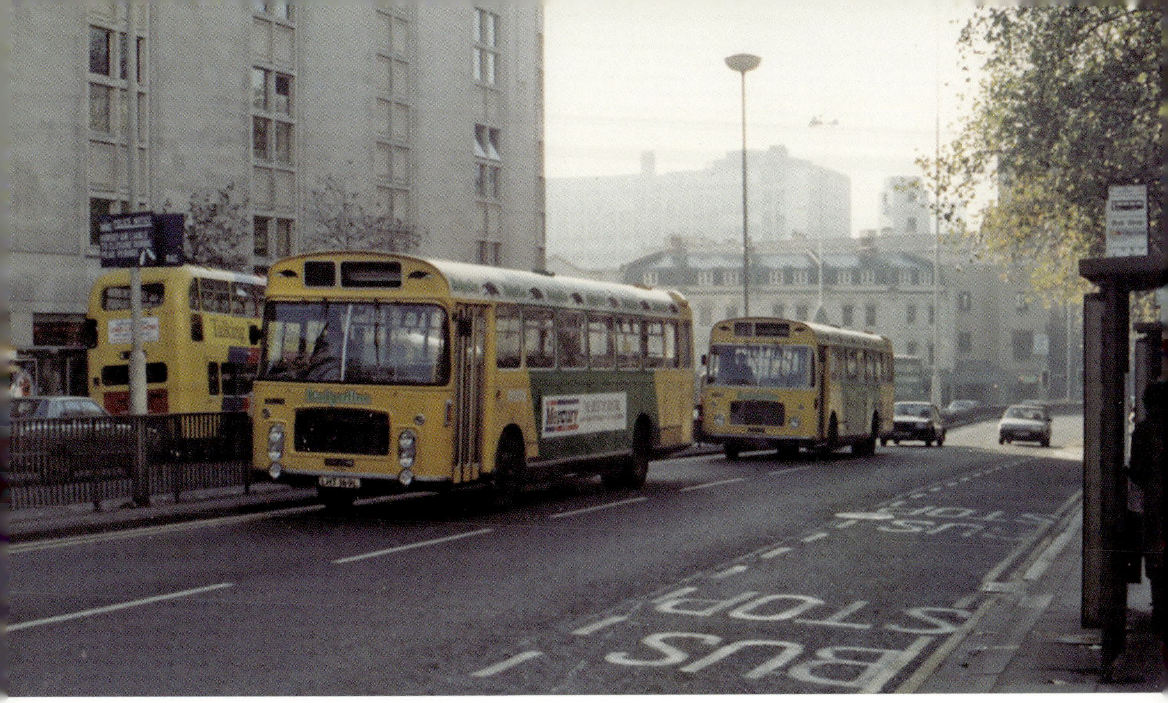

Bristol's country services after privatisation were in the hands of Badgerline. Seen at St James Barton on 23 November 1989 are Bristol REs 1311, LHT 169L, followed by former Cumberland 1260, DAO 293K. Badgerline retained its Bristol REs for a considerable time. Bristol Omnibus and Badgerline received very few secondhand Bristol REs, taking a handful of Plaxton-bodied RELHs plus one with an ECW body from Eastern National and three RELLs from Cumberland.

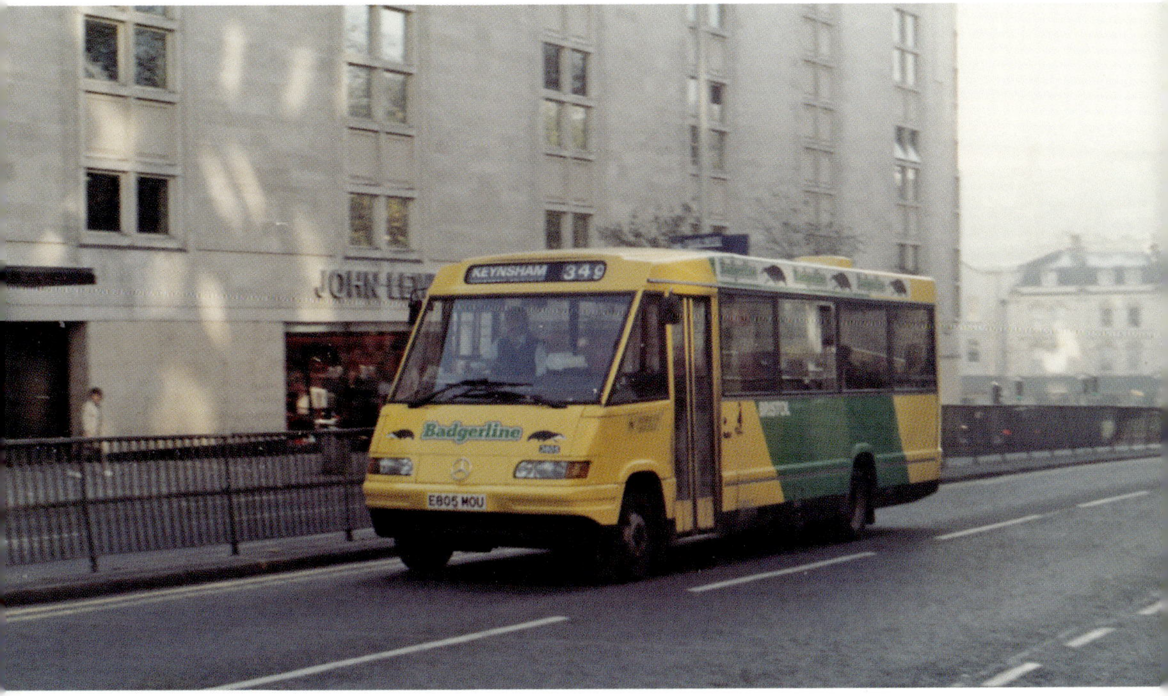

Badgerline did invest in new vehicles, including a single batch of Mercedes-Benz 811Ds with Optare StarRider bodies like 3805, E805 MOU, seen here bound for Keynsham on 23 November 1989.

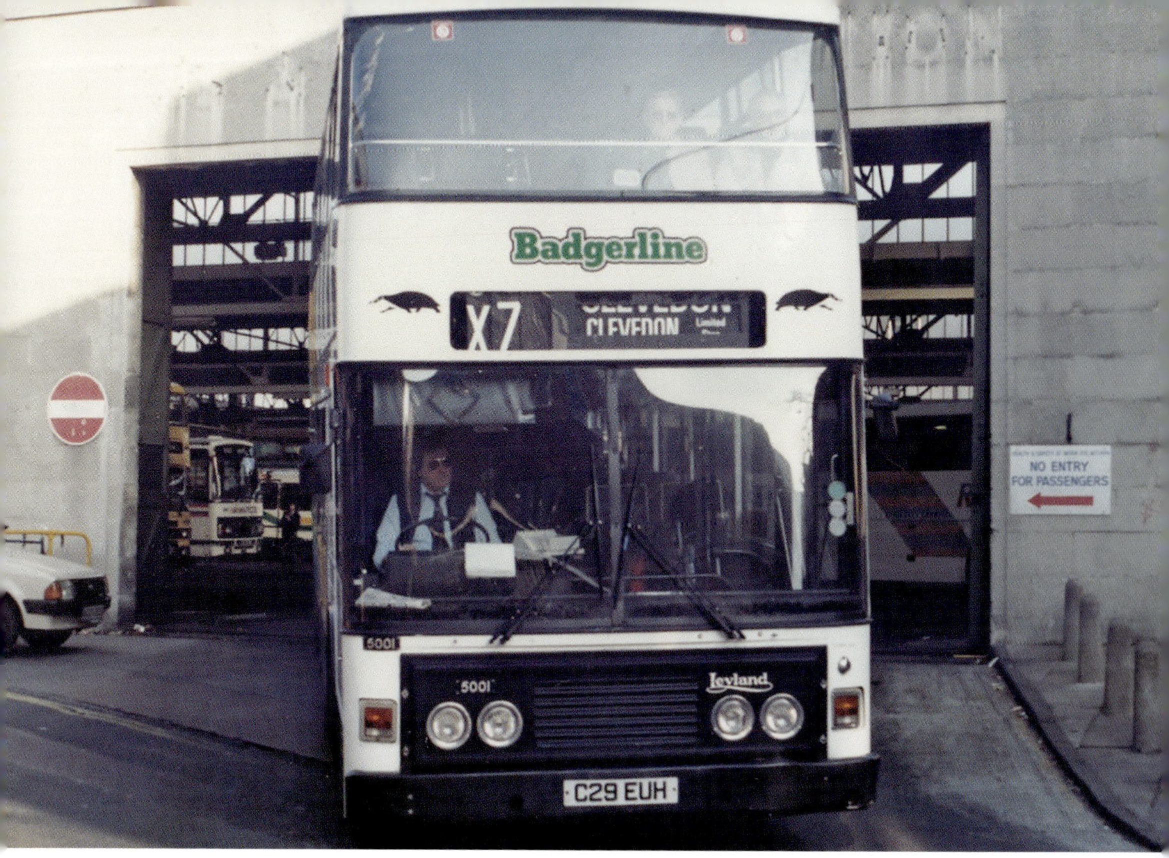

A relatively uncommon vehicle to enter the Badgerline fleet was this East Lancs-bodied Leyland Olympian fitted with coach seats, C29 EUH, numbered 5001. One of two bought new by Rhymney Valley District Council in South Wales, it was actually purchased from G & G of Leamington Spa, and is seen leaving Bristol's Marlborough Street bus station for Clevedon on 23 November 1989.

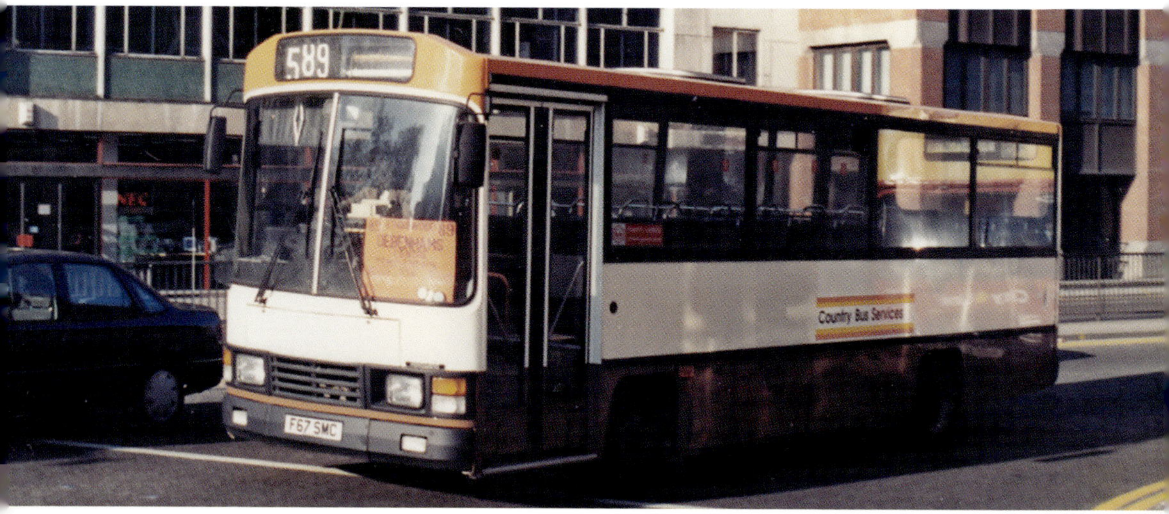

There has always been little in the way of independent bus operation in Bristol, However, Arrowfleet, who traded as Country Bus Services, operated this relatively rare Wadham Stringer Vanguard-bodied Leyland Swift, F67 SMC, on a service from Kingswood. It is seen on St Augustines Place on 23 November 1989. This vehicle ended its days on Jersey.

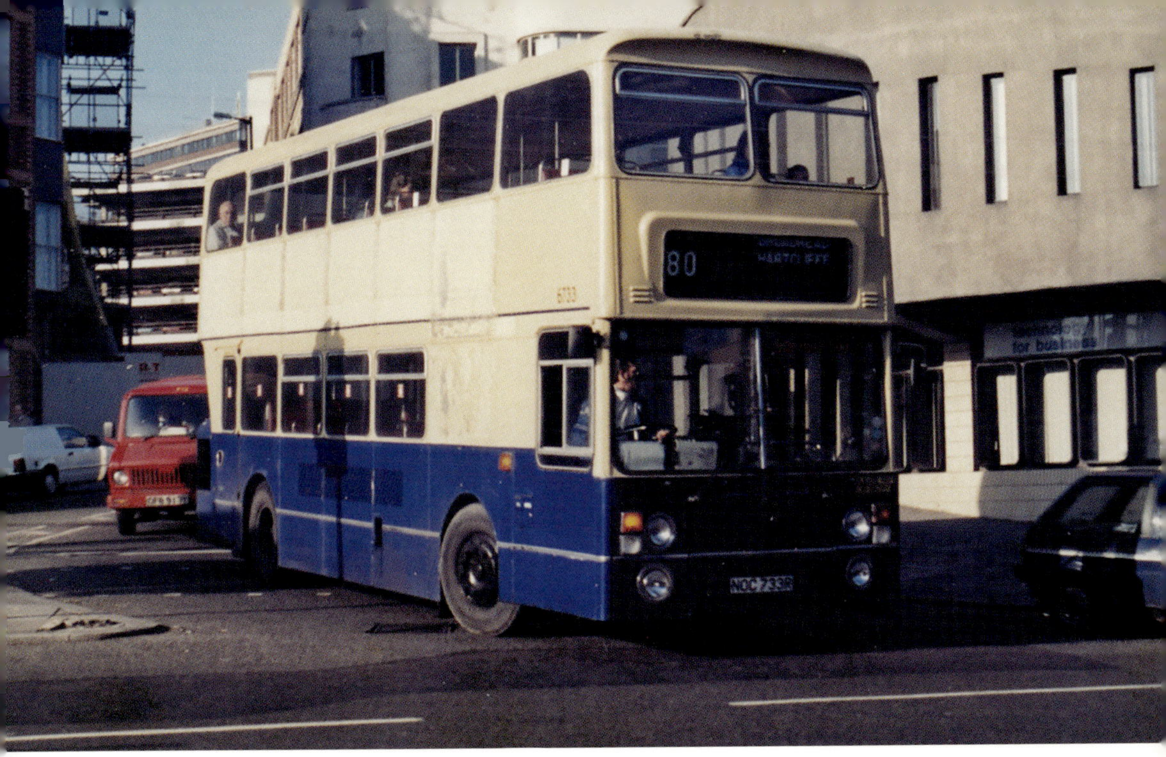

Somerbus of Paulton also operated a service into the centre of Bristol, using this former West Midlands PTE East Lancs-bodied Leyland Fleetline, NOC 733R, bound for Hartcliffe. It still carried its old West Midlands livery and its old fleet number of 6733.

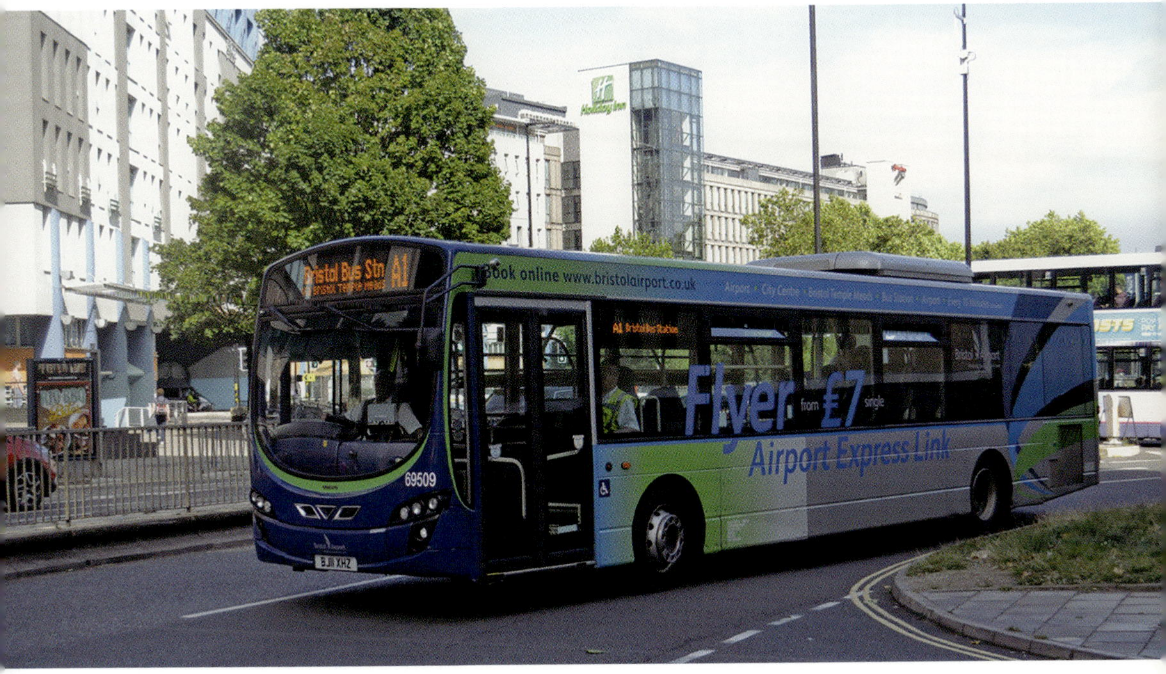

First West of England started an Airport Flyer service connecting the centre of Bristol, Temple Meads station and Bristol Airport. Seen at St James Barton on 11 August 2016, Volvo B7RLE 69509, carrying Wright Eclipse Urban 2 body, is approaching the bus station.

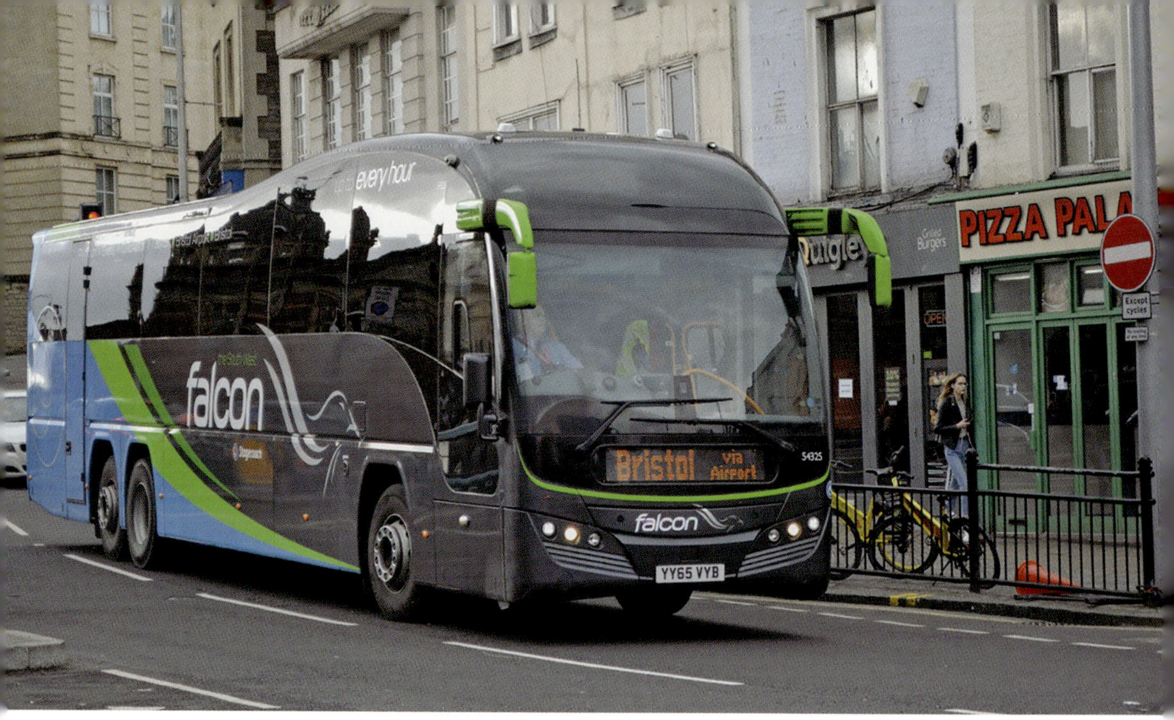

Stagecoach Devon operate to Bristol with their long South West Falcon service from Plymouth. In St Augustines Place and approaching journey's end is Volvo B11R 54325, YY65 VYB, carrying a Plaxton Elite body on 4 February 2018. Stagecoach operations in Bristol and Somerset are relatively few and far between.

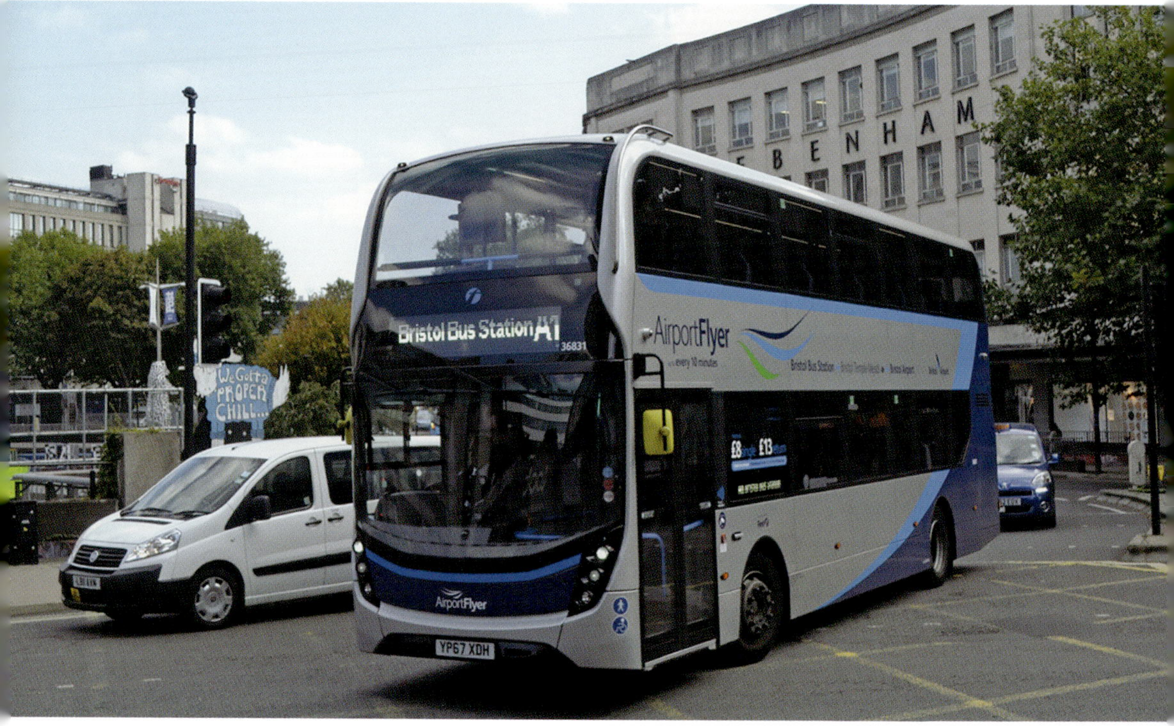

Seen at St James Barton on its final approach to the bus station on 25 September 2018, the Airport Flyer service A1 is now in the hands of double-deckers, and costing an extra pound. 36831, YP67XDH is an Enviro400MMC.

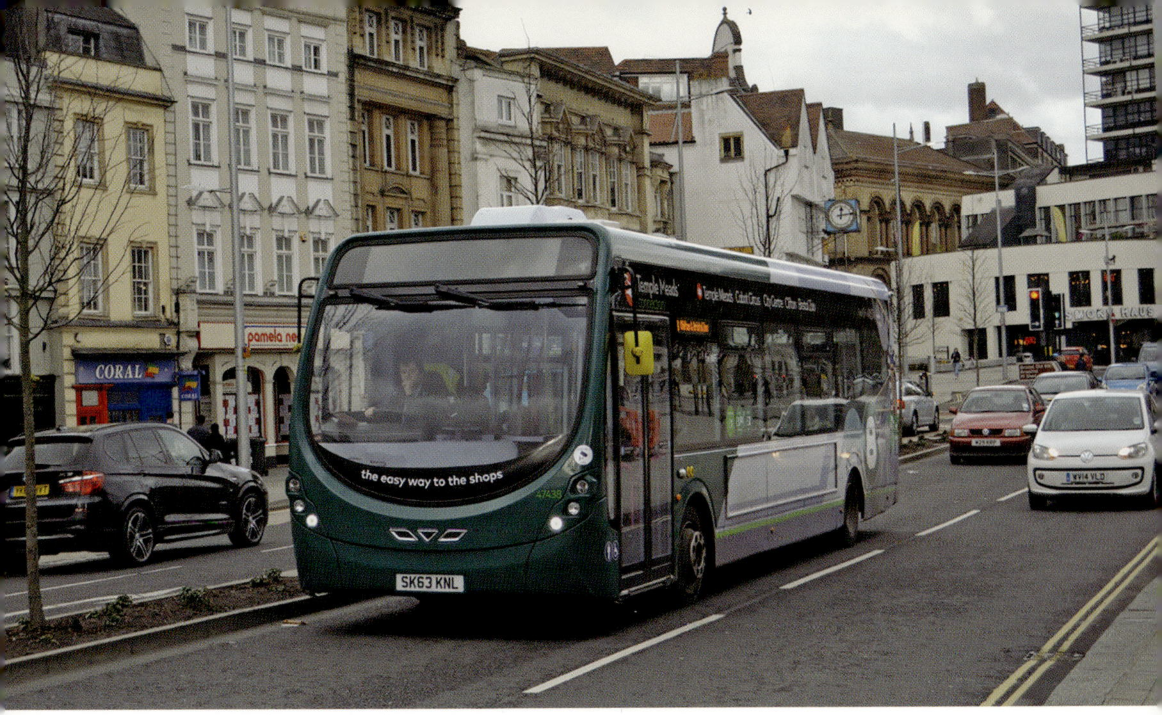

There are still single-deckers on city services in Bristol. Seen in St Augustines Place on 4 February 2018, Wright StreetLite DF 47438, SK63 KNL, is on service 8 from Temple Meads Station to Bristol Zoo.

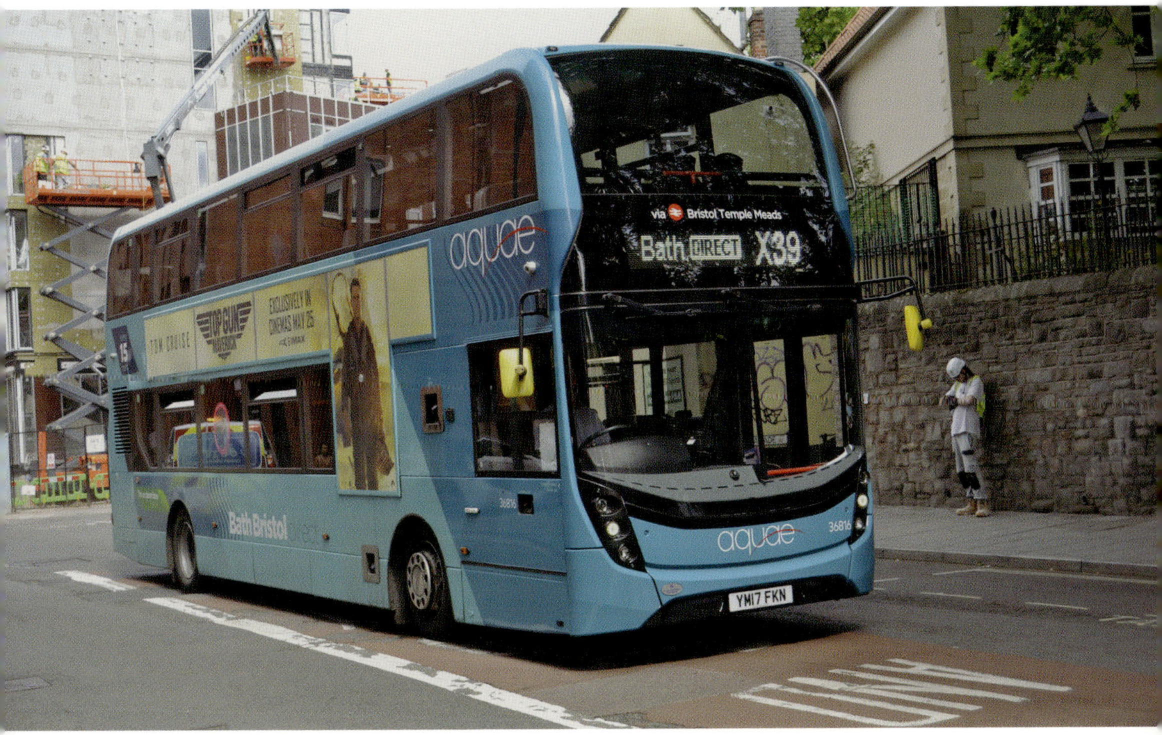

Bristol is now a colourful place for buses. Here First West of England Enviro400MMC 36816, YM17 FKN, is leaving Bristol for Bath on 18 May 2022. This service is marketed as 'Aquae', presumably a reference to Bath's Roman heritage as Aquae Sulis.

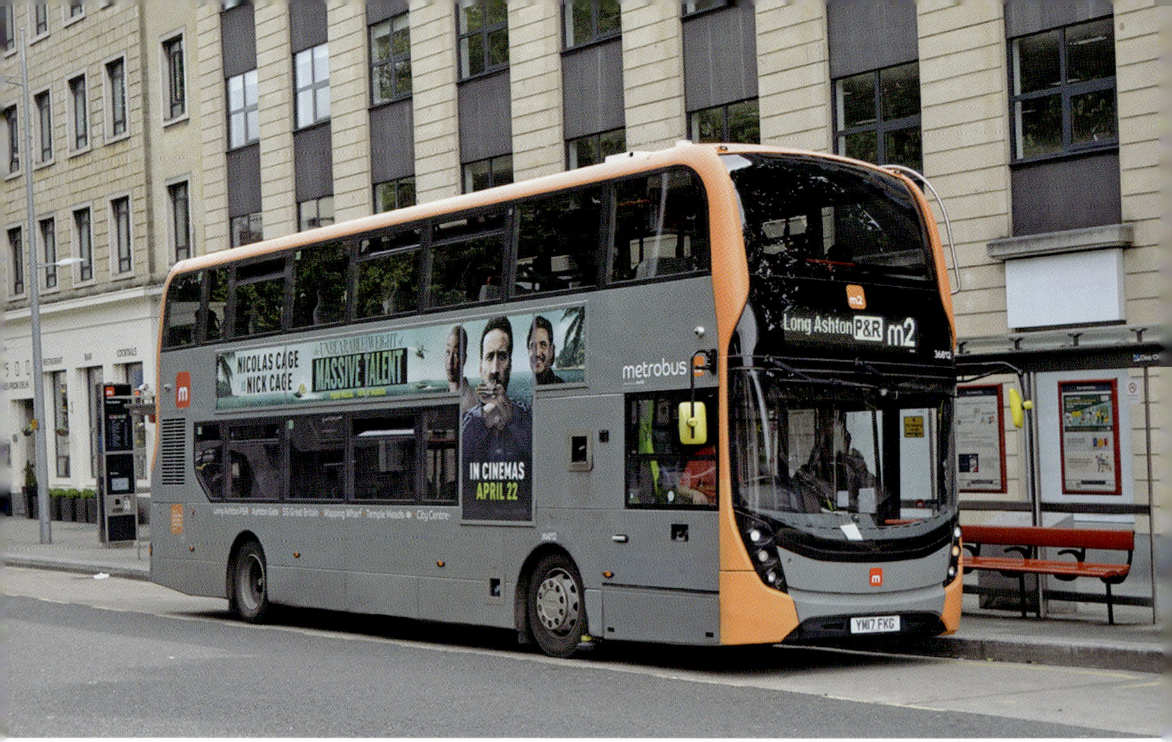

Wearing the colours for Metrobus m2, the Park & Ride service to Long Ashton, Enviro400MMC 36812, YM17 FKG, is seen in St Augustines Place on 18 May 2022.

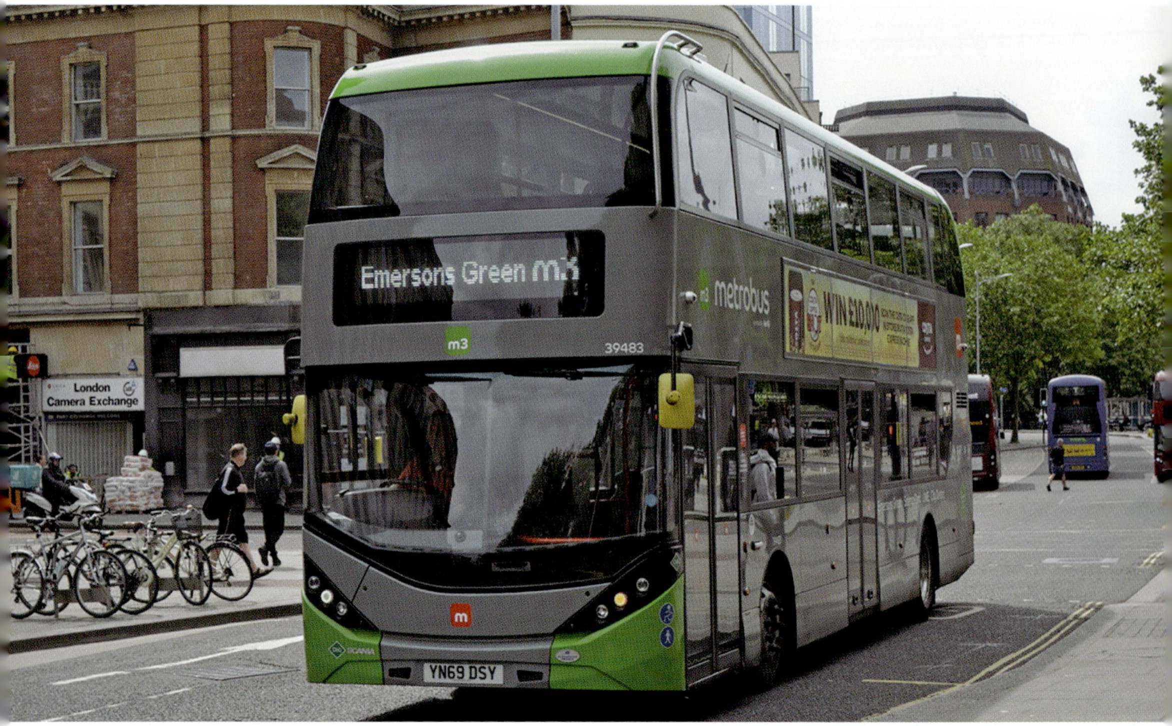

In the m3 variation of the Metrobus livery in Bristol is 39483, YN69 DSY, an Enviro400MMC City on a gas-powered Scania chassis seen in the city centre on 18 May 2022.

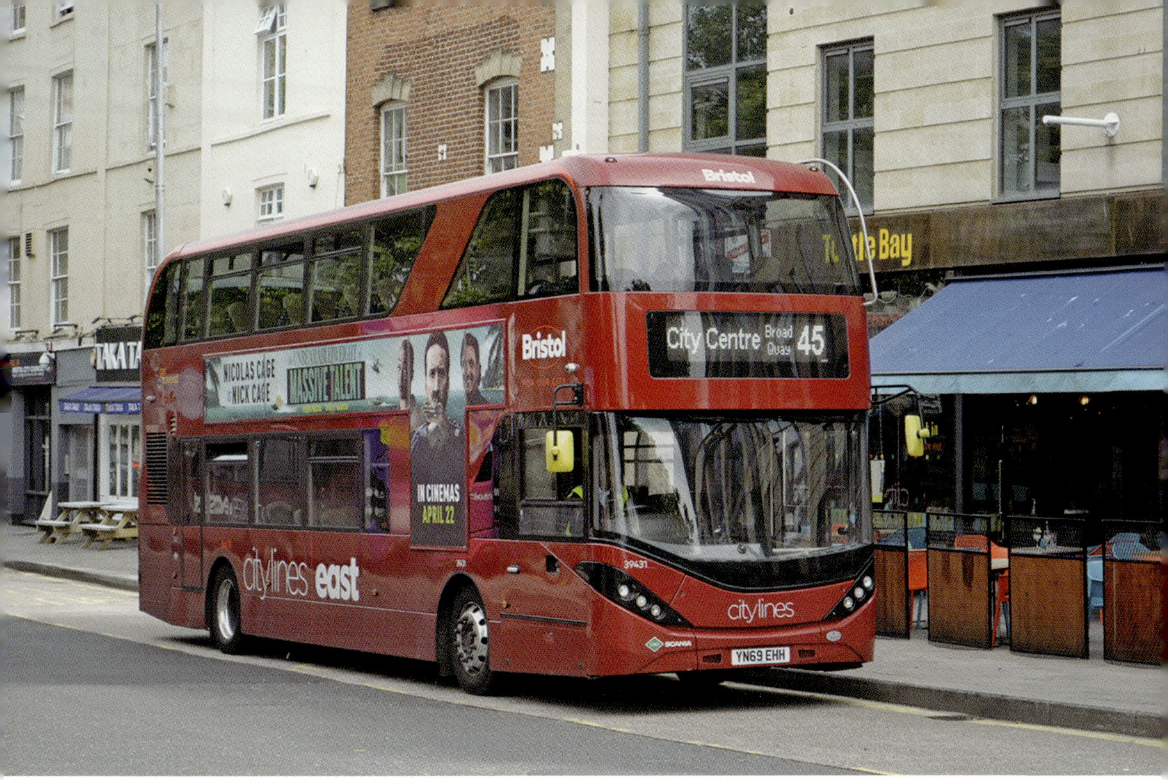

Another Enviro400MMC, another livery! First West of England gas-powered Enviro400MMC 39431, YN69 EHH, and wearing Citylines East colours, is seen on 18 May 2022 in St Augustines Place.

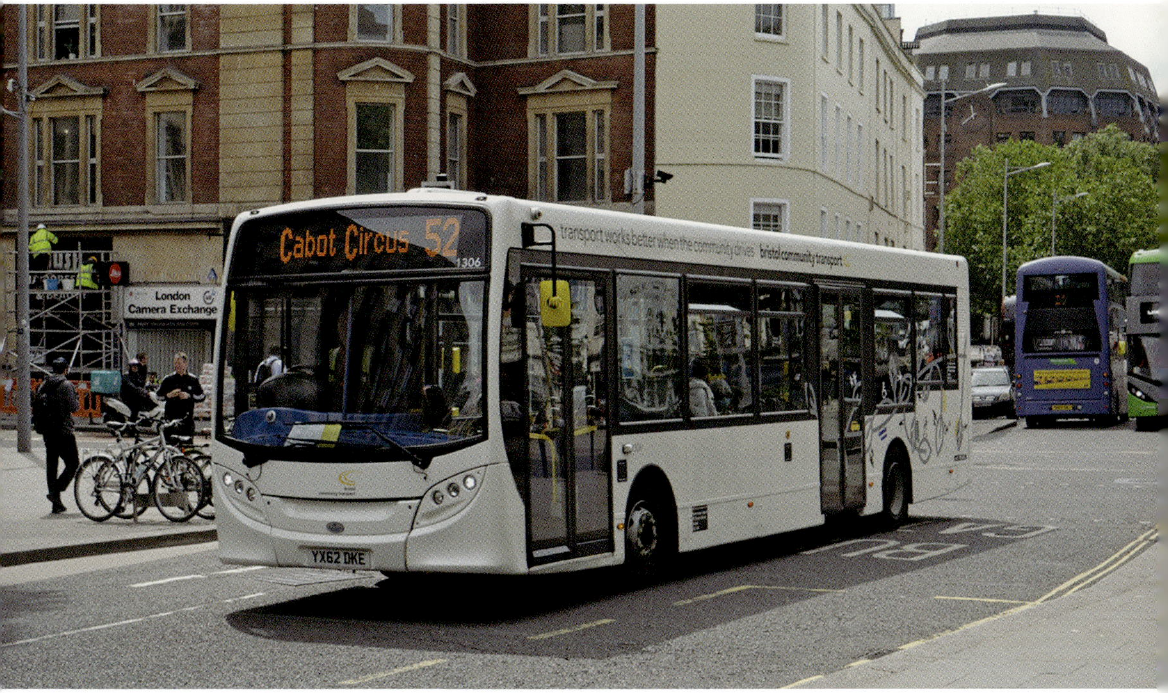

Bristol Community Transport, part of the HCT group, operate a number of services around Bristol. Enviro200 1306, YX62 DKE, is seen here on 18 May 2022, in St Augustines Place bound for Cabot Circus.

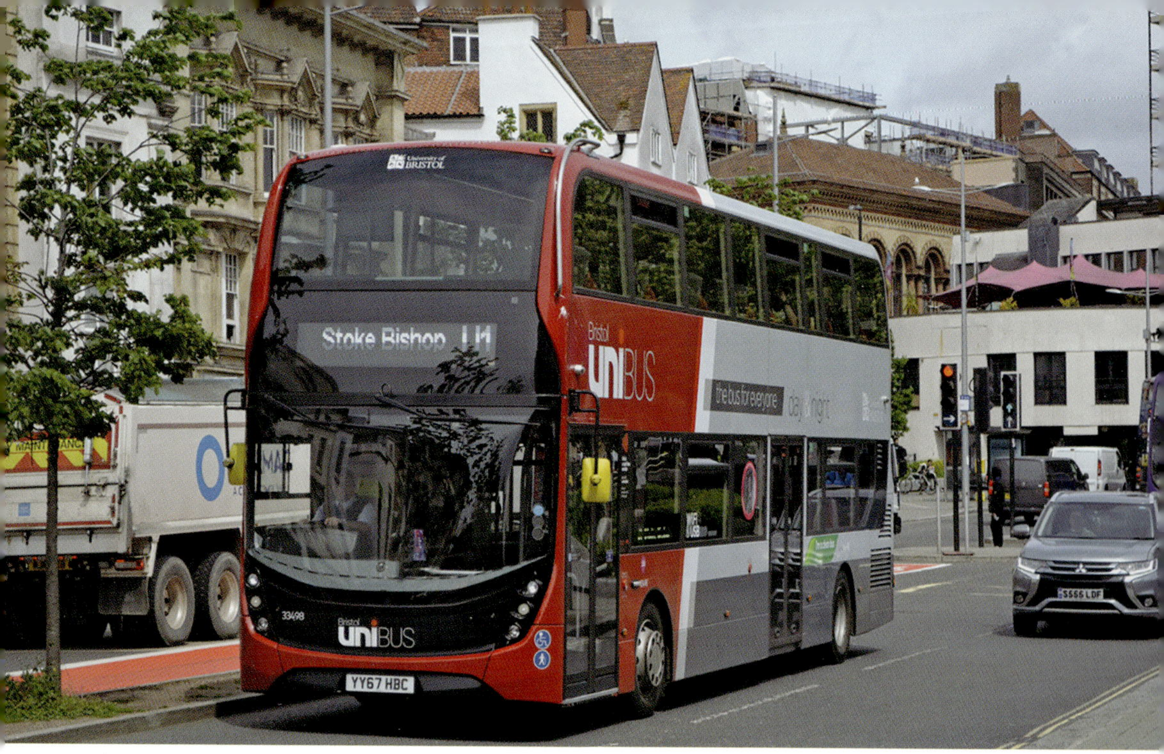

First West of England 33498, YY67 HBC, an Enviro400MMC, is seen here bound for Stoke Bishop on University service U1, 18 May 2022.

BATH

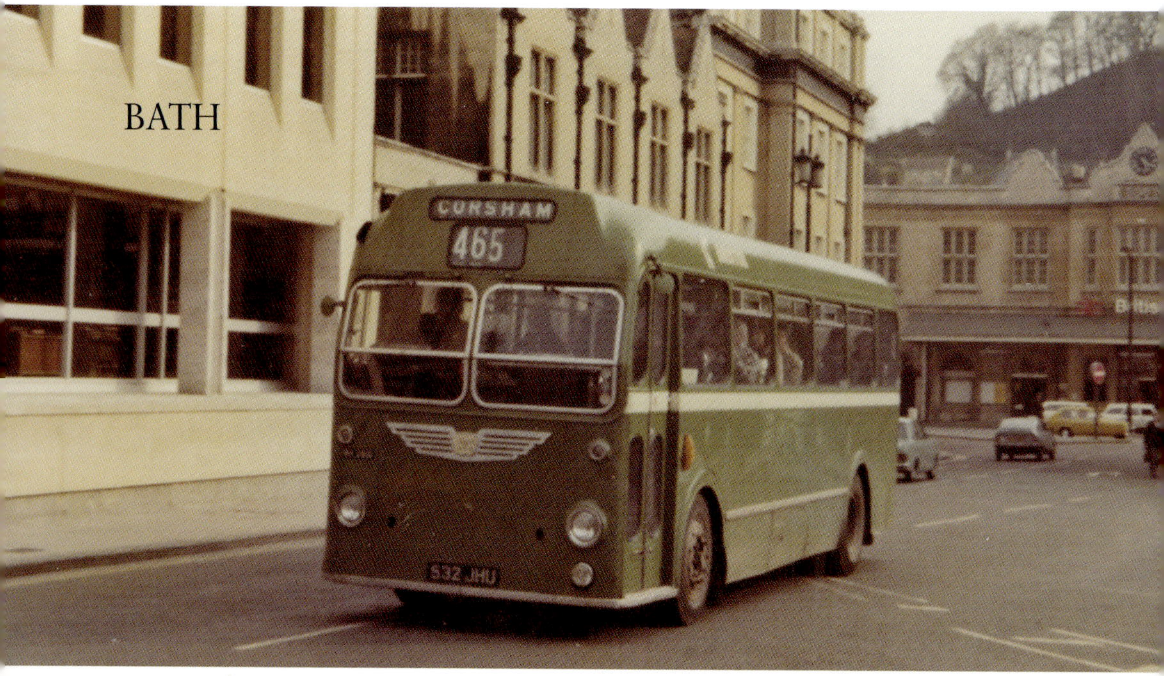

Photographed in 1975, Bristol Omnibus Bristol MW 2510, 532 JHU, is seen here in Manvers Street, Bath, with Bath Spa station behind. Bristol had one of the largest fleets of MWs in the country, in both bus and coach form. This vehicle was new in 1961, being withdrawn from service in 1976. I frequently rode on vehicles like these when travelling to and from school in Wells.

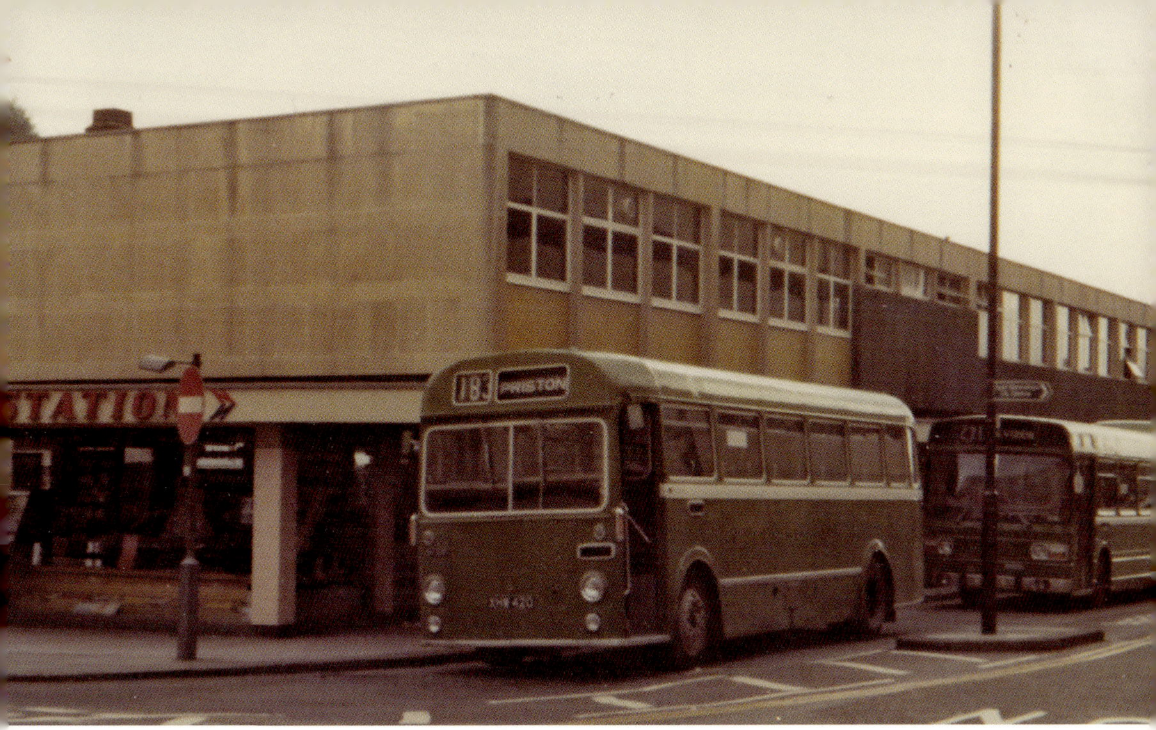

During 1971 Bristol Omnibus started to rebuild some of their Bristol LS types to prolong their lives. This included new engines, modernised interiors and a new windscreen. XHW 420, new in 1957 and formerly numbered 2904 and renumbered 3001, was the second one to be treated and is seen here behind Bath's Manvers Street bus station in 1975. However, only eight vehicles were treated before the programme ceased.

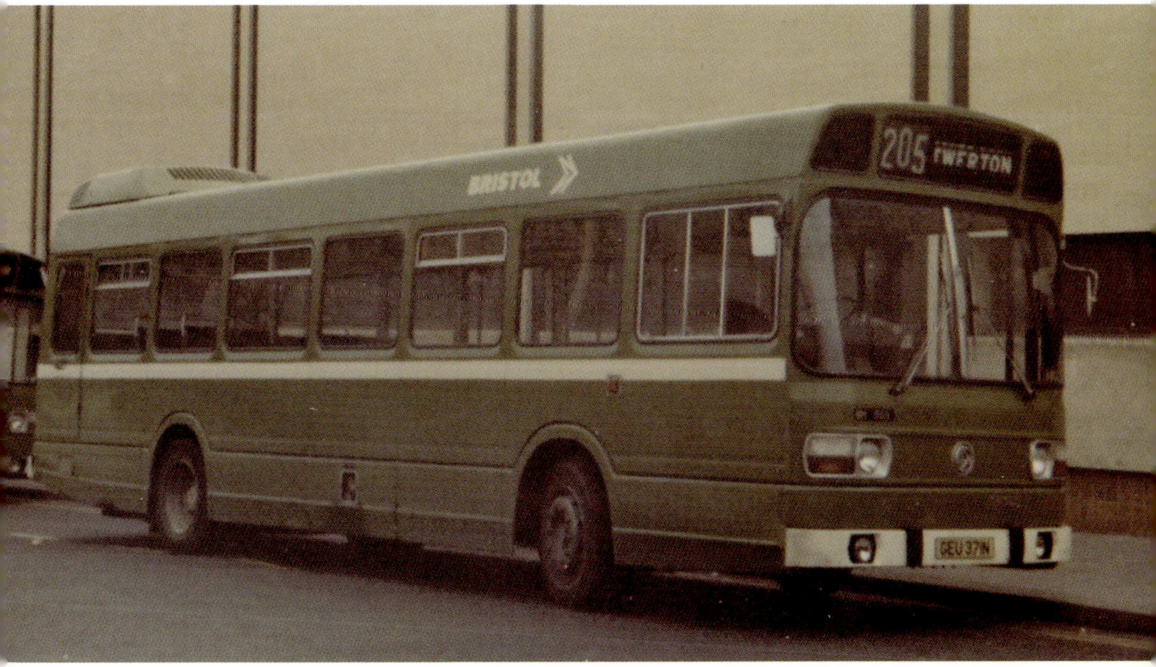

10.3-m Leyland National 559, GEU 371N, was new to Bath depot in 1975. It is seen here behind Manvers Street Bus Station later that year on a city service to Twerton. Most of Bristol's Leyland Nationals were of the 11.3 m type, with a mixture of both single- and dual-doors.

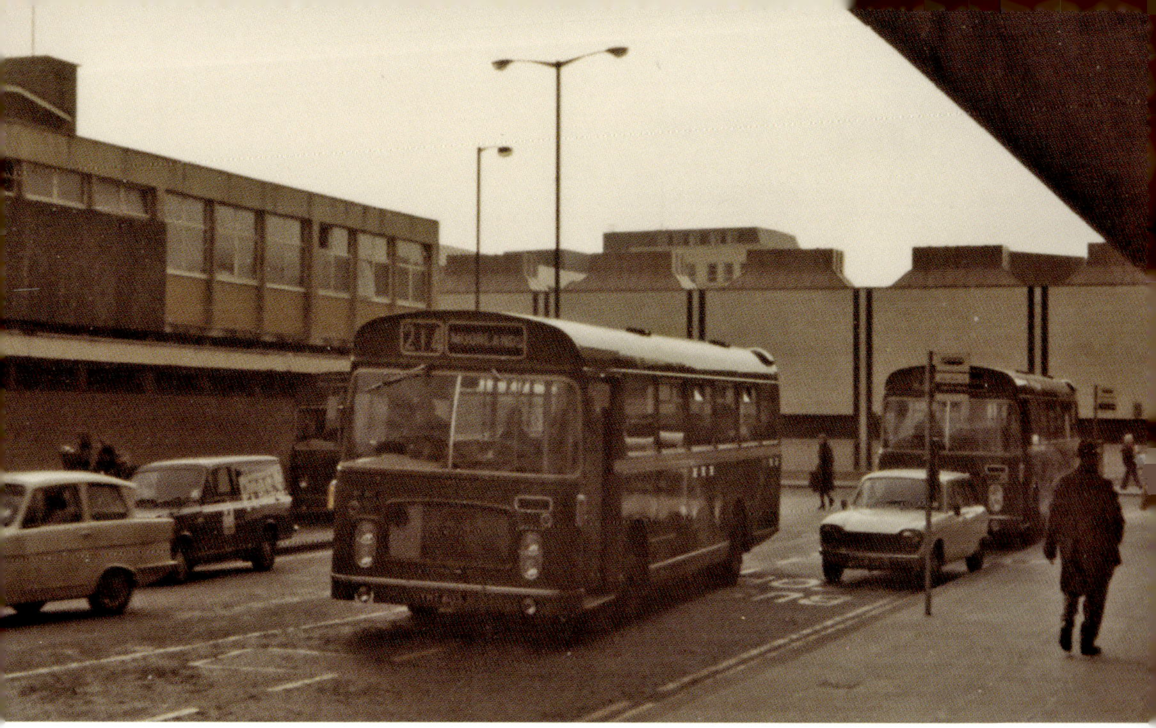

The majority of the Bristol Omnibus fleet of Bristol REs were on the RELL or the RELH chassis. There was, however, a small number of the shorter RESL chassis. Here, Bath depot's 517, YHT 803J, passes Manvers Street Bus Station sometime in 1975.

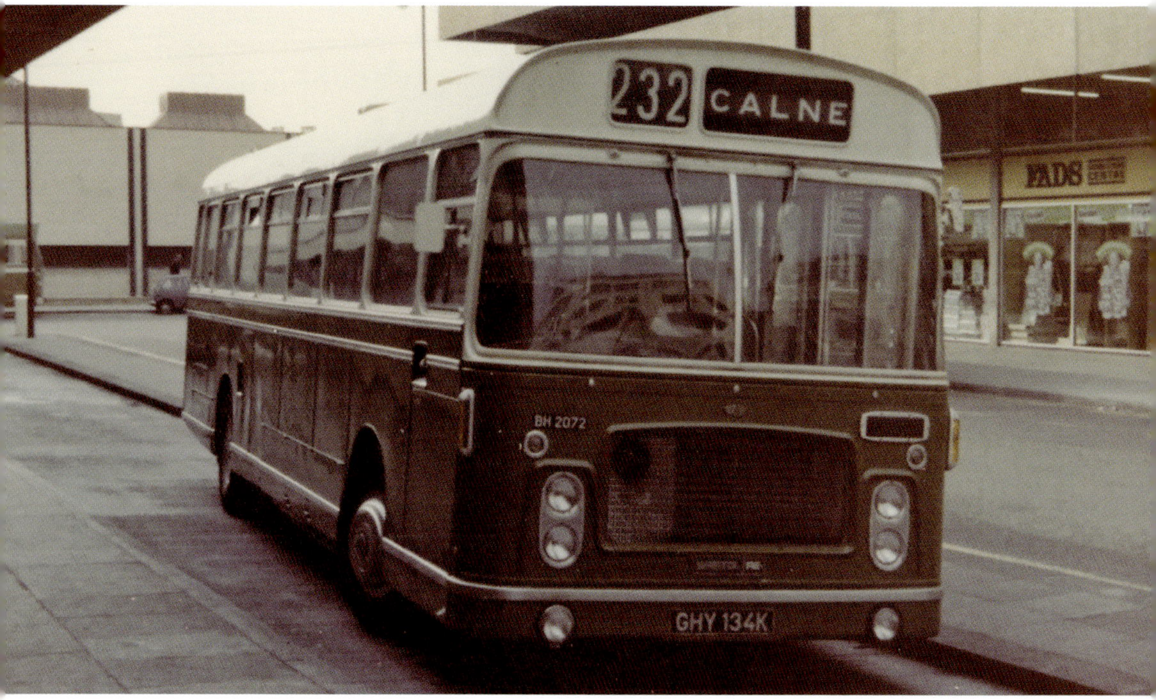

Dual-purpose Bristol RELH 2072, GHY 134K, is pictured here on layover at the back of Manvers Street bus station during 1975. I remember riding on these vehicles a few times from Wells to Bath. They were excellent, comfortable vehicles. This RE eventually moved to that well-known operator of Bristol REs, Northern Bus.

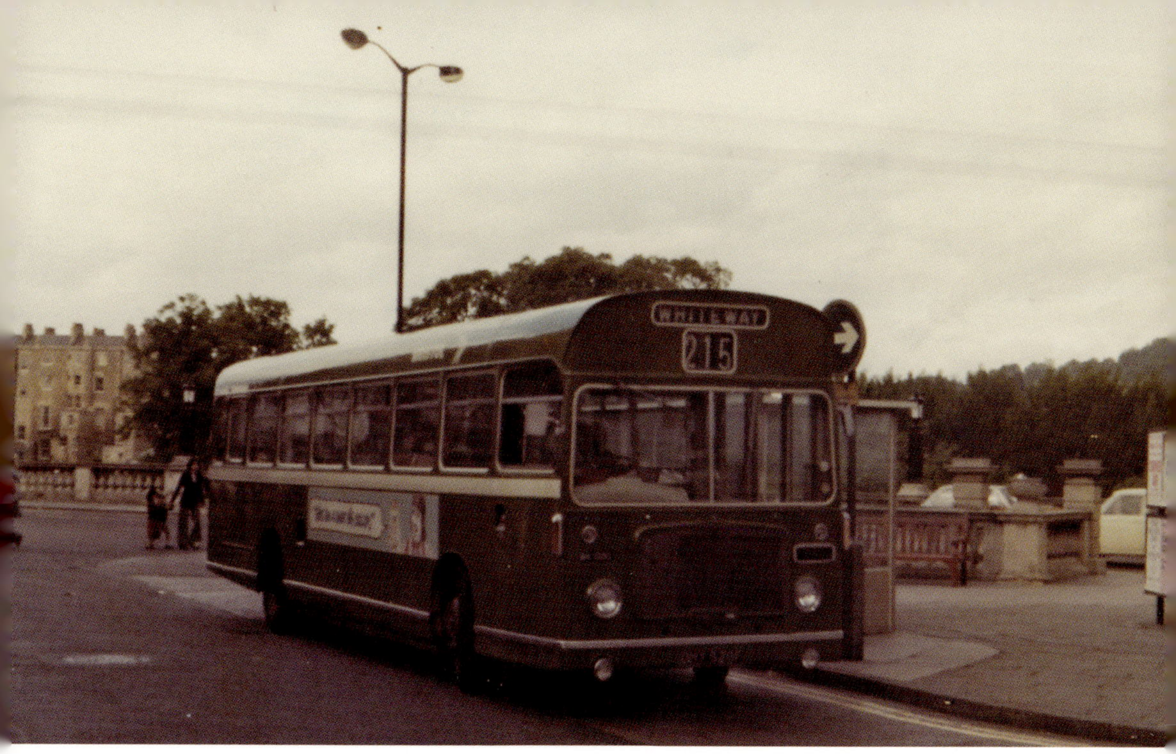

Pictured in North Parade in about 1975, Bristol RELL1090, OHY520F, is on a city service. Bristol Omnibus operated over 400 of these fine vehicles in various forms, the first examples arriving in 1963 for coach work with Bristol Greyhound, and the last in 1974.

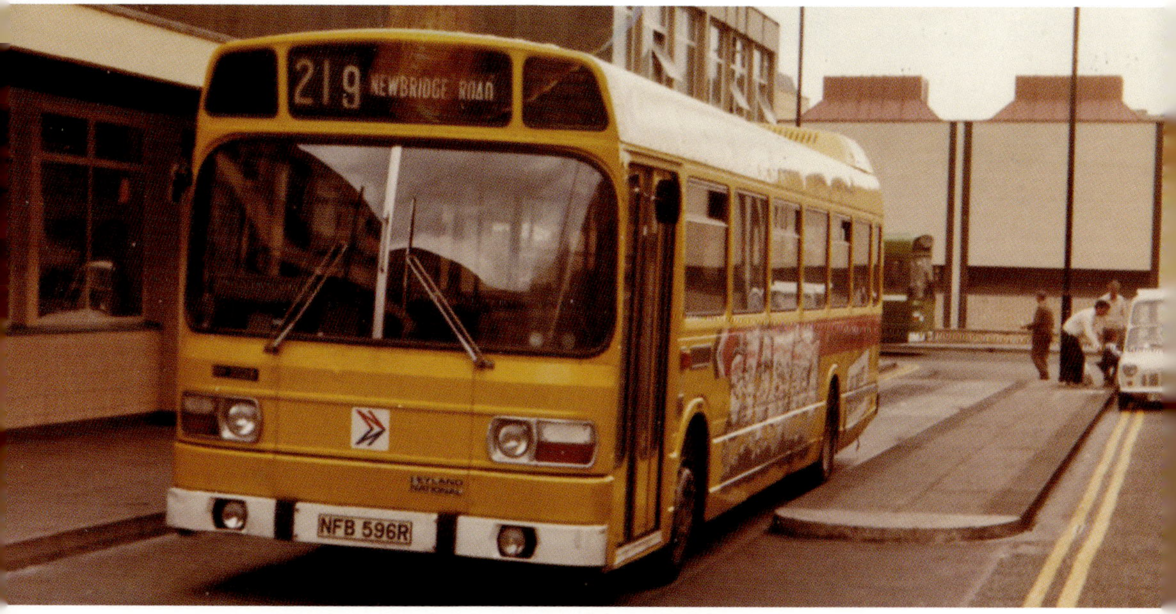

After taking Bristol REs for as long as they could, the Leyland National entered the Bristol fleet in 1973. I well remember the duty inspector at Manvers Street allowing me and my brother to examine one of the first to be delivered in 1973 and taking the time to explain features on it to us. 3028, NFB 596R, was delivered new to Bath depot in 1976, and appropriately carried an 'FB' registration which is a former City of Bath mark. It is seen here at the bus station advertising the company's farecards.

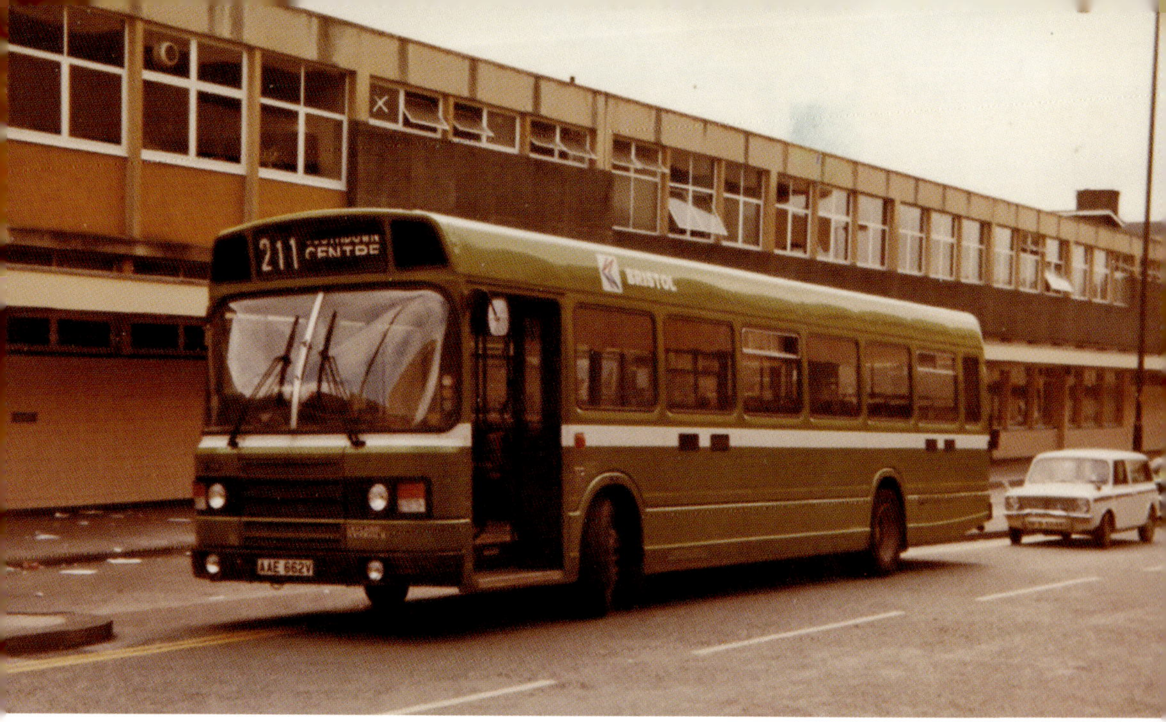

The Leyland National 2 appeared in 1979. It had a front-mounted radiator and a choice of Leyland or Gardner engines. The roof pod was also optional, Bristol's example lacking this feature. 3518, AAE 662V, again seen at the bus station in about 1980, spent all of its working life at Bath, being withdrawn and scrapped in 1998.

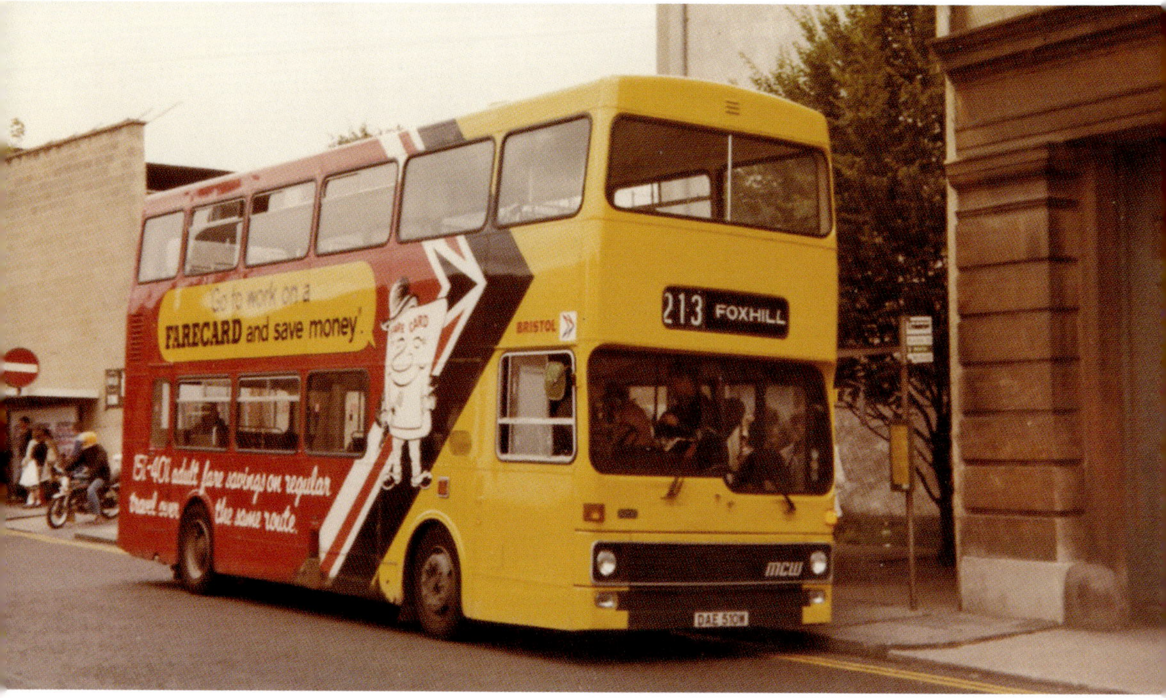

Bristol Omnibus was selected to evaluate the MCW Metrobus alongside its Bristol VRTs, receiving five in 1980, all allocated to Bath. The first of these, 6000, DAE 510W, is seen here in around 1982 wearing a livery to advertise Bristol's farecards in Bath bus station.

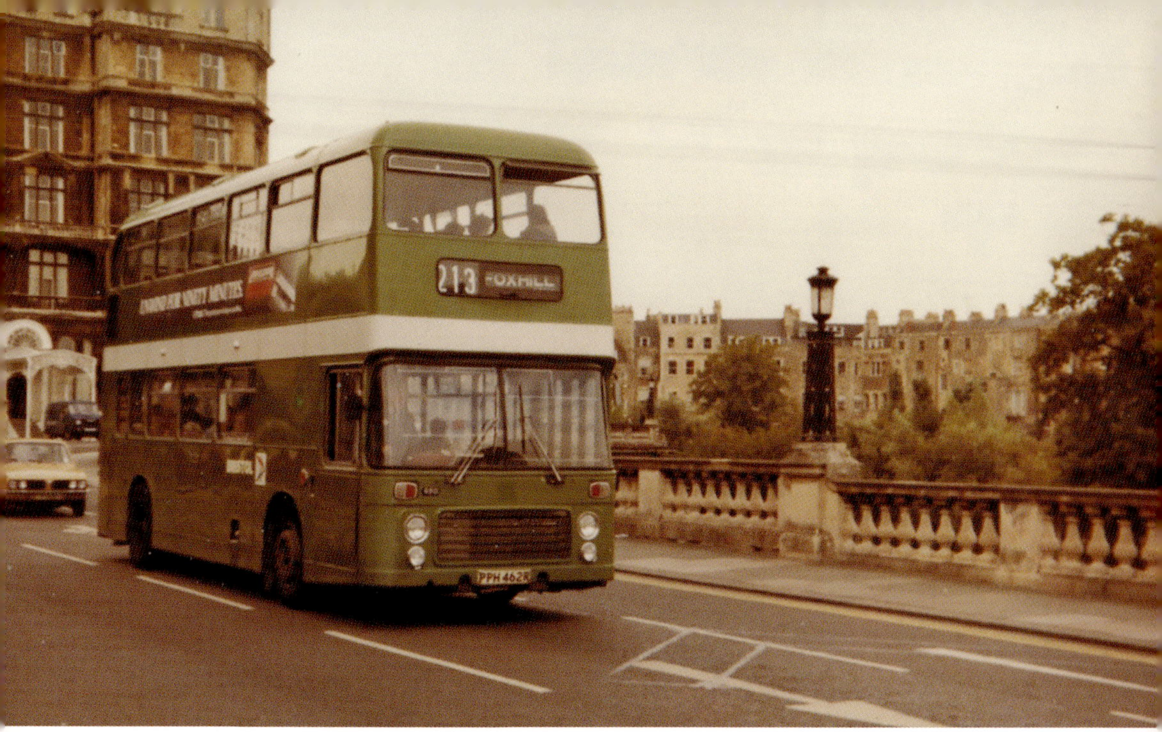

In 1977 London Country took delivery of fifteen high-bridge Bristol VRTs for work in the Grays area of Essex. Totally non-standard to that company they were transferred during 1980 to Bristol Omnibus and allocated to Bath. 6501, PPH 462R is seen here in Pierrepont Street Bath in around 1982. This vehicle later passed to East Yorkshire and is now preserved.

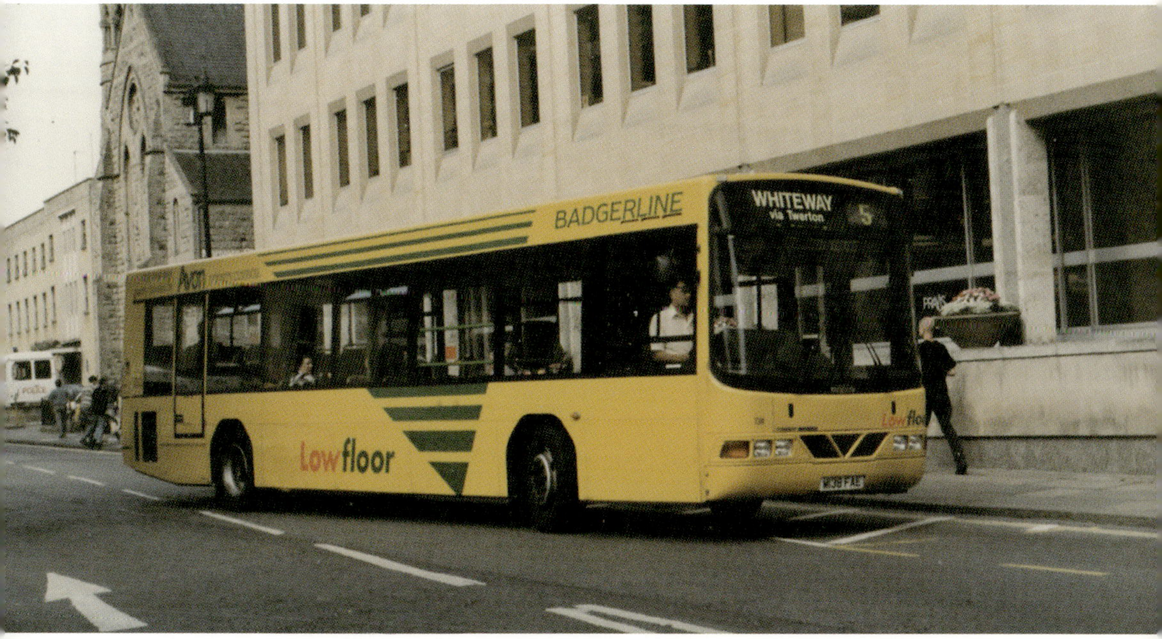

1995 and Bristol Omnibus has become Badgerline. Low-floor vehicles with improved access are beginning to enter service, as shown here by 138, M138 FAE, a Dennis Lance SLF with Wright Pathfinder body, is seen in Manvers Street. Badgerline only ever took this one batch of Lance SLFs, although there was a batch of Dennis Lances with Plaxton Verde bodies.

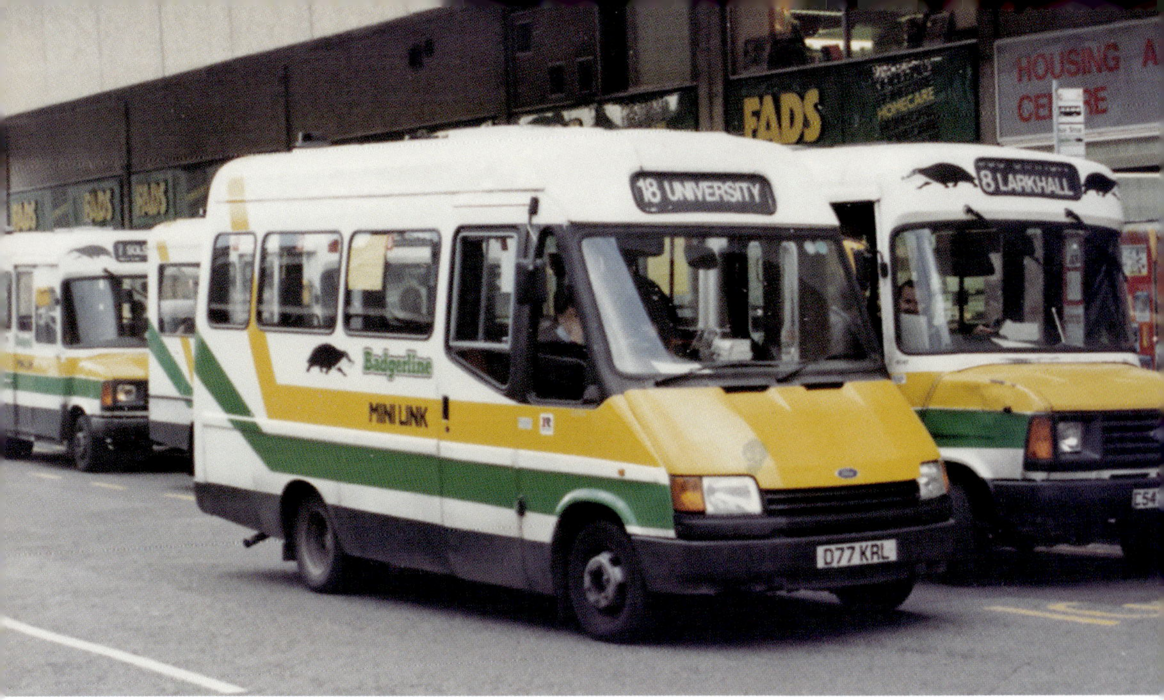

Badgerline, in common with a lot of other companies bought significant numbers of minibuses in its early years, mainly on the Ford Transit chassis. This later model Transit, 4594, D77 KRL, was fitted with a Dormobile body and lasted barely a year with its original operator, Western National, before moving to Badgerline at Bath. It is seen here, among older model Transits, at the bus station and bound for the university on 22 November 1989.

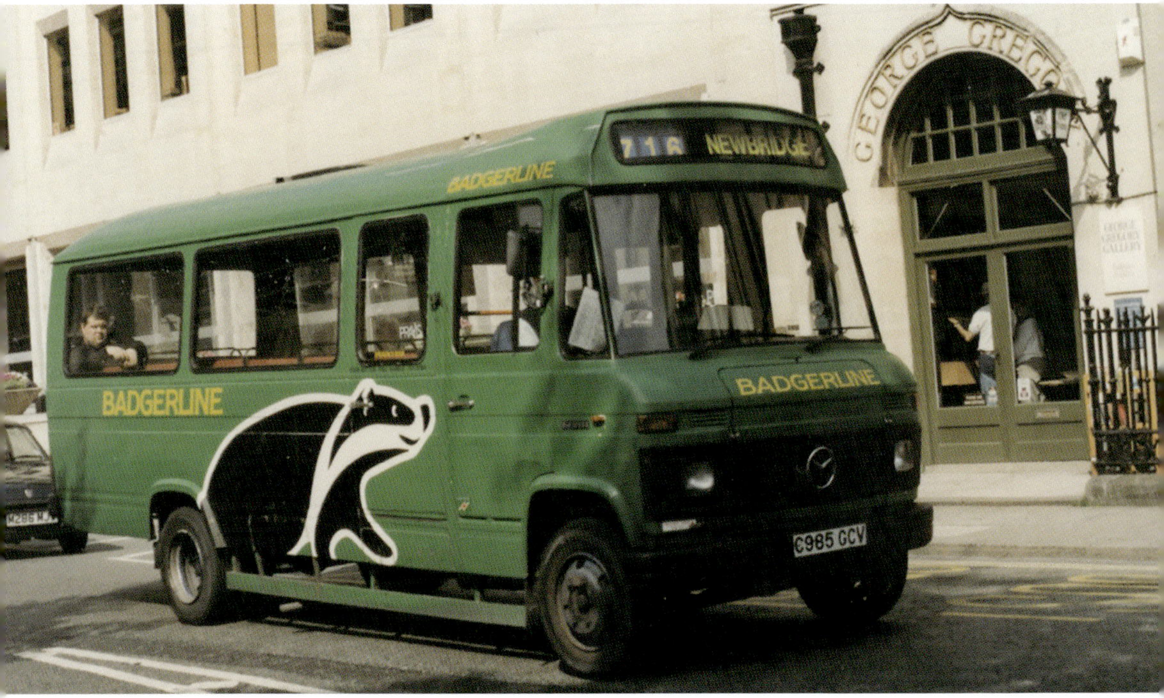

Badgerline also bought a number of Mercedes-Benz L608D and Iveco minibuses, both new and second-hand. 4711, C985 GCV, carrying a Robin Hood body, was delivered new to Western National in 1986, moving to Badgerline at Bath in 1994. It is seen in Manvers Street soon after heading for Newbridge.

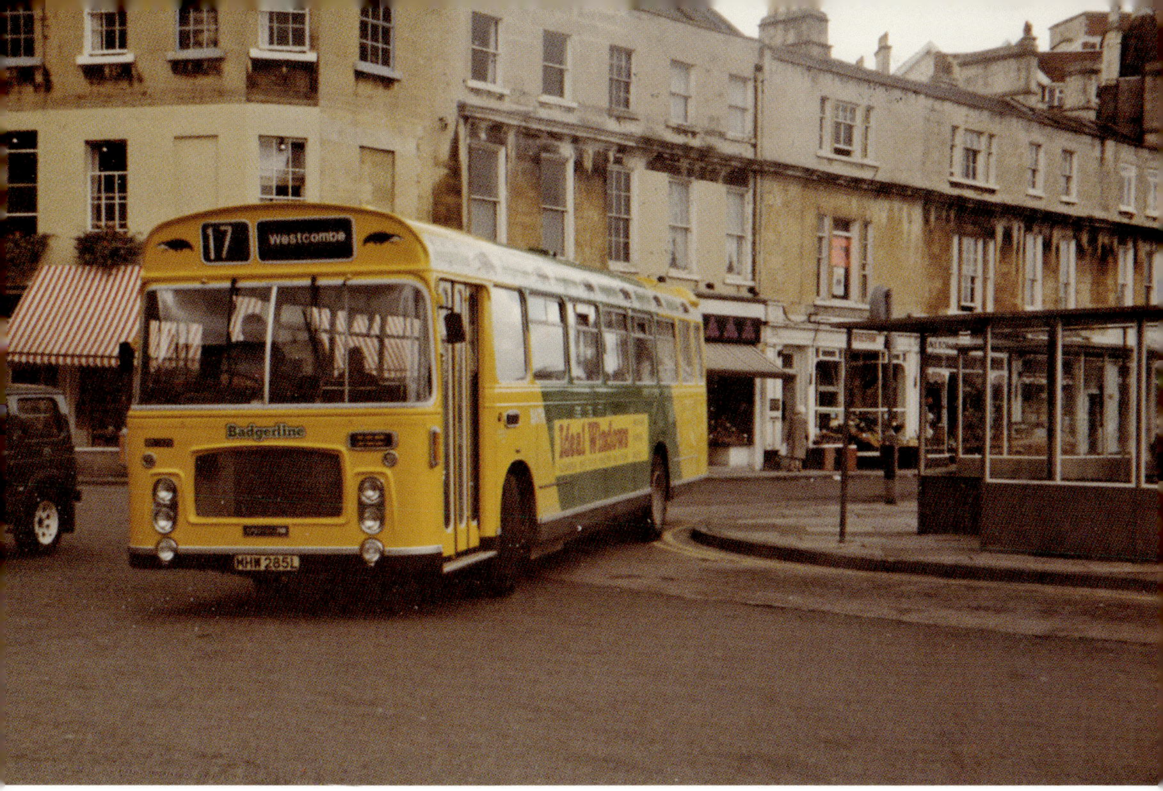

Bristol may have become Badgerline, but there are still Bristol REs to be seen, such as 1325, MHW 285L, seen at North Parade in 1985 working a city service to Westcombe.

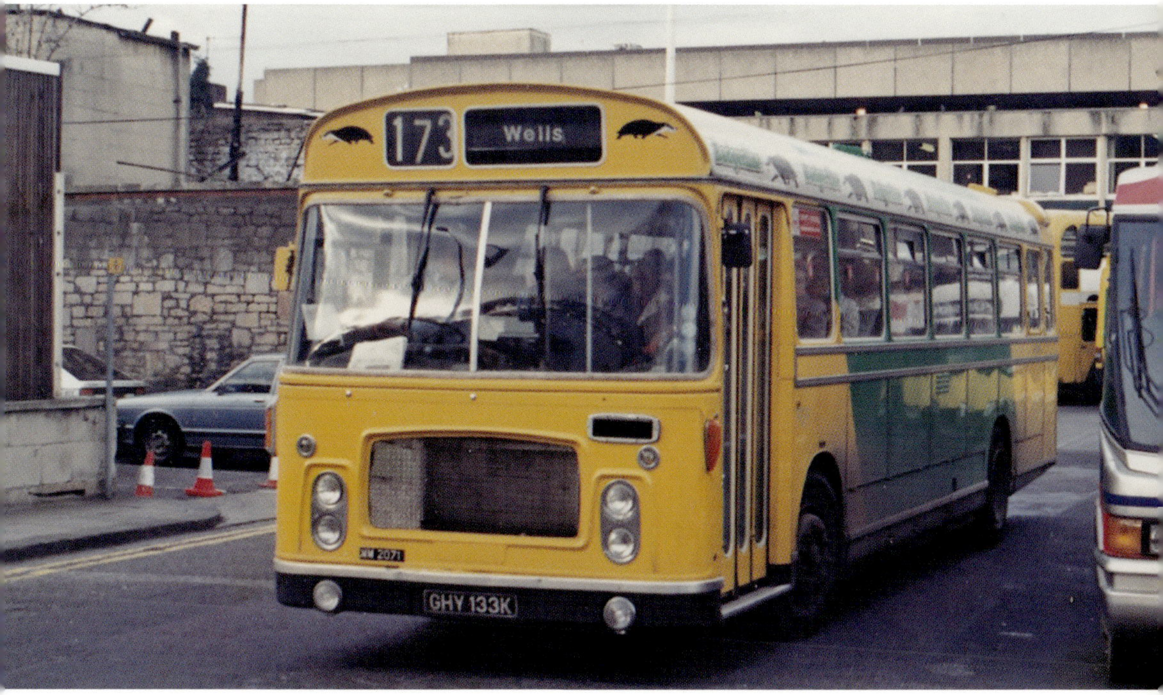

The main centre of Badgerline's Bristol RE operation was Wells. Here RELH 2071, GHY 133K is leaving the bus station for Wells, but wearing the allocation code for Weston-super-Mare depot.

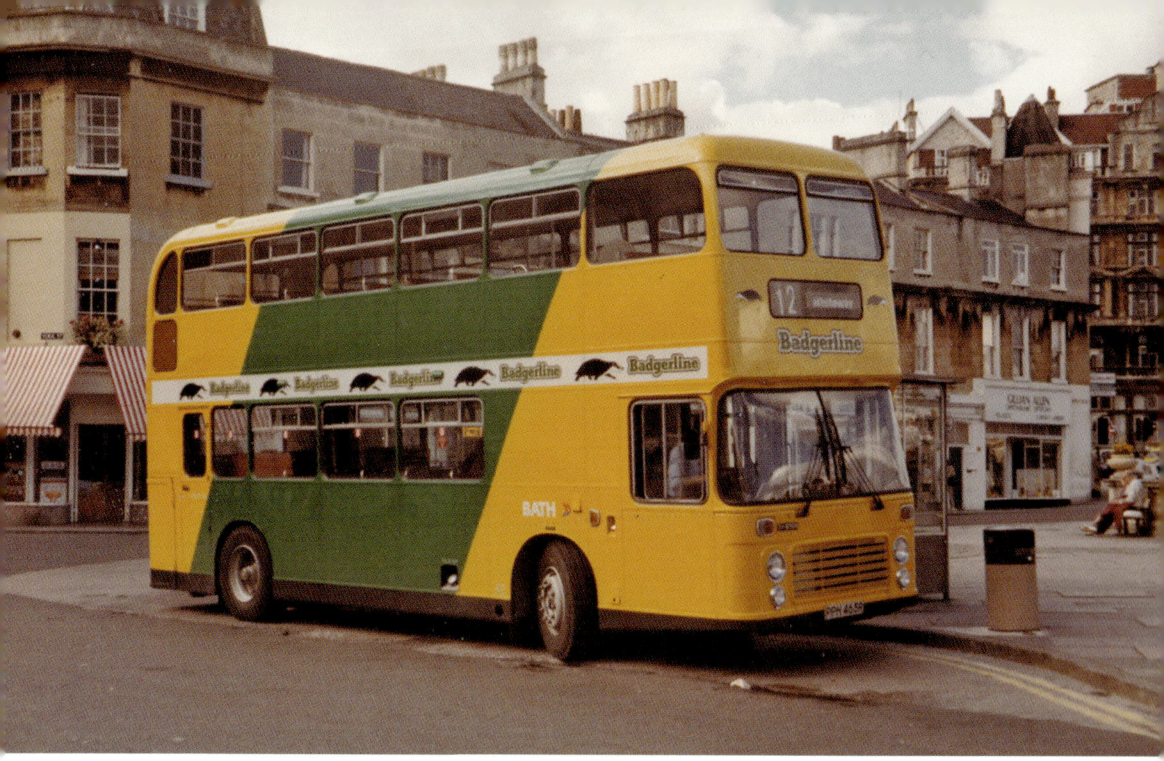

Here we see another one of the former London Country Bristol VRs, this time 6504, PPH 465R, at North Parade in about 1985, and still carrying the NBC logo on its Badgerline livery.

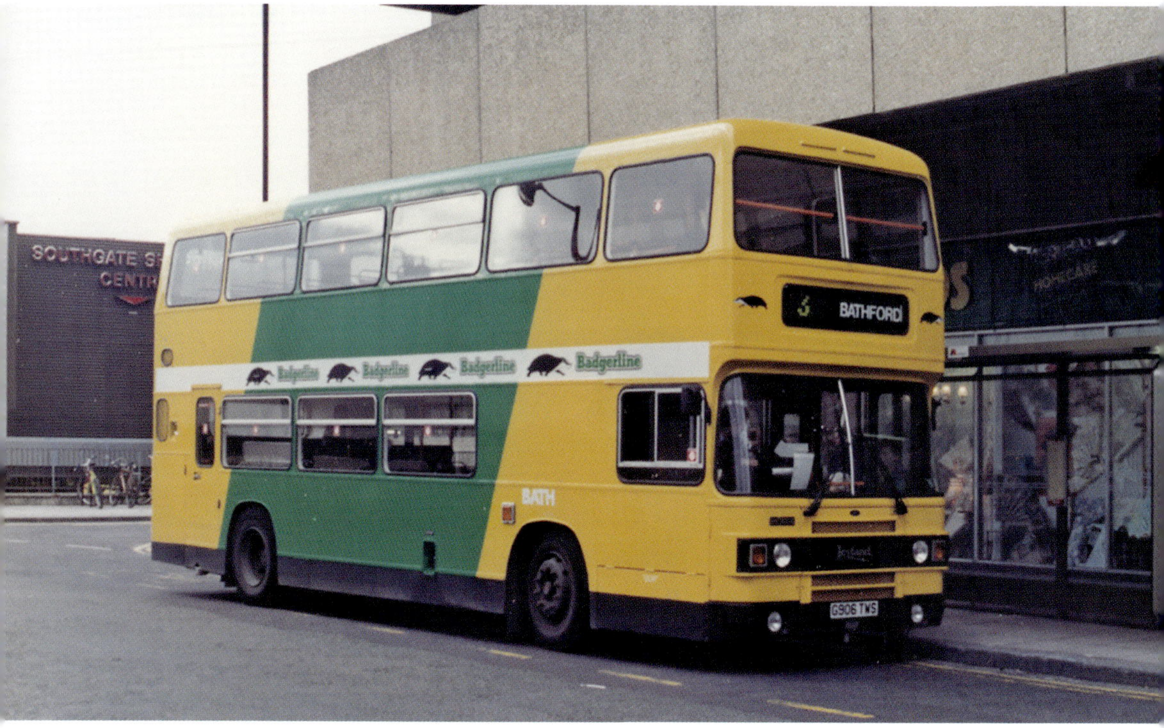

Badgerline bought ten all-Leyland Olympians 1989, all based at Bath depot. 9006, G906 TWS is seen at the bus station on 22 November 1989. The whole batch eventually found their way to Southern National.

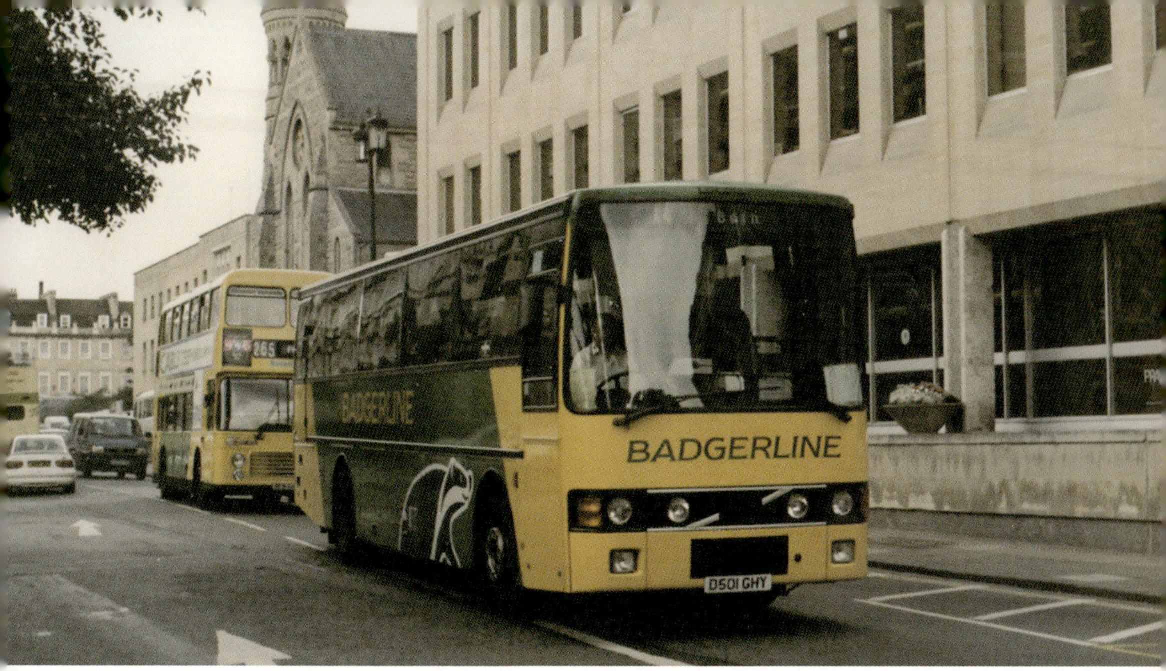

Badgerline took a large number of Volvo B10Ms during 1987 – including single- and double-deck buses and coaches. Here, Van Hool Alizee-bodied 2501, D501 GHY, is approaching the bus station on service X4 from Salisbury. Originally in National Express livery, it is now wearing bus livery.

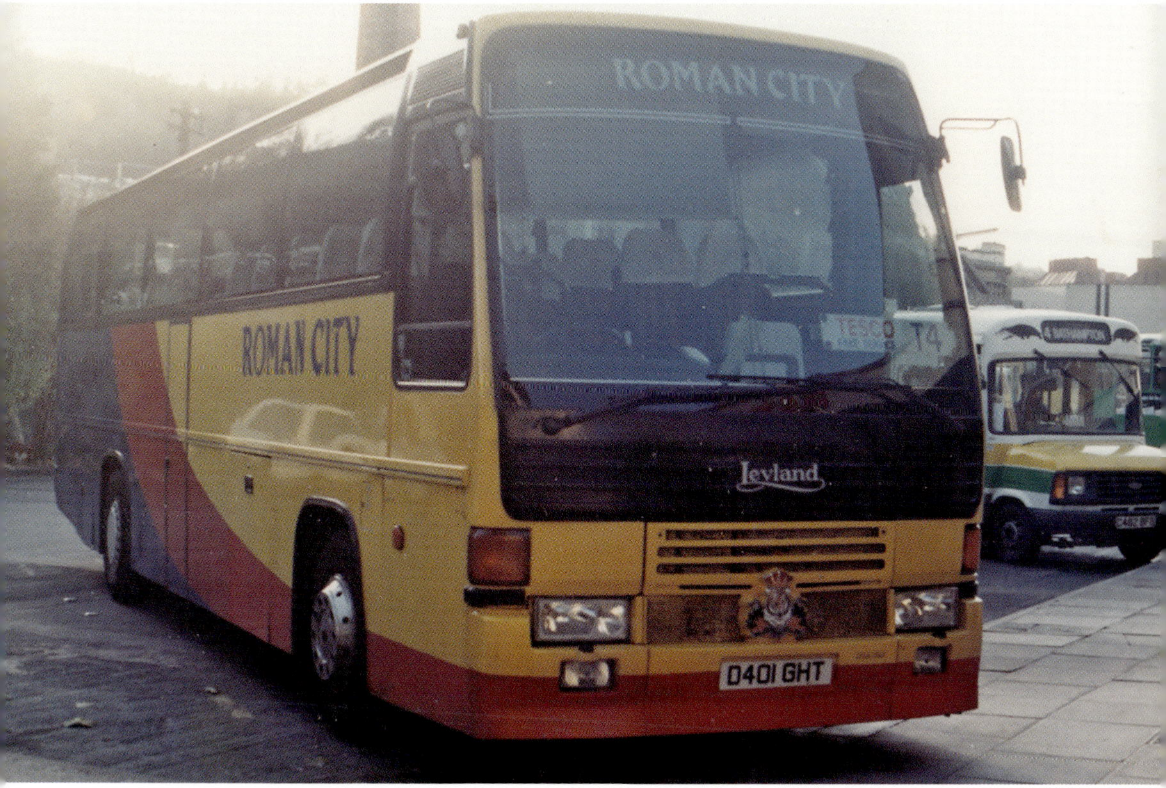

Roman City coaches was formed in 1948 and ceased trading in 1986, with the name passing to Badgerline. Seen in the bus station on 22 November 1989 is 2401, D401 GHT, a Leyland Royal Tiger with Leyland Doyen body.

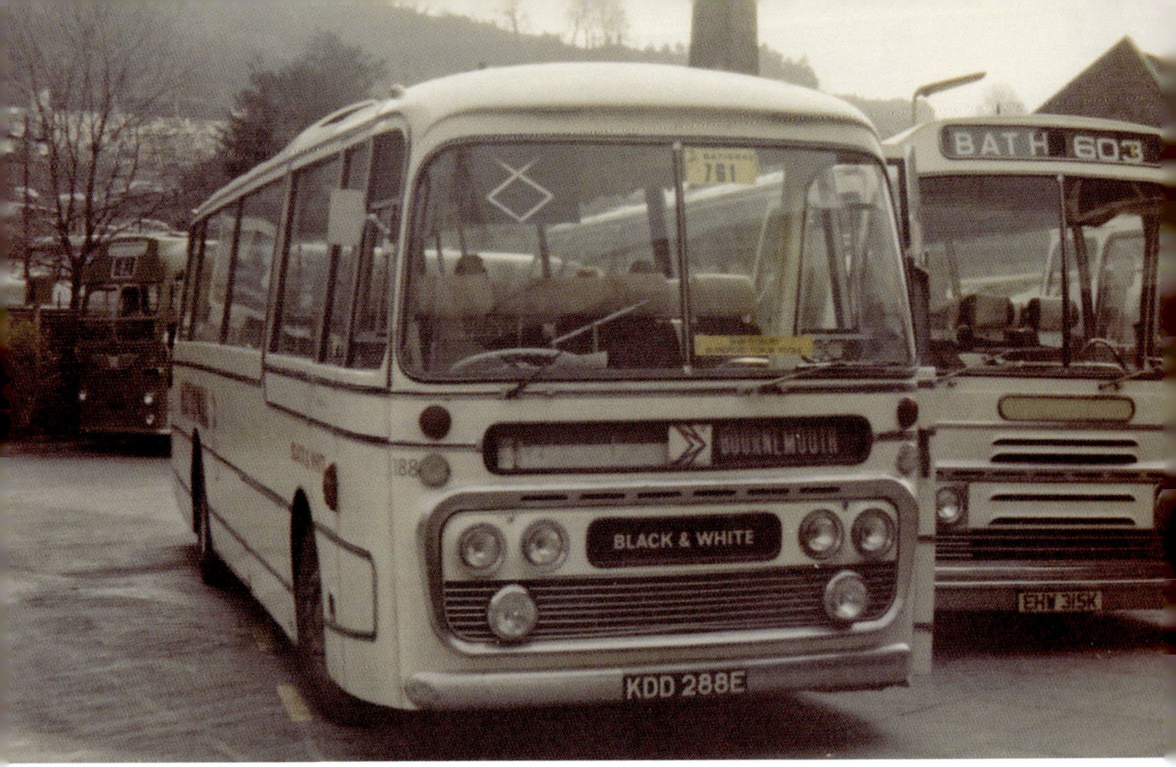

An earlier marque of Leyland is National Travel South West 188, KDD 288E, a Leopard PSU3 with a Plaxton Panorama body, new to Black & White Motorways and still showing evidence of its original owner. It was caught in Bath bus station during 1975, bound for Bournemouth on National Express 761.

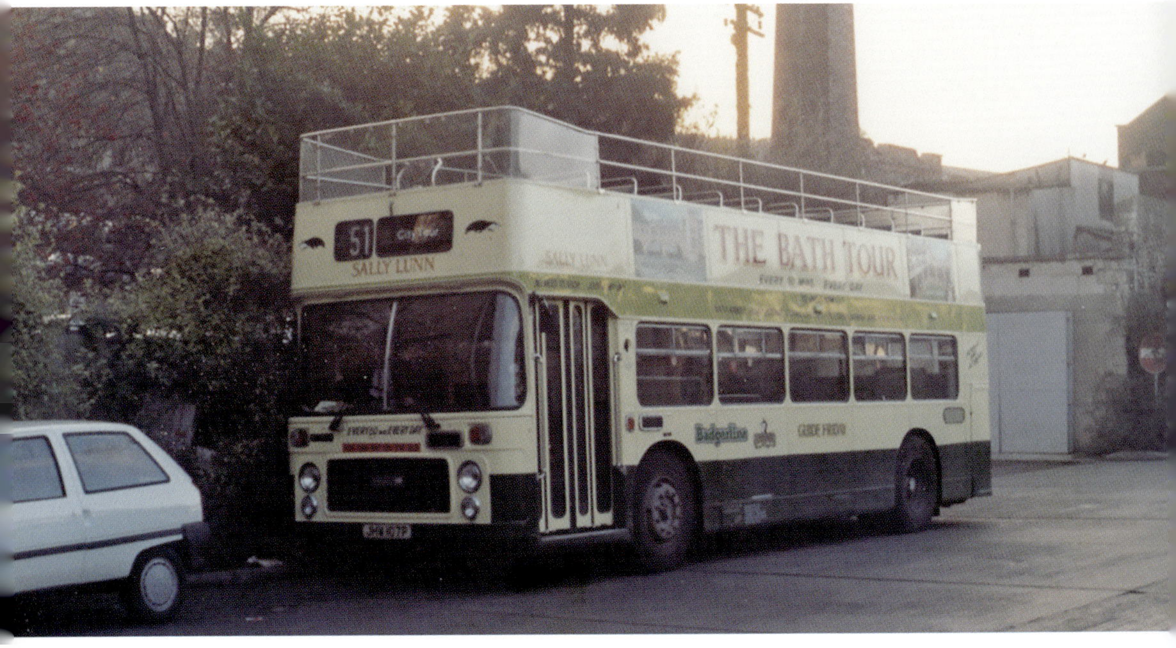

With its beauty and world heritage status Bath has long been a tourist destination, and open-top sight-seeing tours of the city are popular. Parked in the bus station on 22 November 1989 is Bristol VRT 8615, JHW 107P, in the livery of tour-provider Guide Friday. This vehicle was new as a dual-door bus for Bristol City services, numbered C5033 and converted to single-door open-top in 1985.

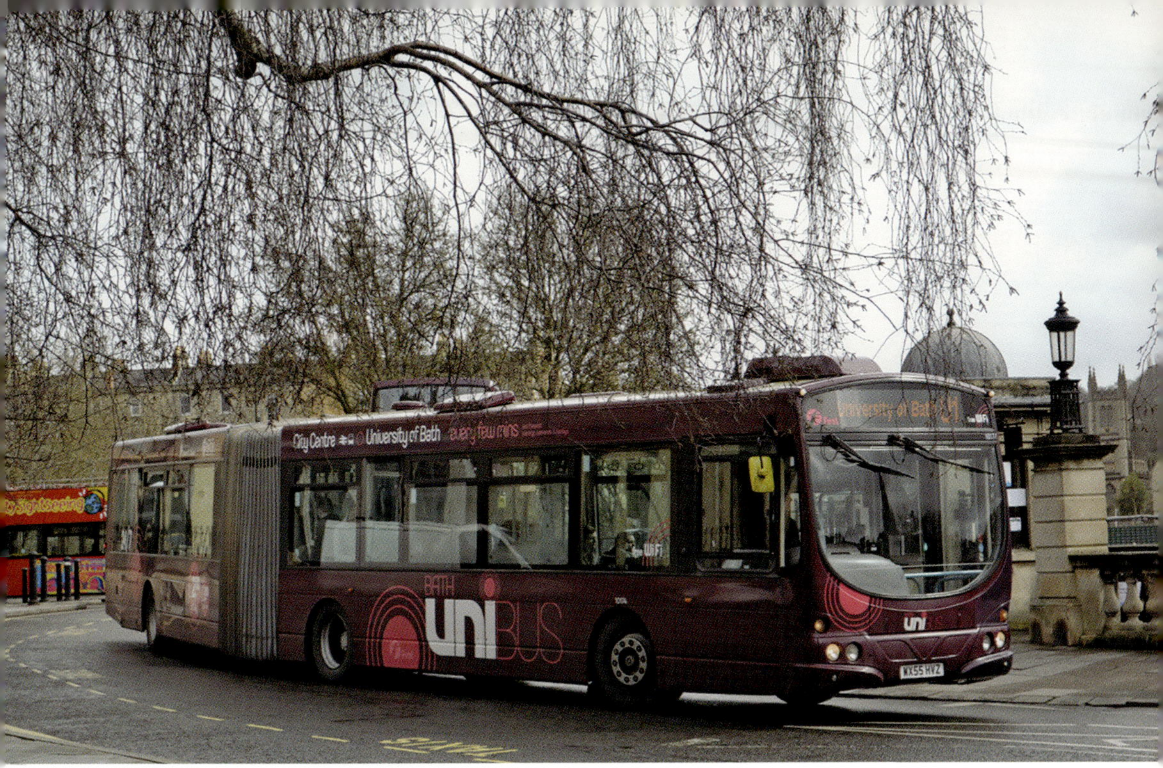

A complete contrast to the Ford Transit heading to the university pictured earlier, First West of England introduced articulated Wright-bodied Volvo B7LAs to the university services, branded as Unibus. 10174, WX55 HVZ, is seen here near the Bath Abbey on 3 April 2018.

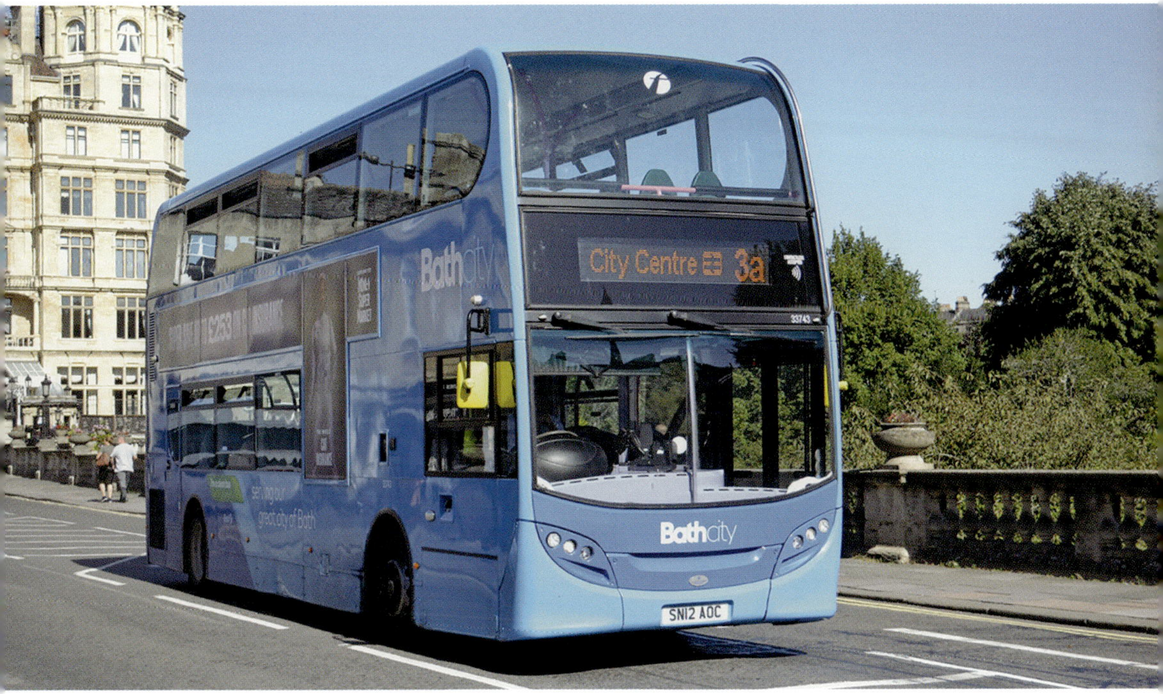

Caught at more-or-less the same spot in Pierrepont Street as Bristol Omnibus Bristol VRT 6501 is First West of England Enviro400 33743, SN12 AOC, wearing the Bath City livery on 21 September 2021.

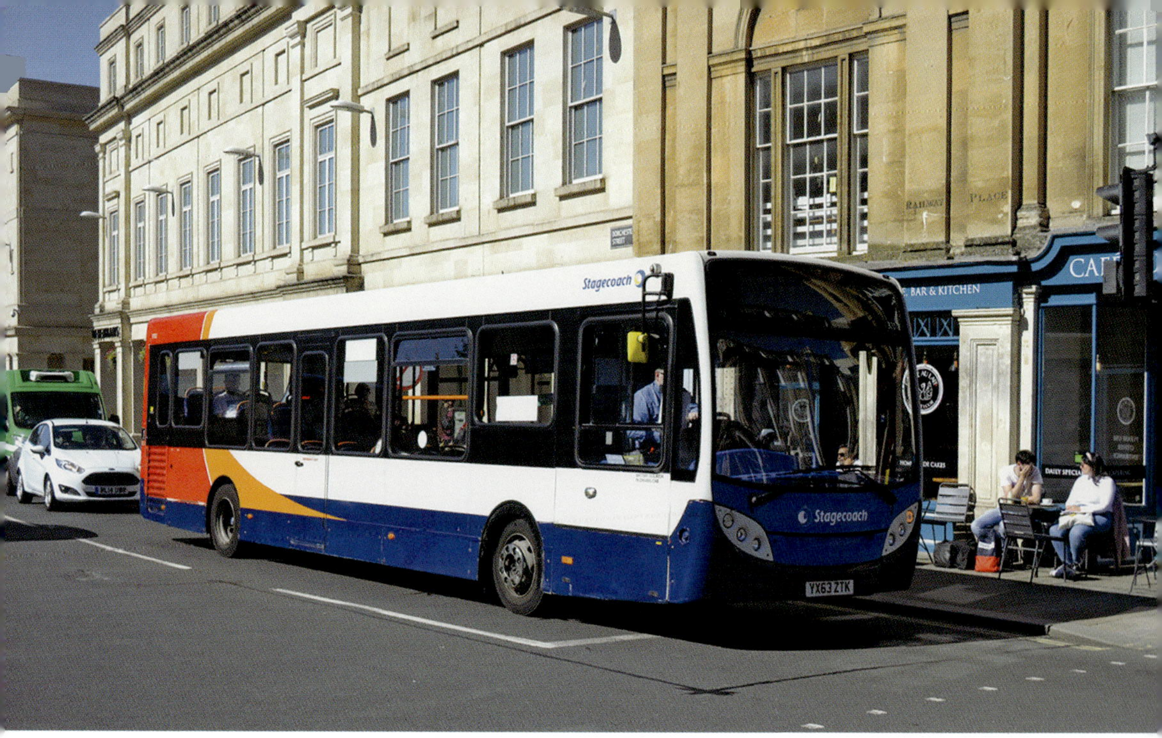

Stagecoach West work into Bath with service 620 from Old Sodbury. Seen on 21 September 2021 is Enviro200 37012, YX63 ZTK. Stagecoach are the third operator of this route, having taken it over from Wessex Bus, who in turn took it over from Cotswold Green.

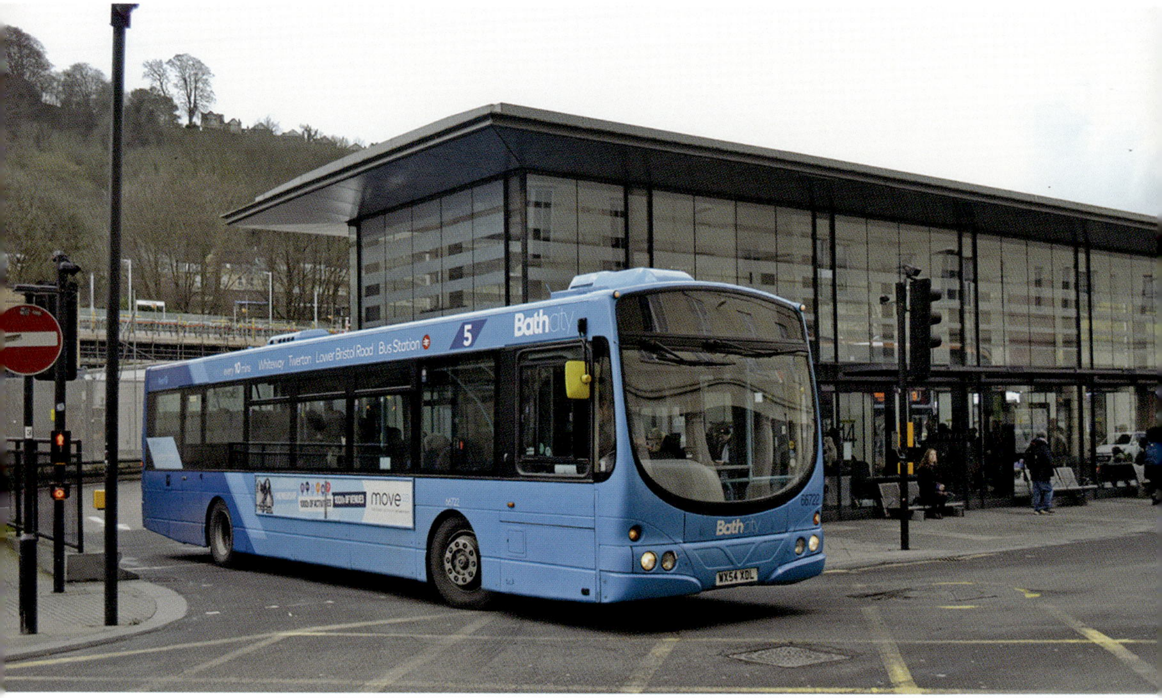

The bus station in Manvers Street closed in 2007 and the site has now been extensively developed. A new bus station was opened in nearby Dorchester Street in 2009. Seen leaving the new facility on 3 April 2018 is Wright Eclipse Urban-bodied Volvo B7RLE 66722, WX54 XDL, on city service 5 to Whiteway.

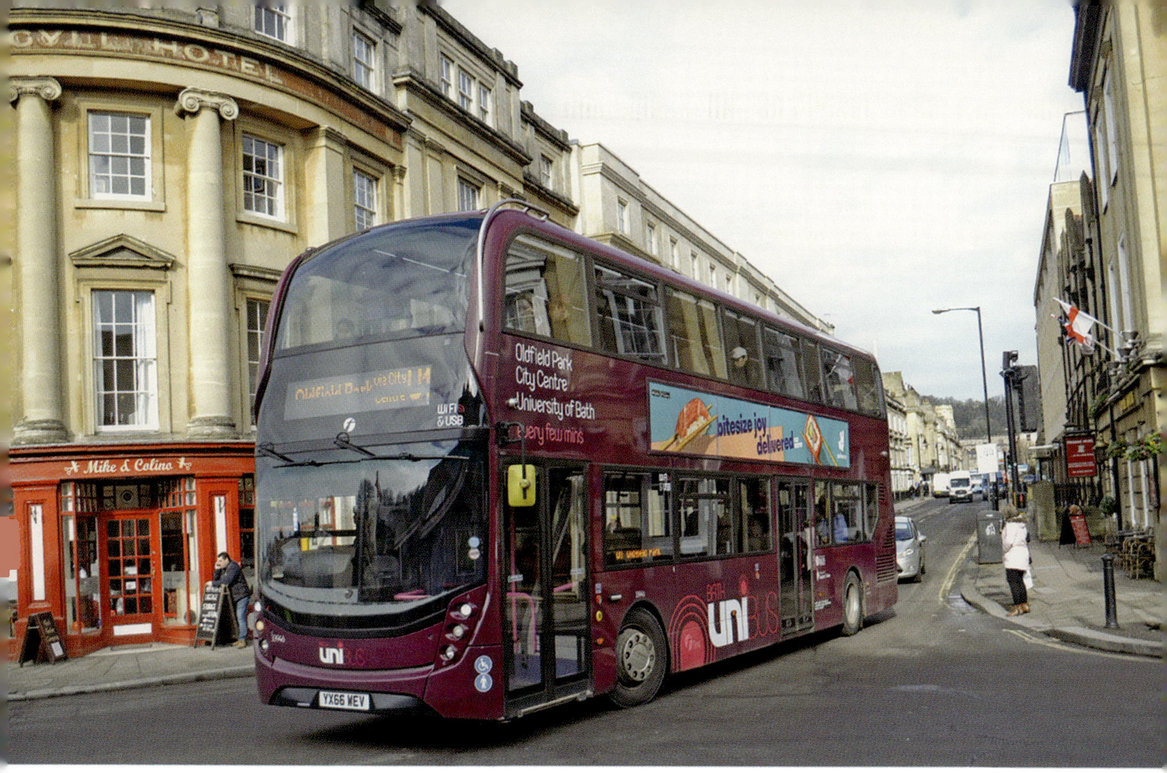

Turning out from Manvers Street into Dorchester Street, just by Bath Spa station, is First West of England 33946, YX66 MEV, an Enviro400MMC on university service U1 on 11 February 2019. These vehicles replaced the articulated Volvo B7LAs.

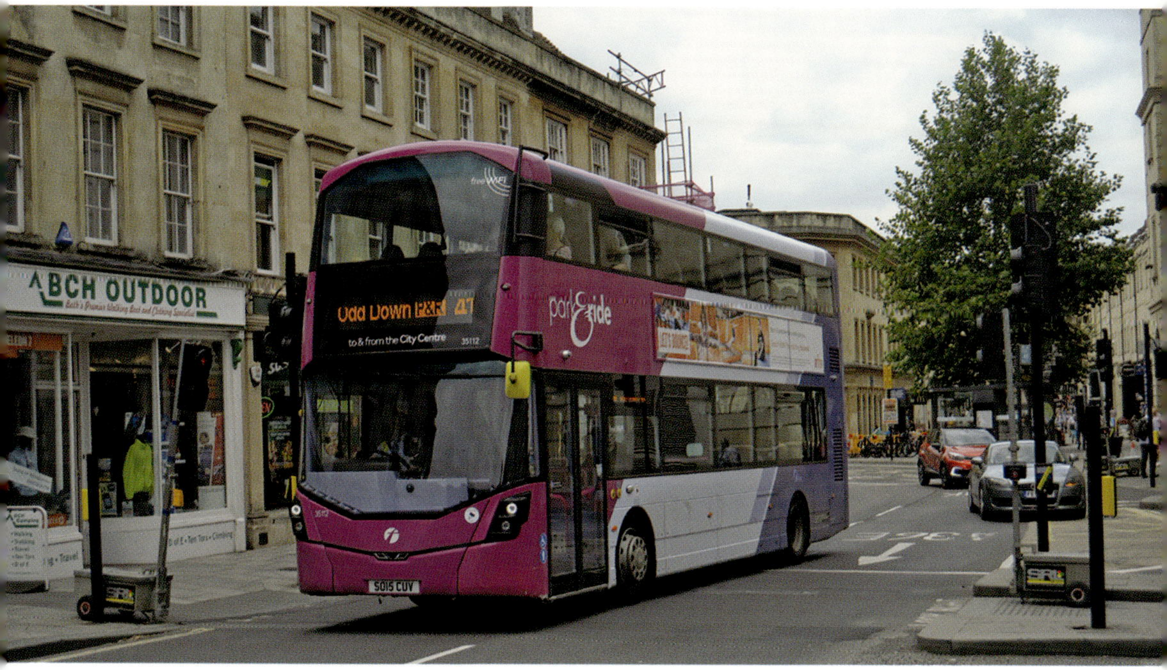

Seen in Southgate Street, Wright StreetDeck 35112, SO15 CUV is working the Park and Ride service 42 to Odd Down on 8 August 2019. Park and Ride vehicles now carry the blue Bath City livery and this vehicle has since been transferred away from Bath to Bristol's Hengrove depot.

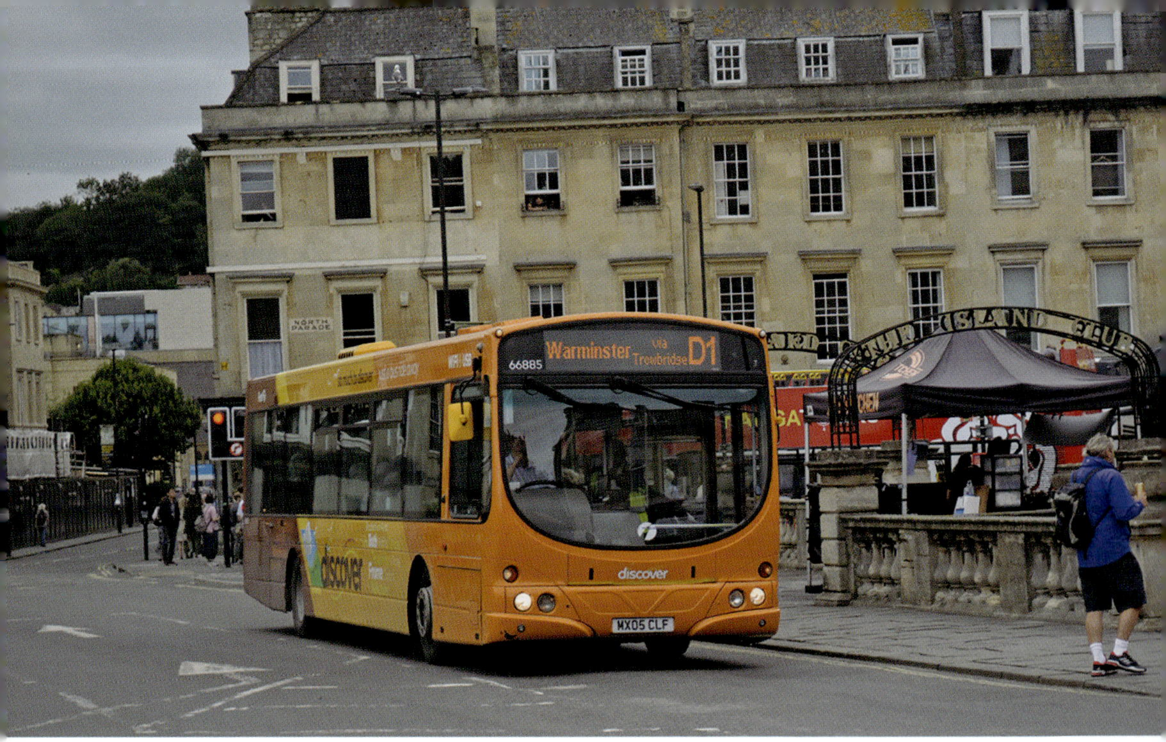

In 2018 First West of England branded their services towards Frome, Melksham, Warminster and Salisbury as Discover and repainted a number of single-deckers into this special livery. Caught at North Parade on 8 August 2019, Volvo B7RLE with Wright Eclipse Urban body 66885, MX05 CLF is seen bound for Warminster.

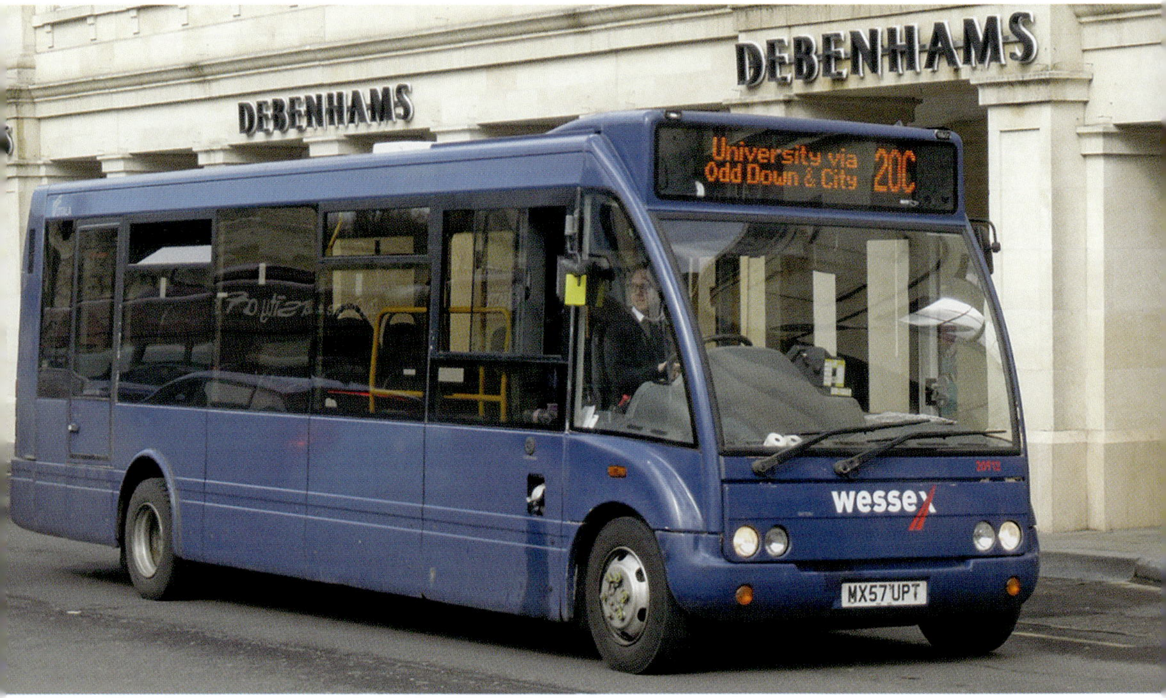

As well as First West of England, Wessex Bus, part of Rotala, operated a number of services across both Bristol and Bath until they ceased operations at the end of 2018. Seen in Dorchester Street on 3 April 2018 is Optare Solo 20912, MX57 UPT.

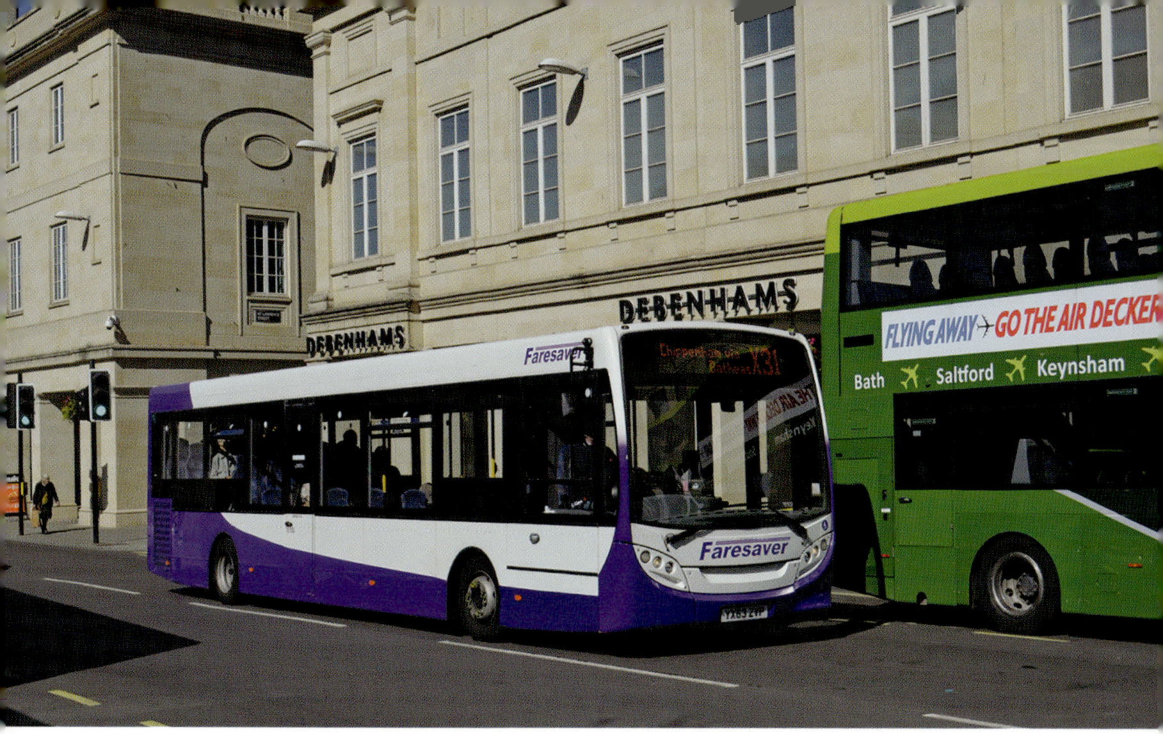

First West of England gave up a number of their services into Wiltshire, and local operator Faresaver of Chippenham took them over. Enviro200 YX63 ZVP, bought from Weavaway of Newbury, is seen here on 20 September 2021 on service X31 to Chippenham.

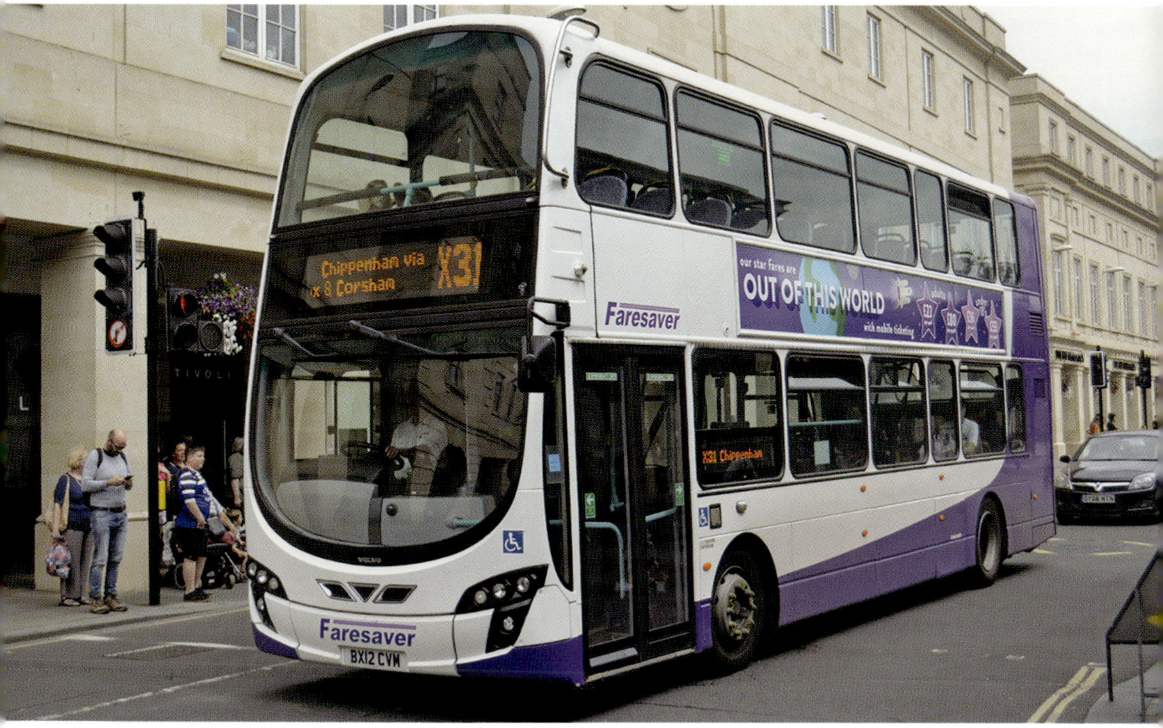

Double-deckers also feature in the Faresaver fleet. Seen on 8 August 2019, BX12 CVM is a former First London Volvo B9TL with Wright Eclipse Gemini 2 body seen at the bus station while working the X31 Chippenham service.

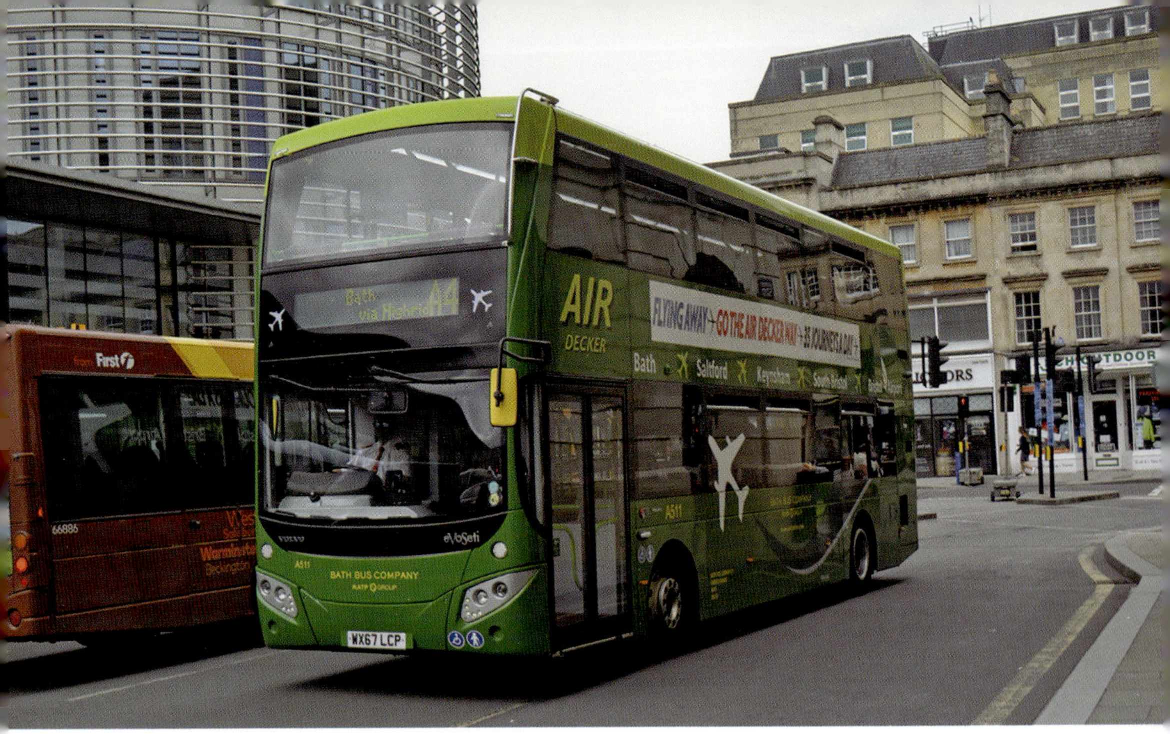

Bath also now has a service direct to Bristol Airport, operated by the Bath Bus Company, part of the RATP group. Their A511, WX67 LCP, a Volvo B5TL with Egyptian-built MCV body is seen in Dorchester Street on 20 September 2021.

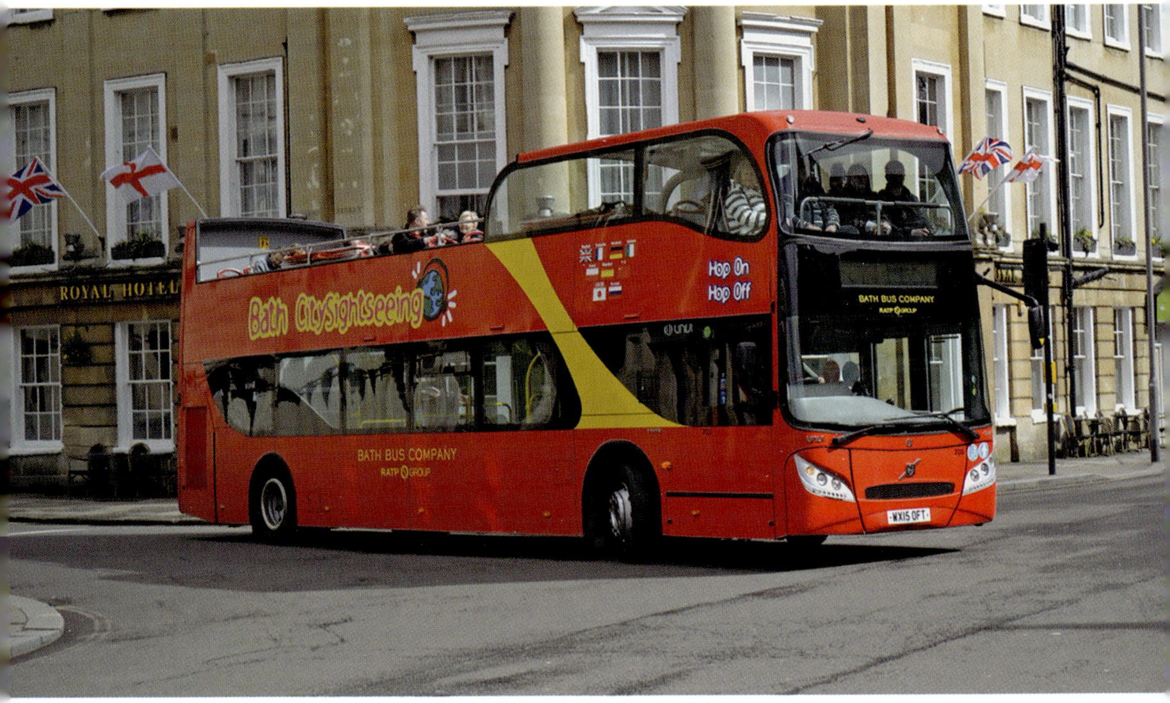

The Bath Bus Company also operate sight-seeing tours around the city. Contrasting with Bristol VRT 8615, Volvo B5TL 703, WX15 OFT, with Spanish-built UNVI Urbis bodywork, is seen turning onto Dorchester Street on 3 April 2018.

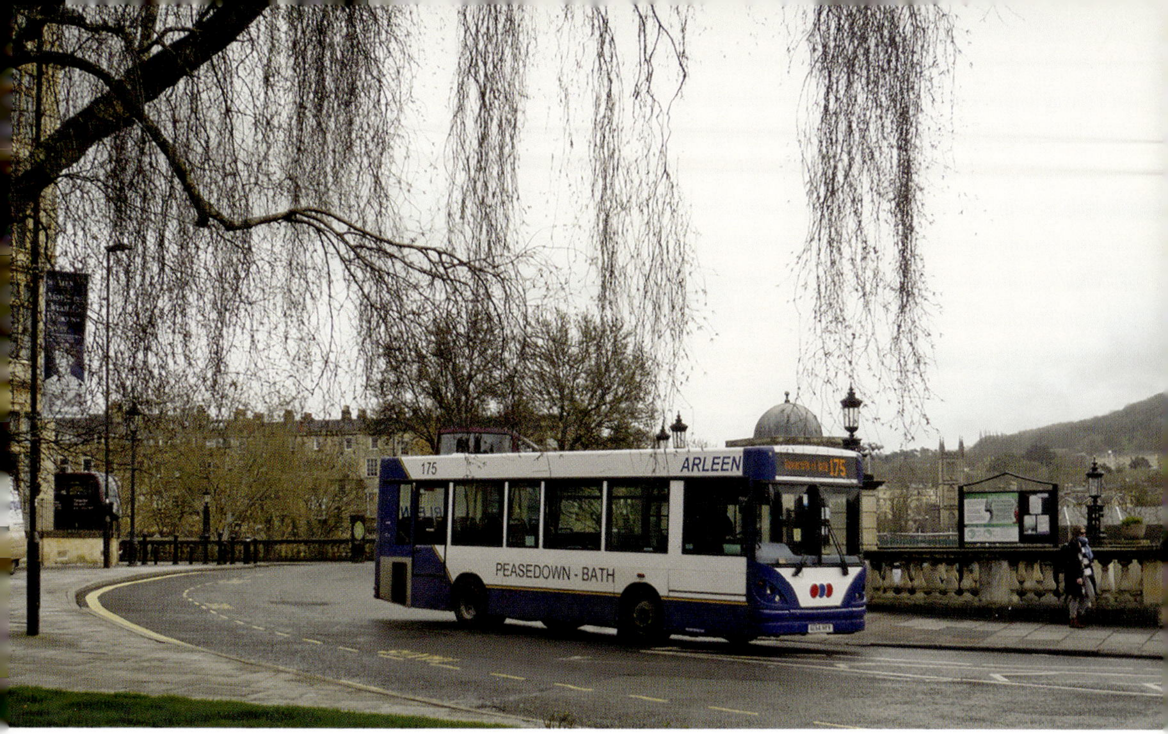

Arleen Coaches of Peasedown St John was founded in 1965 and started operation of service 175 into Bath from Peasedown in 2018. In my schooldays in Wells, the 175 was the Wells to Bath service. Arleen purchased this much-travelled Dennis Dart SLF with Caetano Nimbus body, AE54 HYV, to work the route. It is seen on 3 April 2018 near Bath Abbey.

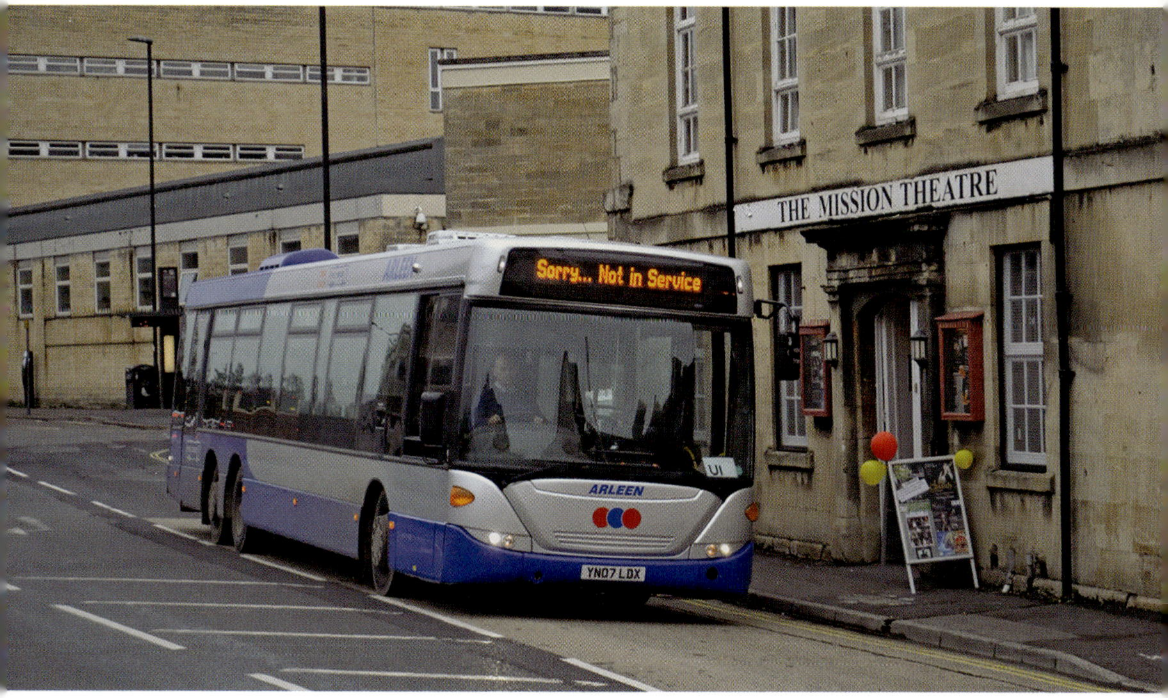

Arleen bought this three-axle Scania, YN07 LDX, from DRM of Bromyard, new to Nottingham City Transport, in 2019 to replace the Dart. It is seen laying over in Corn Street on 1 November 2019.

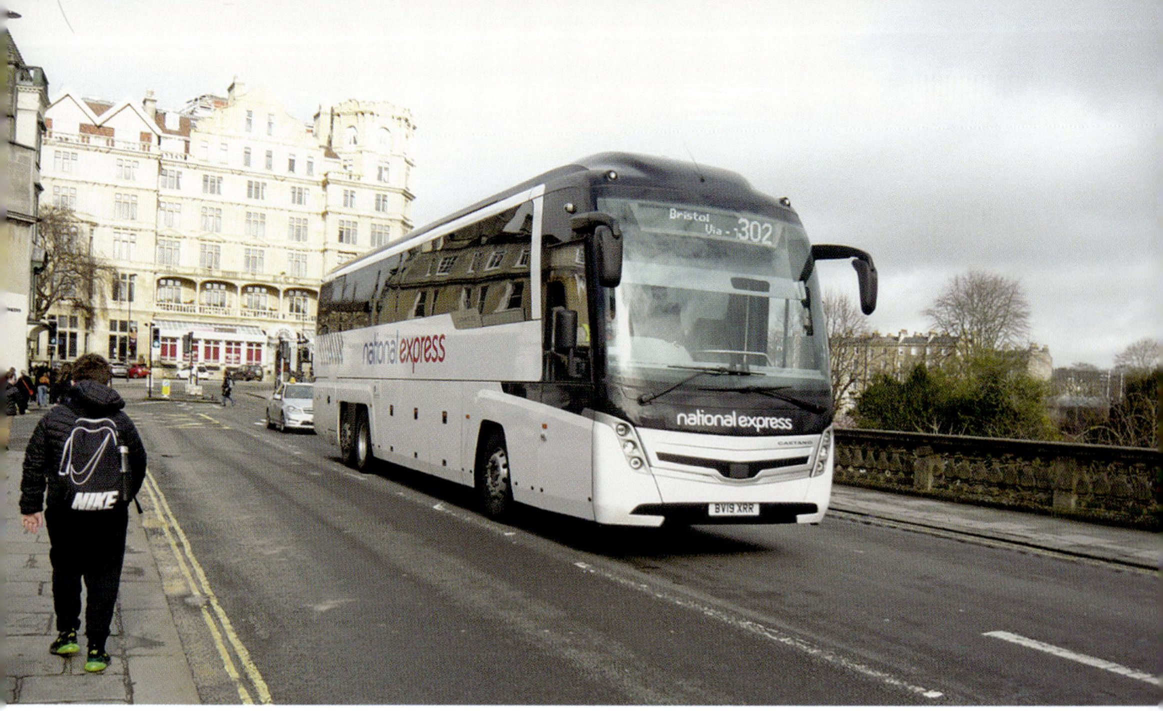

A contrast to the former-Black & White Leyland Leopard illustrated earlier in this book is a modern National Express coach from Edwards of Avonmouth, BV19 XRR, a Caetano Levante 3-bodied Scania, seen in Pierrepont Street on 23 February 2020 on National Express 302 to Bristol from Northampton.

WELLS

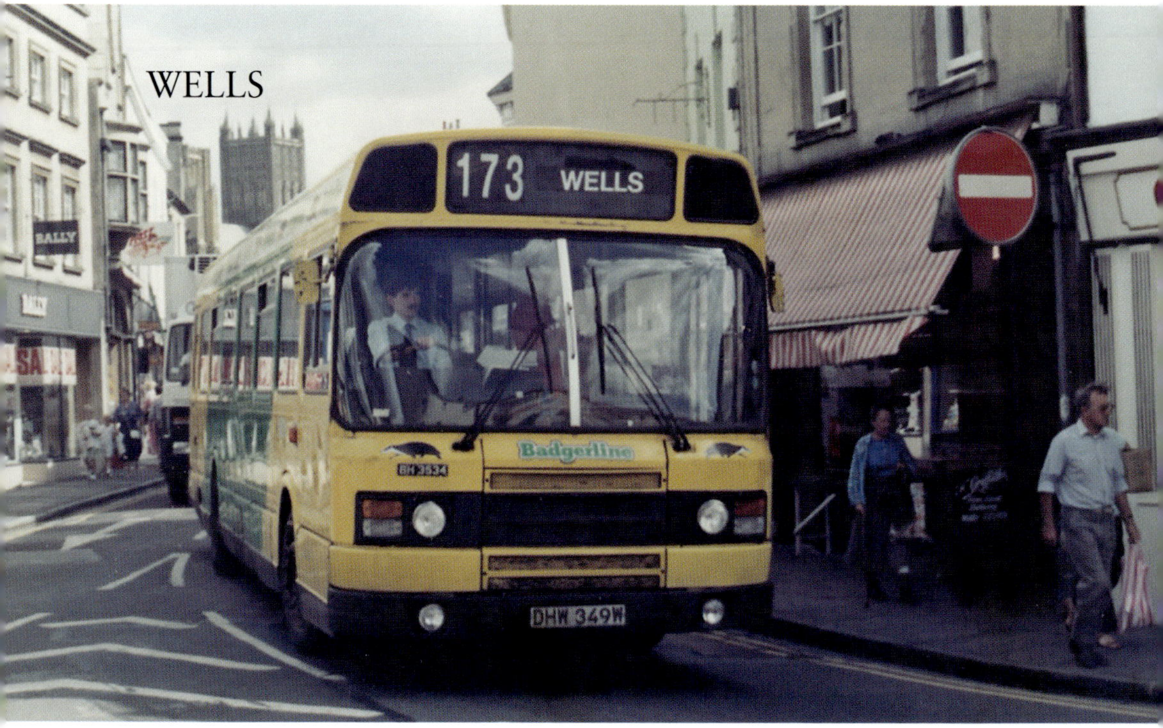

With the central tower of the magnificent thirteenth-century cathedral in the background, Badgerline Leyland National 2 3534, DHW 349W, is in Wells High Street, arriving from Bath.

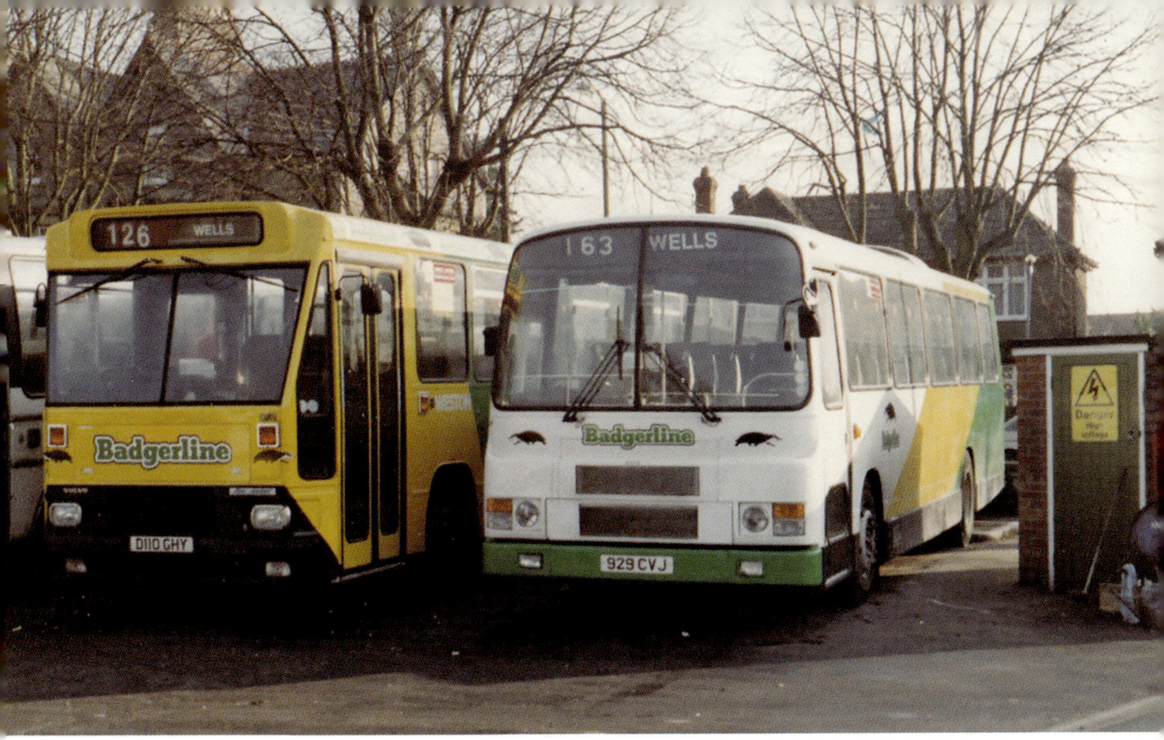

Badgerline 2079, 929 CVJ, is a vehicle with an interesting history. New to Tillings Transport in 1973 as VHK 177L, it was rebodied in 1981 with this prototype ECW B51 body. It was the only RE to carry this style of body, this style being mostly found on Leyland Leopards and Leyland Tigers. Transferred to Badgerline in 1985, it naturally gravitated to that centre of Bristol RE operation, Wells, where it is seen resting in the depot on 27 October 1988.

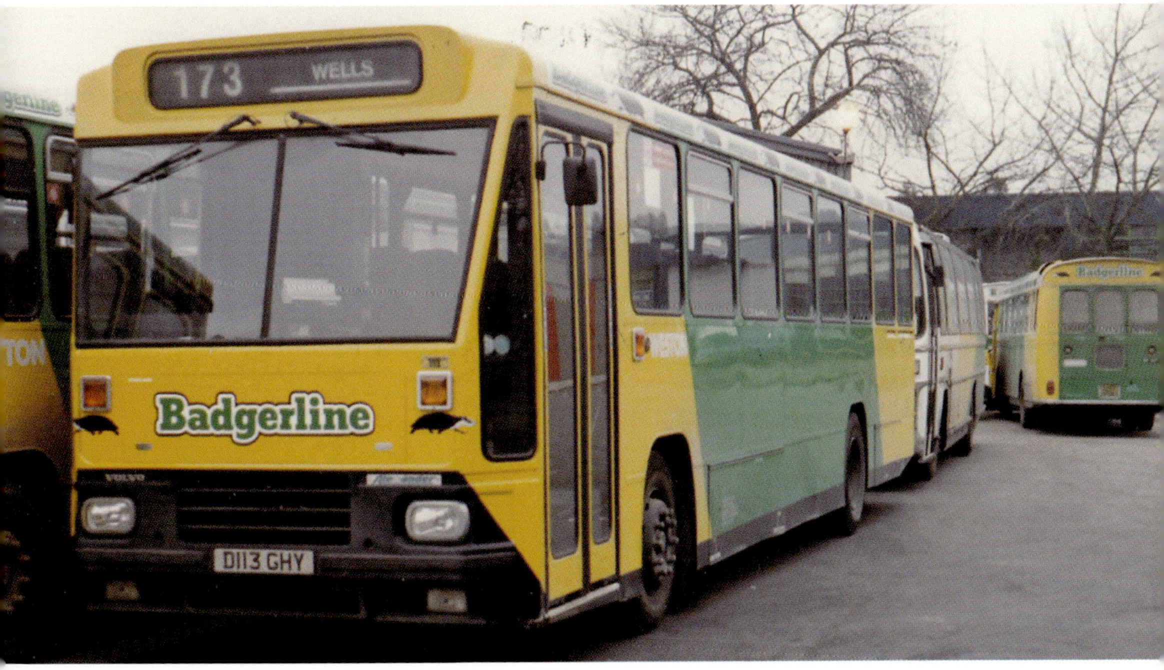

Parked in Wells depot on 1 January 1989 is Badgerline 113, D113 GHY, a Volvo B10M with angular Alexander P-type body. It was one of a large number of Volvo single-deckers and double-deckers with Alexander bodies and coaches with Van Hool bodies delivered around 1987.

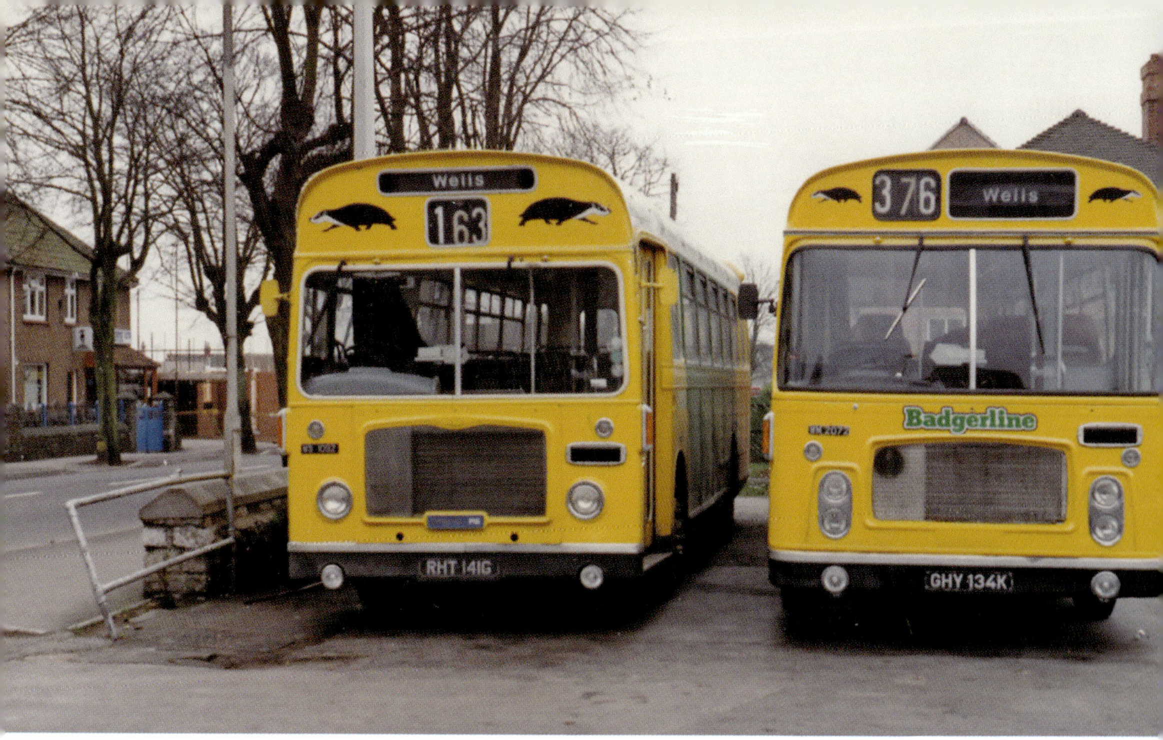

Also on 1 January 1989 we see Bristol RELL 1092, RHT 141G and Bristol RELH 2072, GHY 134K, previously illustrated in NBC green. As previously mentioned, Wells was very much the centre of Badgerline Bristol RE operation, and these vehicles remaining in front-line service for a quite a long time. This depot is one of the few in the country to still be on its original site, having opened in Priory Road a hundred years ago, in 1922.

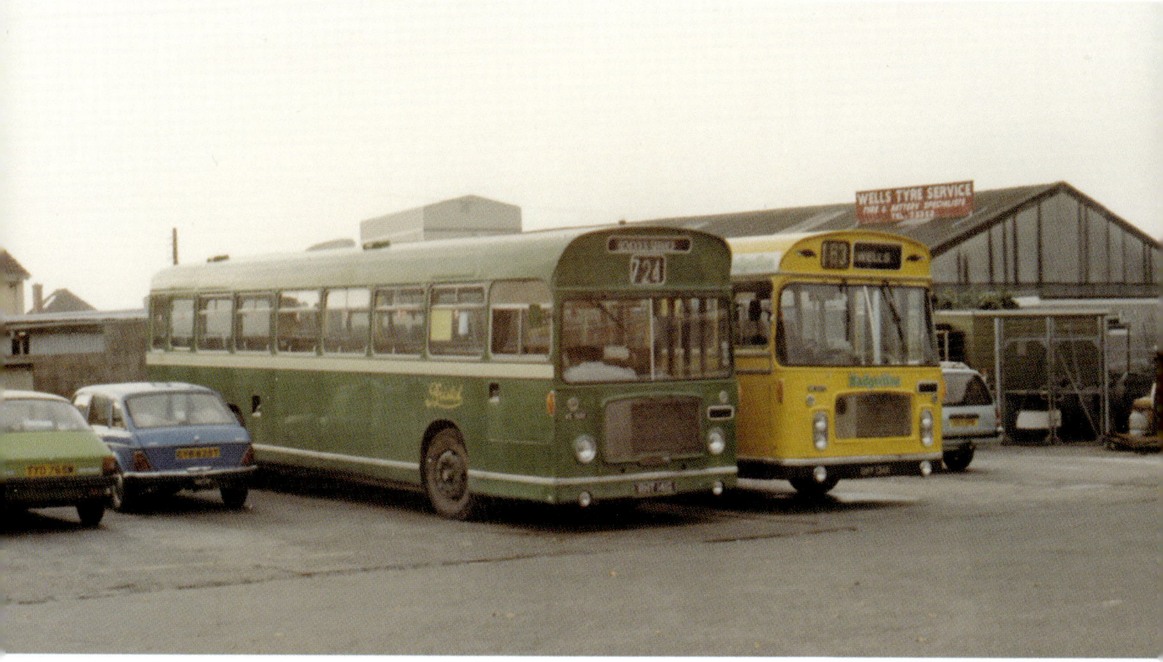

During 1989, 1092 was repainted into its original Tilling Green livery. It is seen here parked in Wells depot on 20 October 1990 next to an RELH. This vehicle subsequently passed to that keen user of Bristol REs, Northern Bus, and was sadly scrapped after suffering accident damage.

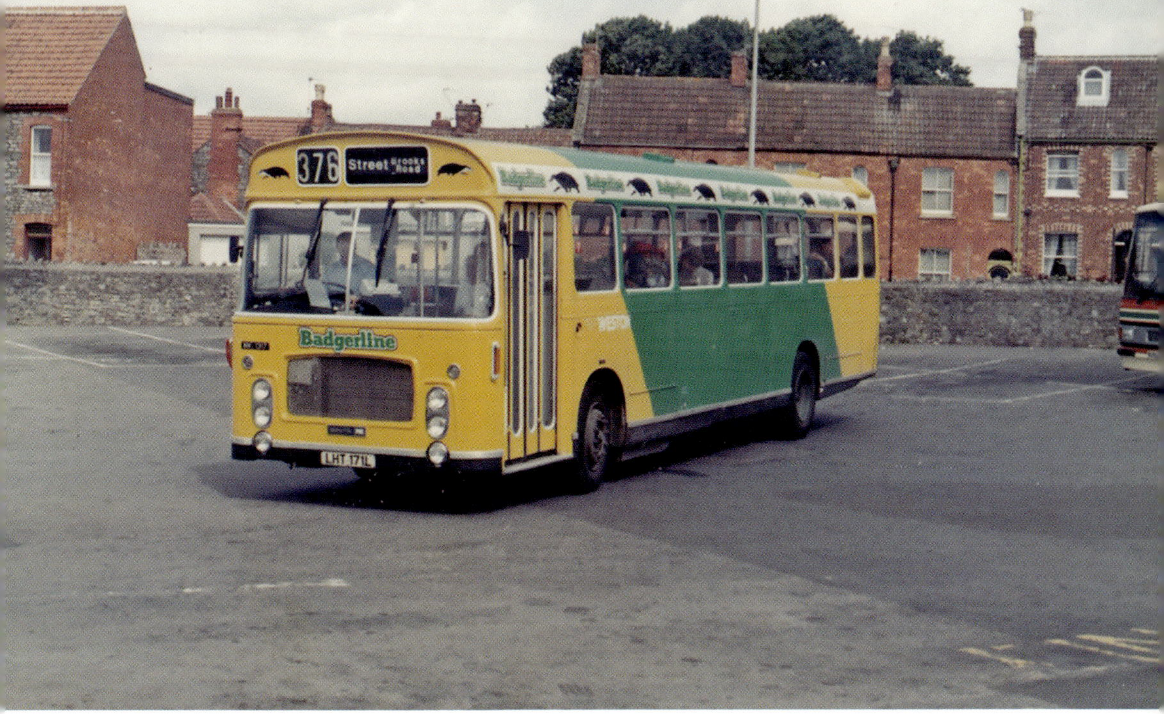

Departing Wells bus station on 16 August 1989 is Bristol RELL1317, LHT 171L, bound for Bristol on service 376. Bristol REs first took over this service in 1968. Happily, this vehicle is now preserved.

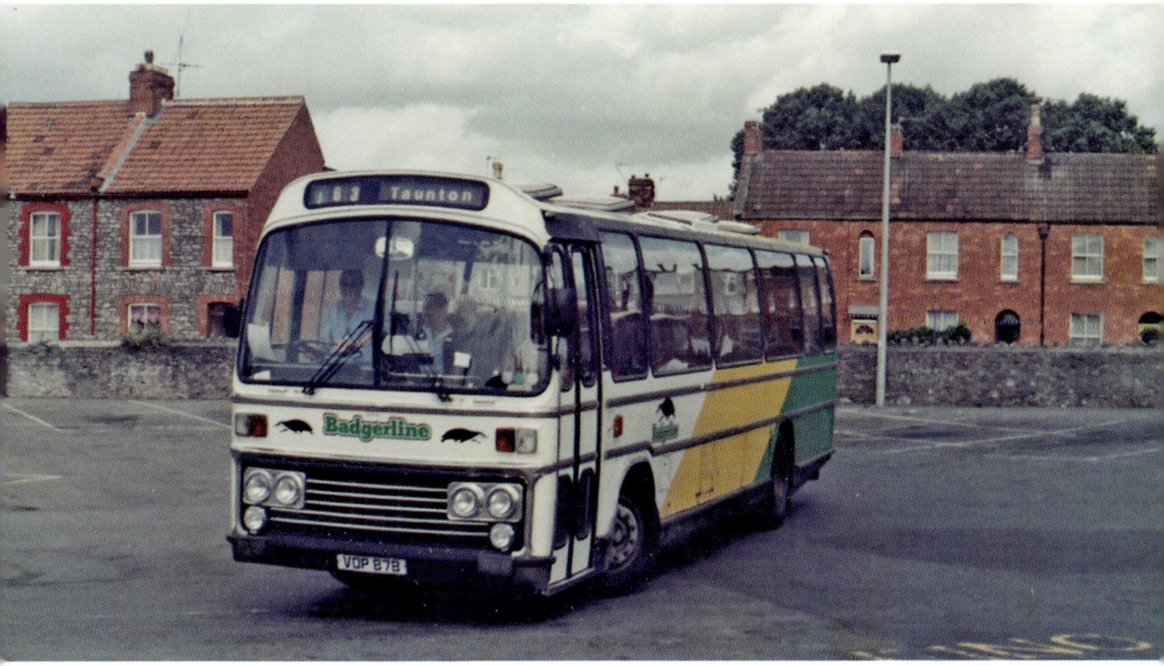

Badgerline 2099, VOP 878, was new as ROU 347S. A Leyland Leopard with Plaxton Supreme Express body it is seen on 16 August 1989 leaving Wells for Taunton on service 163. When I was at school in Wells the 163 was the Wells to Shepton Mallet service, and often worked with the two Bristol FLFs then based in Wells.

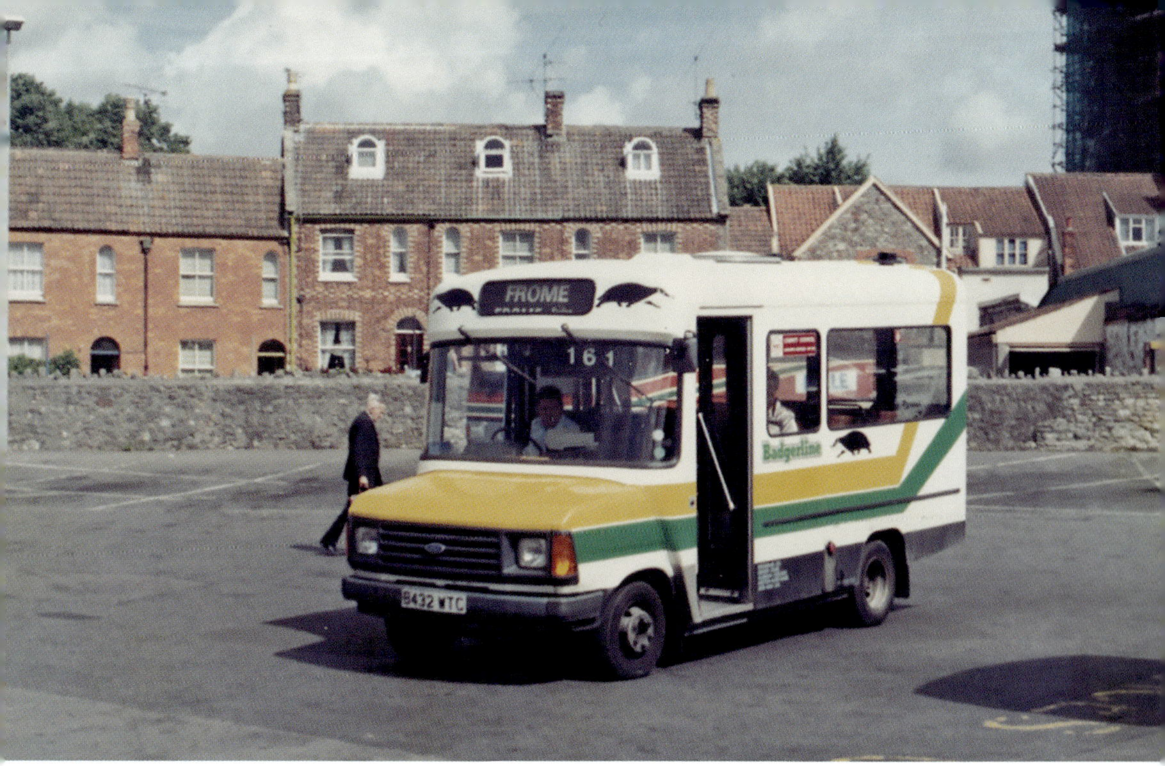

Like many other operators, Badgerline bought a large number of minibuses in the early 1980s; these vehicles were sometimes derided as 'bread vans'. Dormobile-bodied Ford Transit 4432, B432 WTC, is seen here on 16 August 1989 leaving Wells for Frome.

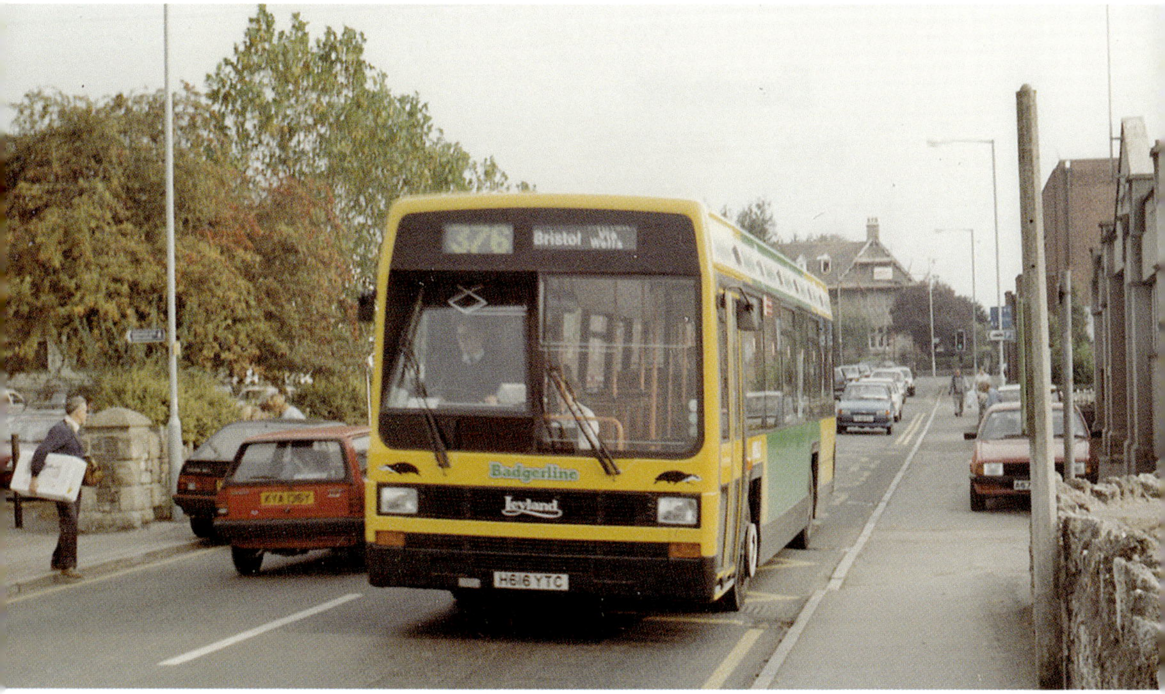

20 October 1990 found two-month-old Leyland Lynx 3616, H616 YTC, operating the 376. Badgerline only ever took this one batch of Leyland Lynxes.

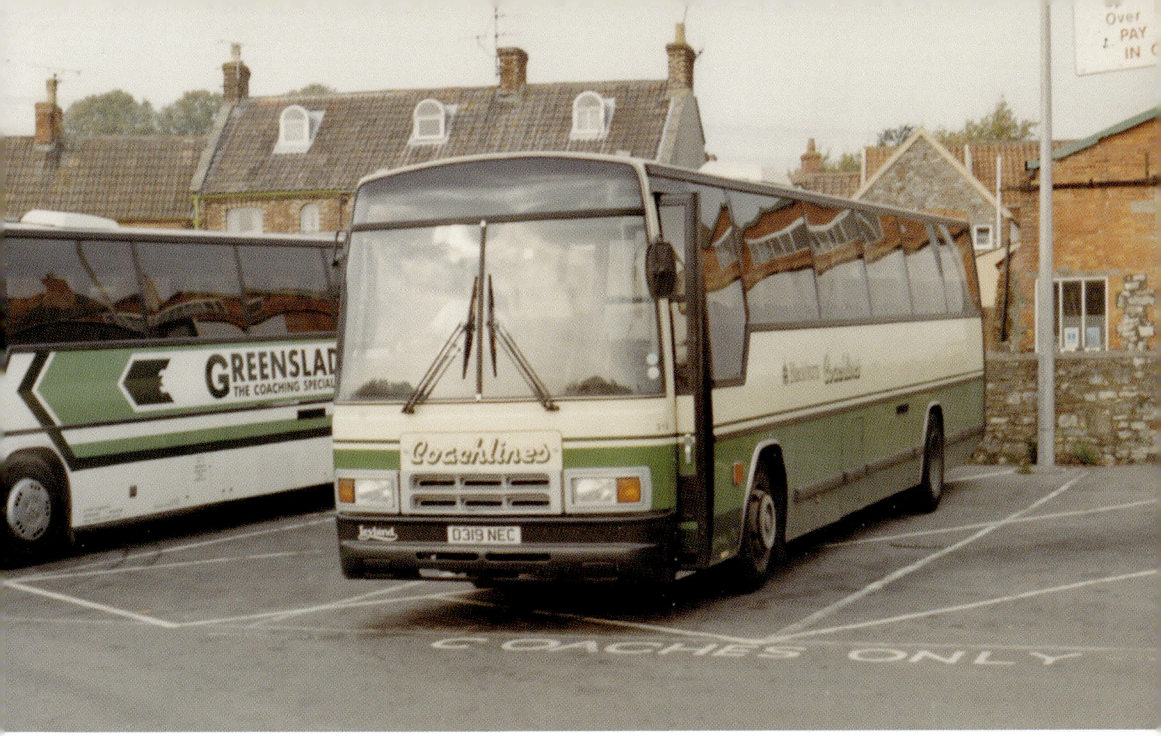

Wells, with it's amazing Gothic cathedral, historic Bishop's Palace and Vicar's Close, dating from the mid-fourteenth century and claimed to be the oldest purely inhabited street in Europe, has long been a popular tourist destination. Visiting from the north-west on 20 October 1990 was Blackburn Corporation's Leyland Tiger 319, D319 NEC, fitted with Plaxton Paramount 3200 III body.

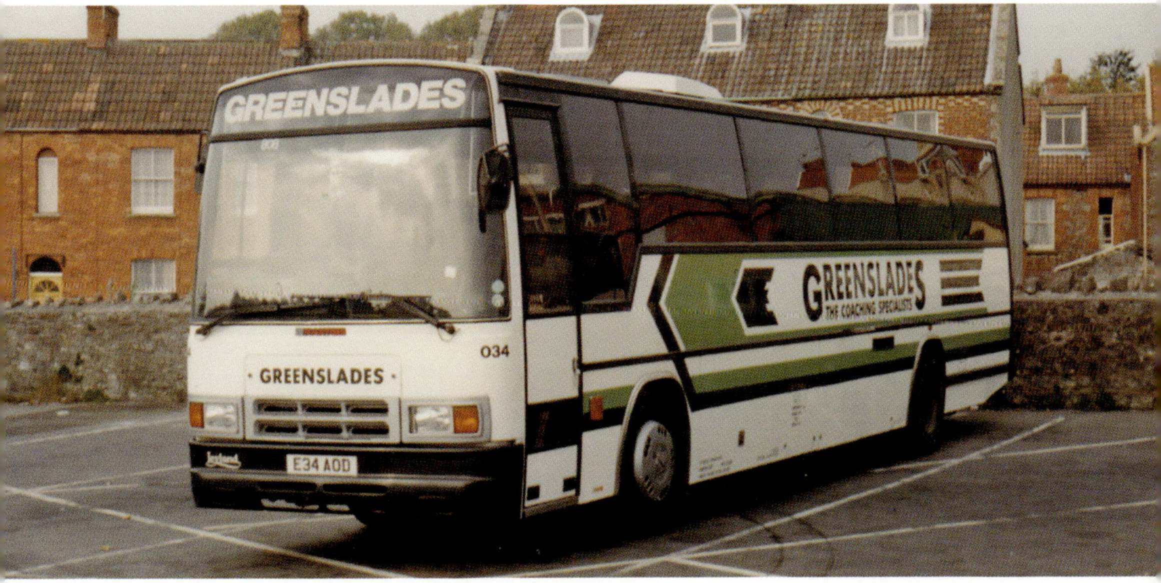

Greenslades was formed in 1912, becoming Greenslades Tours in 1933. In 1953 it became part of British Electric Traction (BET), joining the National Bus Company in 1969 as part of Western National before passing to the newly reformed Devon General upon privatisation in 1983. In 1987 the firm was bought by Nightingale Coaches of Exmouth. Seen in Wells bus station, again on 20 October 1990, E34 AOD, another Leyland Tiger, shows a few detail differences on its Plaxton Paramount 3200 III body when compared with the Blackburn Tiger in the previous image.

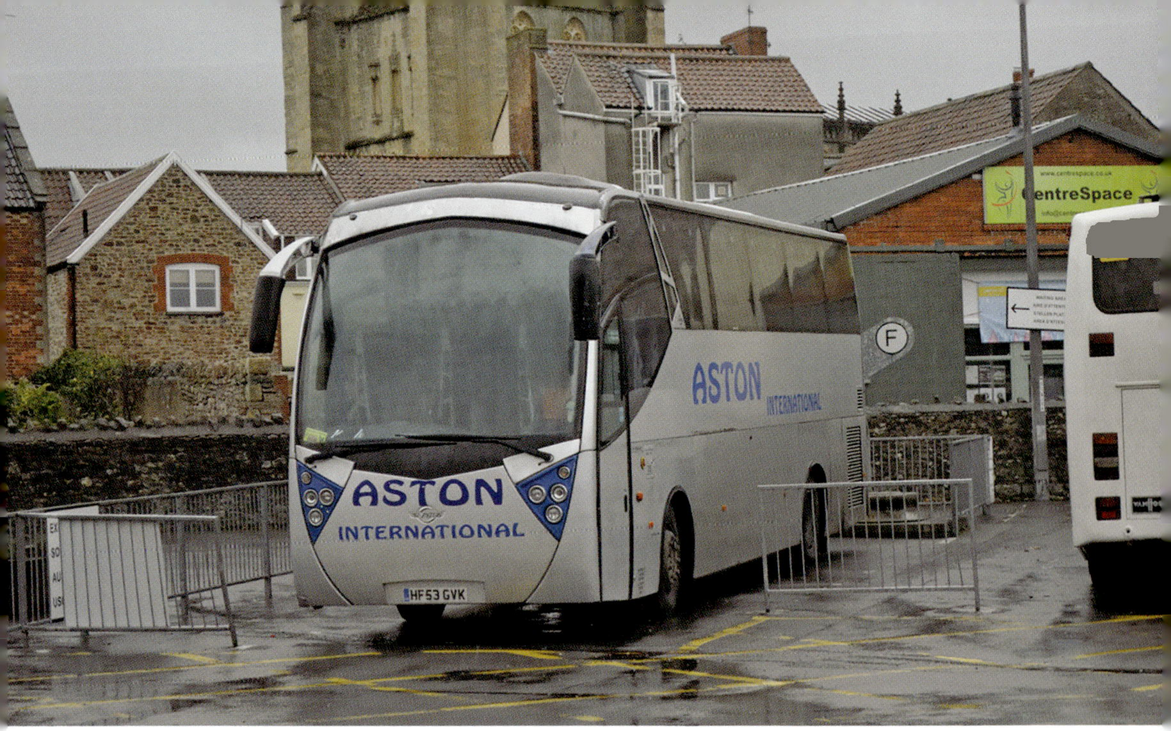

18 December 2018 saw school children from all over Somerset gathering at Wells Cathedral for an end-of-term carol service. One of the vehicles used to convey them was this rather unusual looking Ayats Atlantis, HF53 GCK, new to Seaview of Parkstone but serving here with the now-defunct fleet of Astons, based in the village of West Pennard.

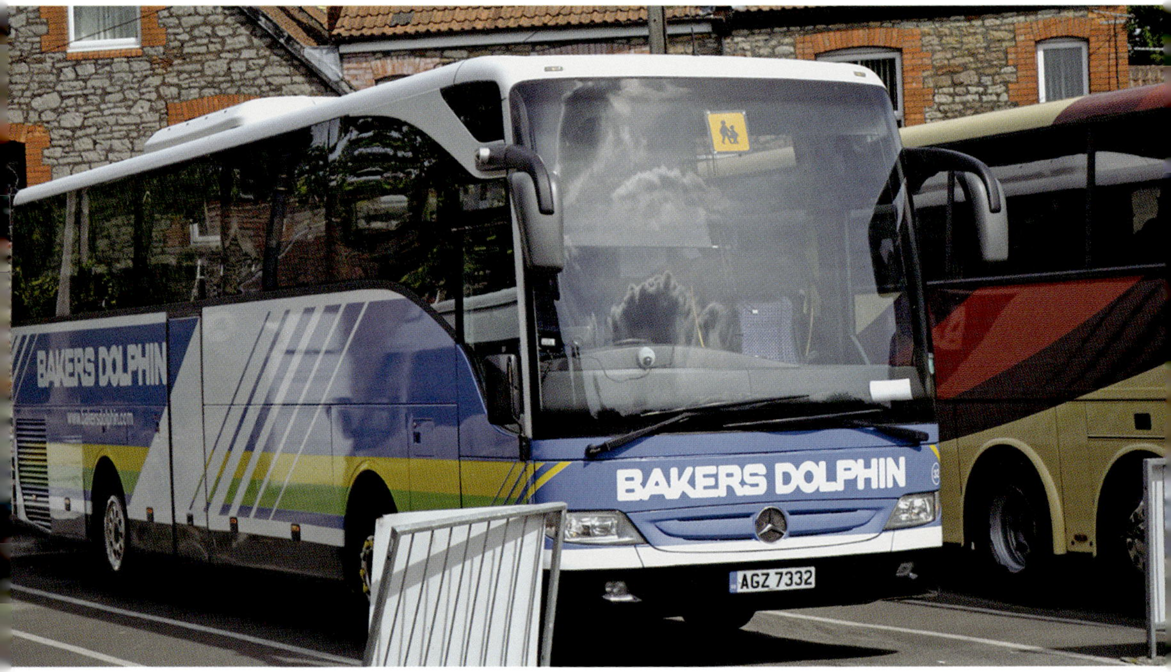

Bakers Dolphin are a very old and long-established name in Somerset, working from their base in Weston-super-Mare. Established as far back as 1889, their blue and yellow coaches, and their up-market Gold Service vehicles, are a familiar sight all over the country. Mercedes-Benz Tourismo AGZ 7332, new to Swans of Chadderton as BJ08 KNK, is seen on a local excursion to Wells on 15 June 2018.

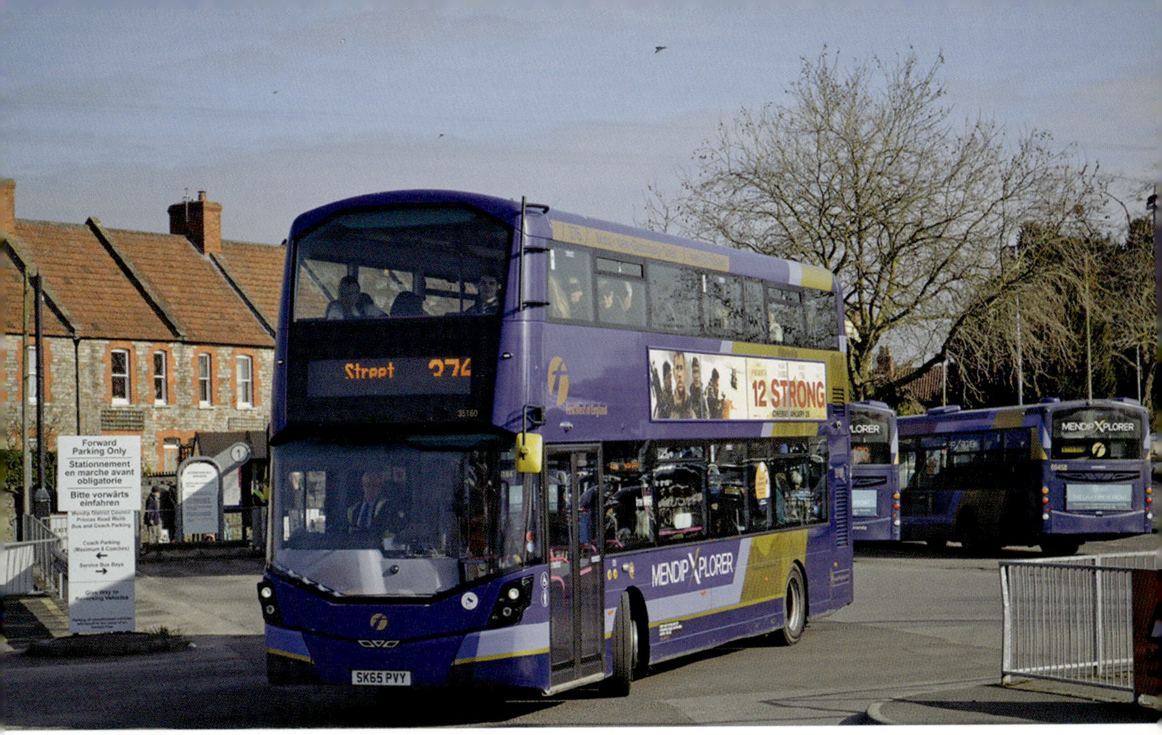

Due to their scenic nature, operating across the top of the Mendip Hills, First West of England services working out of Wells depot are branded as 'Mendip Explorer' and wear this smart livery of blue and gold. In 2015 a batch of new Wright StreetDecks was allocated to Wells for service 376. Here 35160, SK65 PVY, is leaving Wells for Street on 21 February 2018.

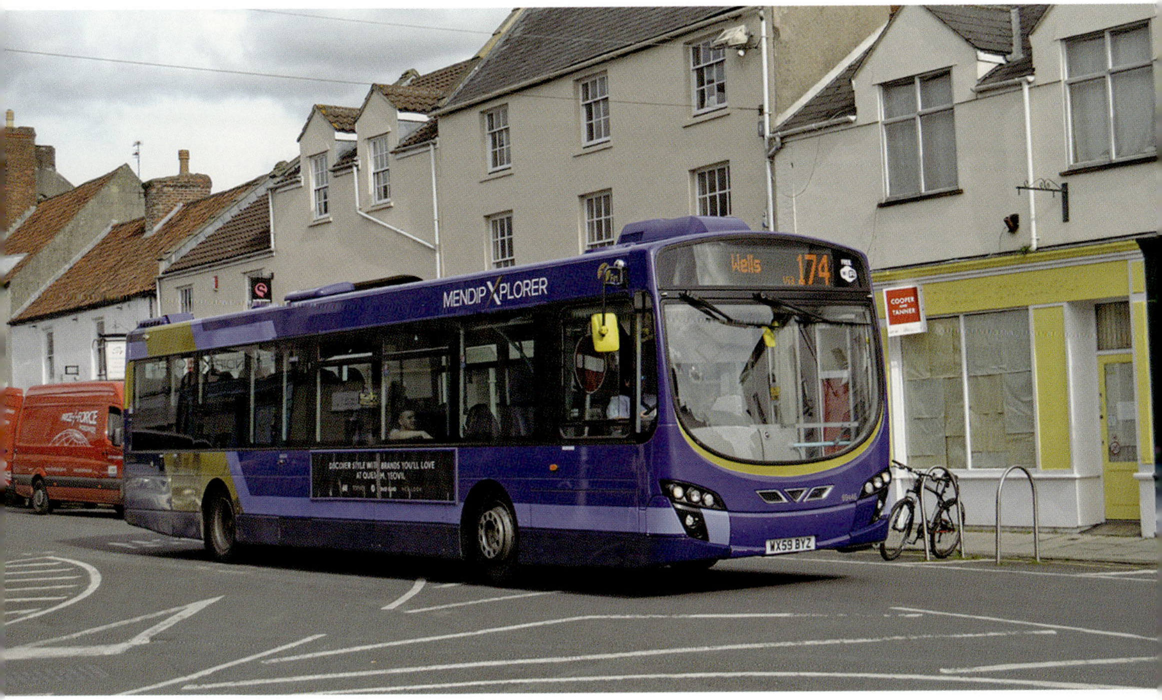

Arriving in Wells on service 174 from Bath via Shepton Mallett, 69446, WX59 BYZ, a Volvo B7RLE with Wright Eclipse Urban 2 body is seen on 6 October 2017.

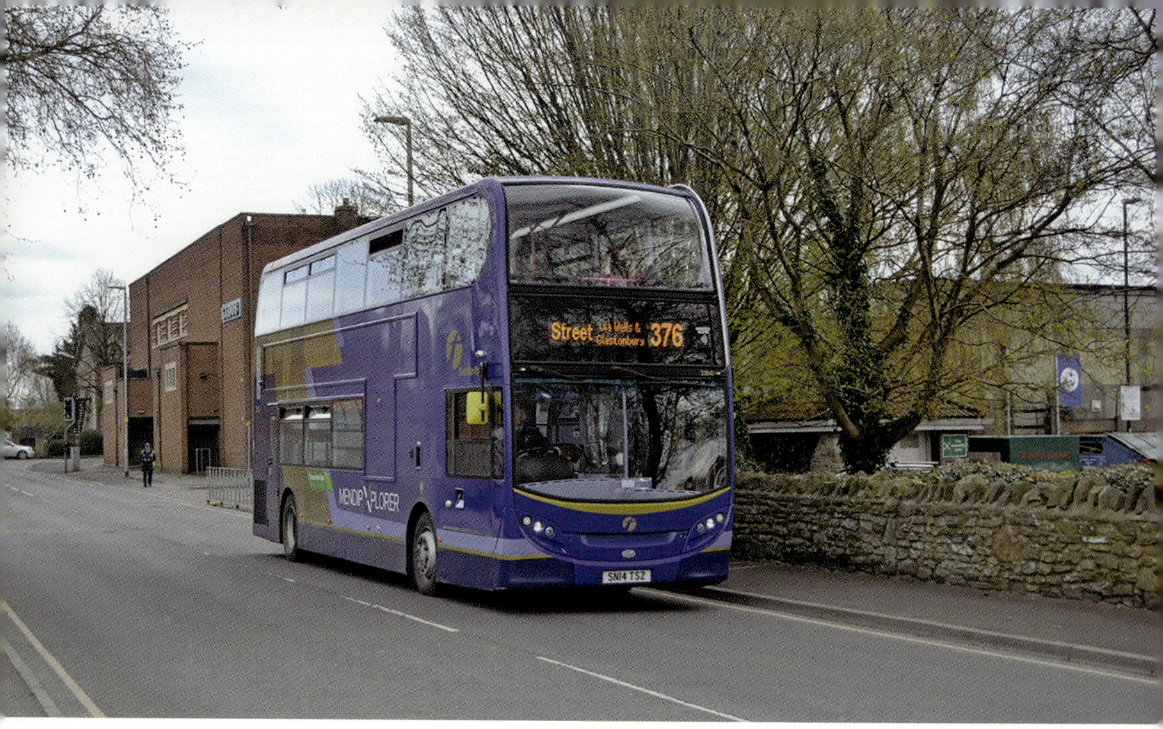

The Wright StreetDecks and Volvo B7RLEs were replaced at Wells by a mixture of Enviro400s and Wright Gemini-bodied Volvos, so that Wells is now a 100 per cent double-decker depot. Enviro400 33840, SN14 TSZ, is seen here on 12 April 2021, arriving in Wells on its way to Street on service 376.

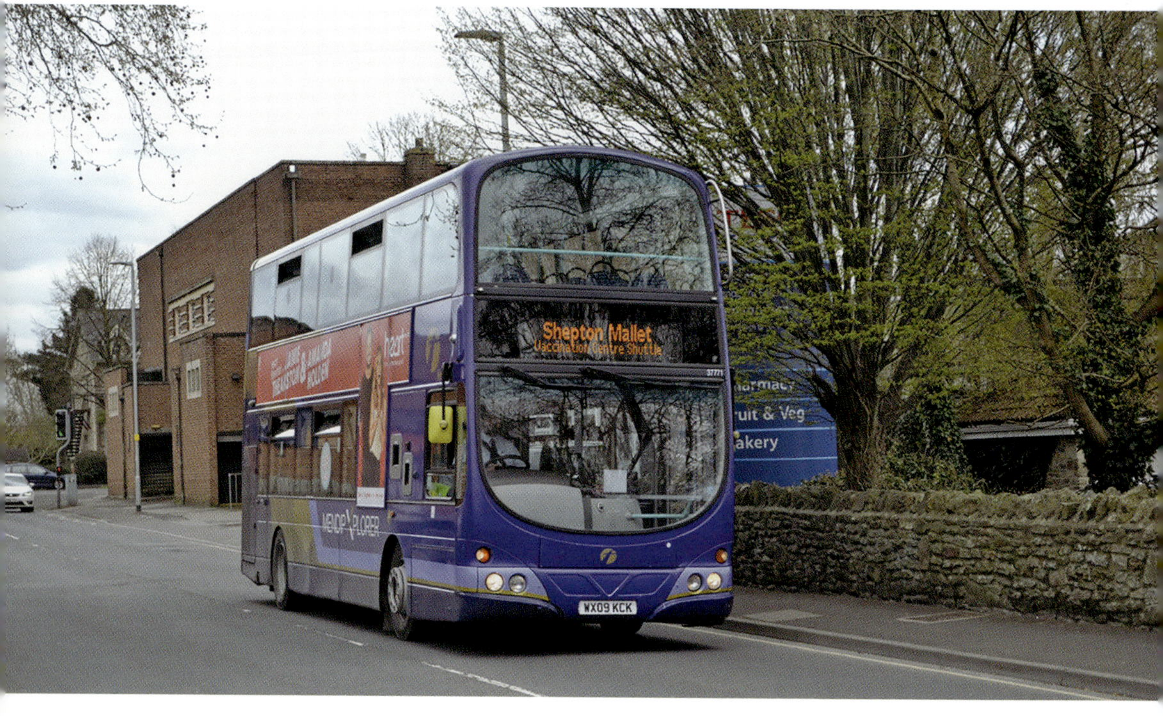

A symbol of the times during 2021… Wright Eclipse Gemini 2-bodied Volvo B9TL 37771, WX09 KCK, is arriving in Wells on 12 April, working a shuttle service to the COVID-19 vaccination centre at the Royal Bath and West Showground at Shepton Mallet.

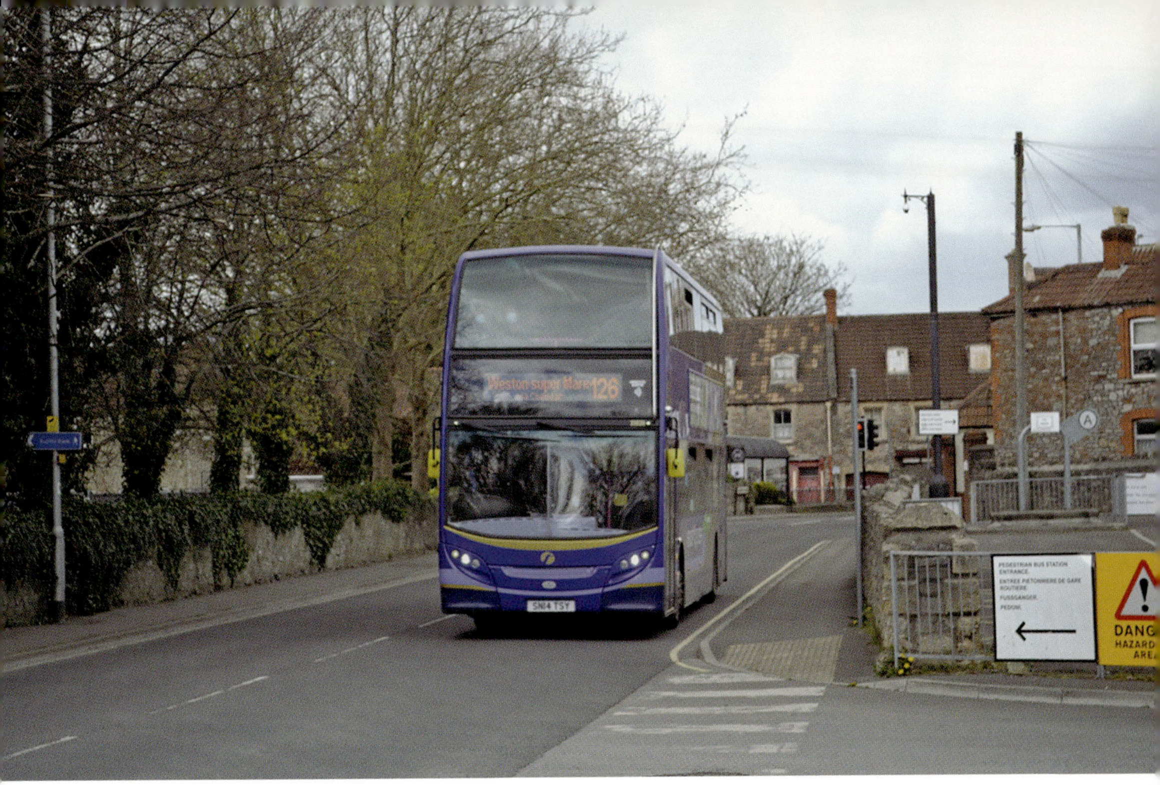

The last Wells area route to move to double -decker operation was the 126 to Weston-super-Mare. Enviro400 33839, SN14 TSY, is arriving in Wells on 12 April 2021.

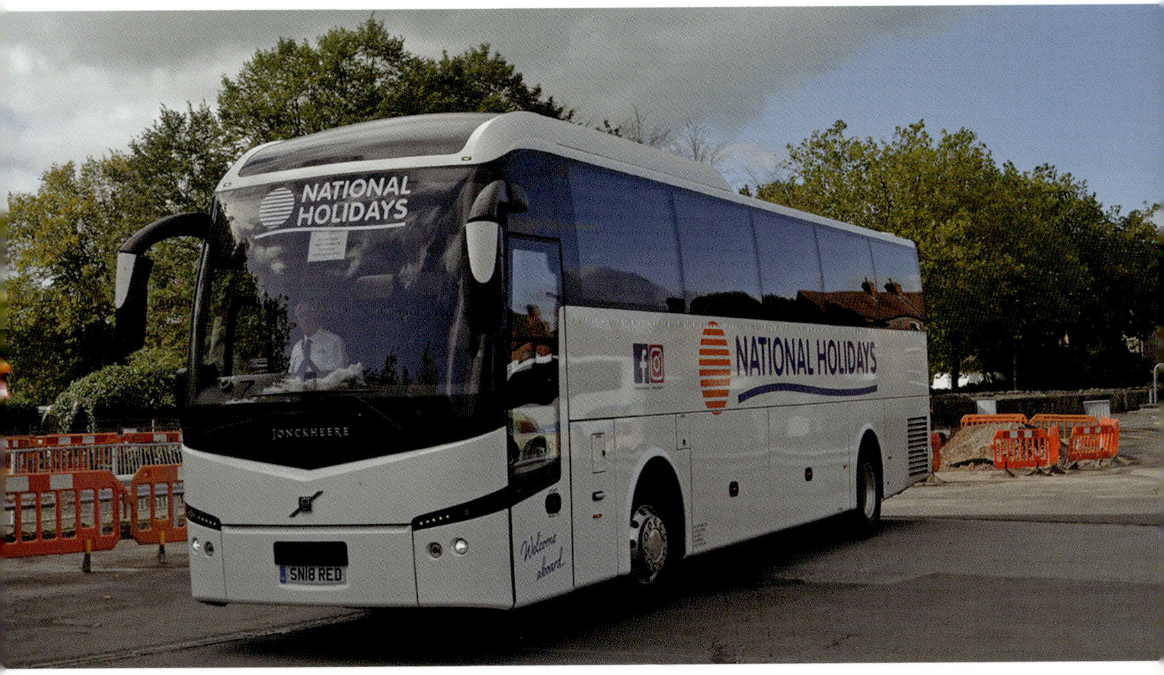

A visiting coach in Wells on 20 October 2021 was this Volvo B11R, SN18 RED, with Jonckheere JHV body from the fleet of Redline of Penwortham, near Preston, engaged on National Holidays tour work. It's really good to see the revival of coach tours and holidays after the restrictions of the pandemic.

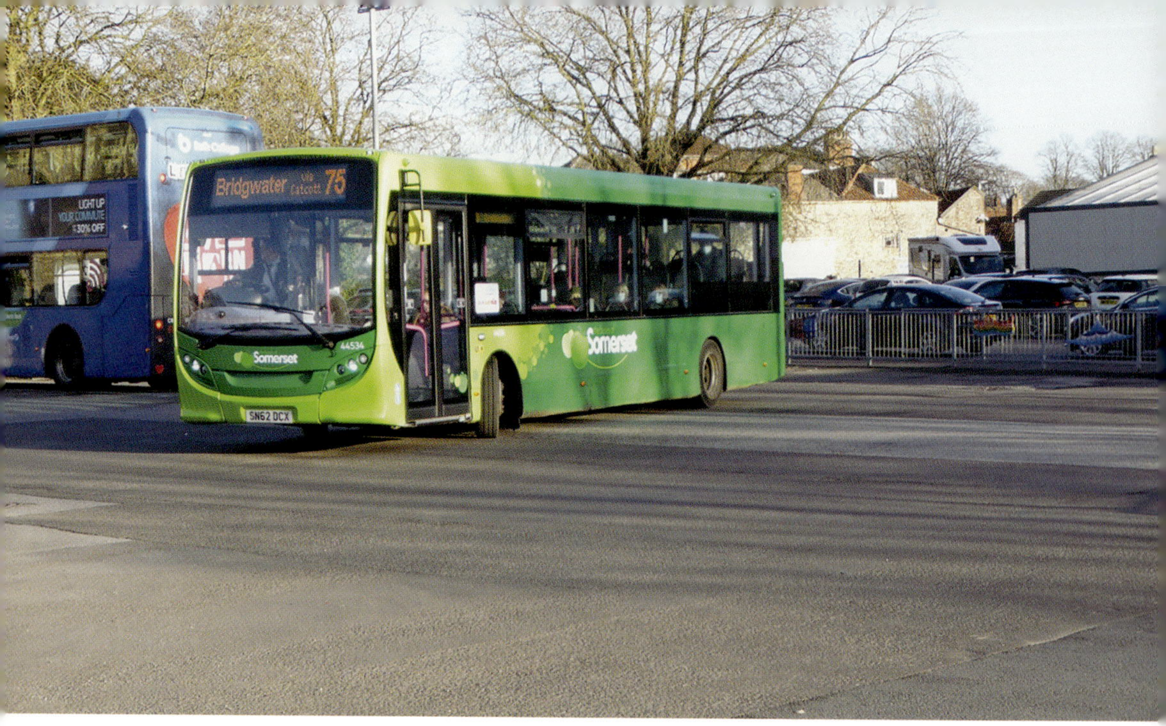

Buses of Somerset work into Wells from Taunton, Bridgwater and Yeovil, their green livery contrasting with the Mendip Explorer blue. Enviro200 44534, SN62 DCX, reverses off stand at the bus station to return to Bridgwater on service 75 on 5 January 2022, working via the village of Catcott, where my father was once the vicar.

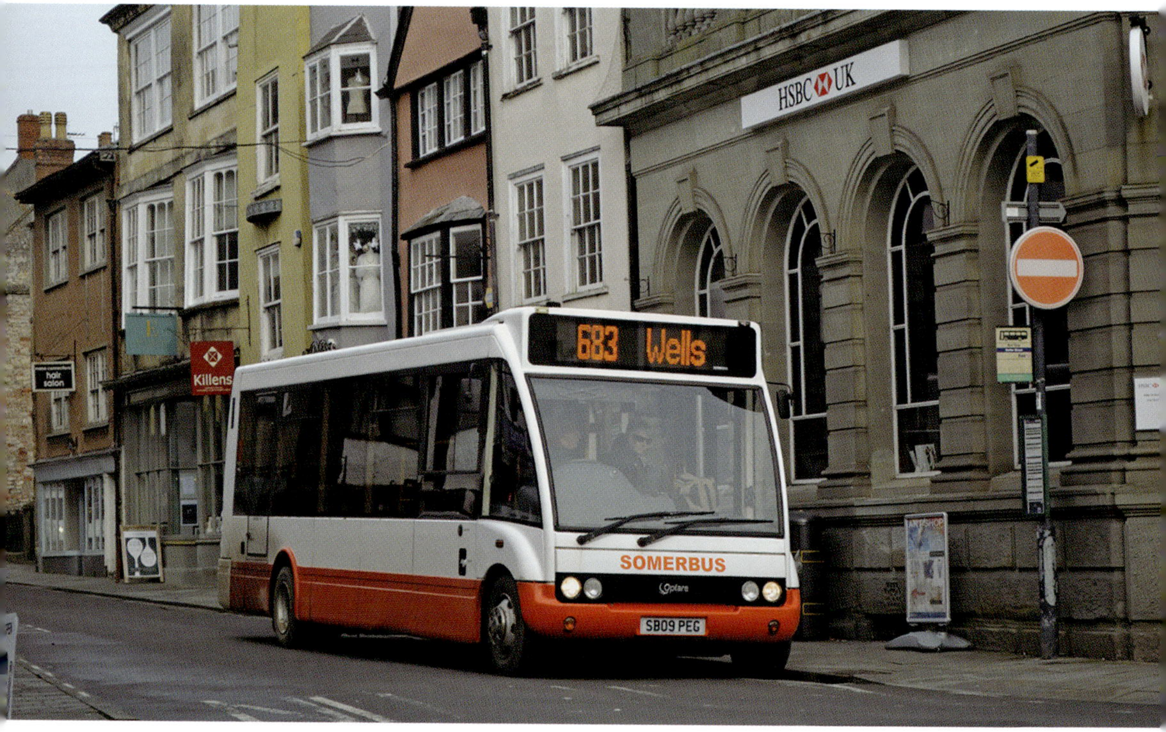

Somerbus of Paulton operate a single return journey every Tuesday to Wells from Keynsham, normally with Optare Solo SB09 PEG. It is seen here in Sadler Street, Wells, on 29 January 2019.

WESTON-SUPER-MARE

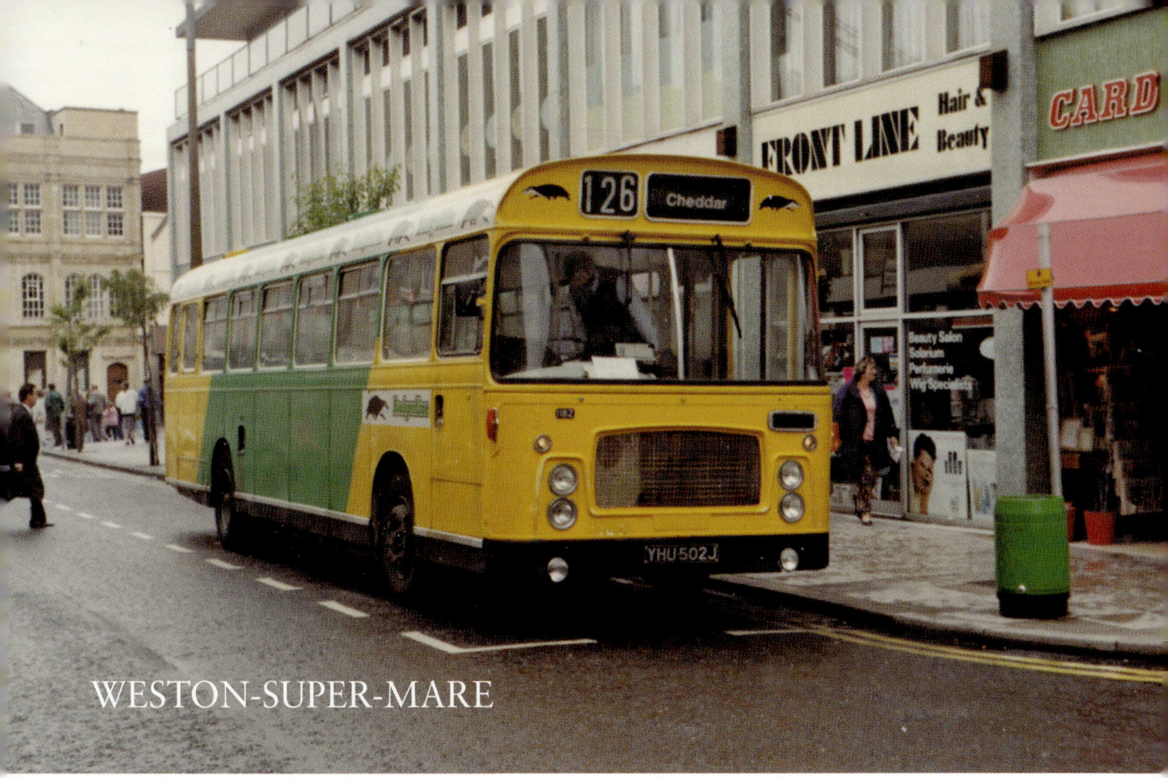

As mentioned previously, Badgerline retained Bristol REs in frontline service for quite some time. Weston-super-Mare-based 1182, YHU 502J, is seen here in Union Place with a 126 working to Cheddar on 4 July 1990.

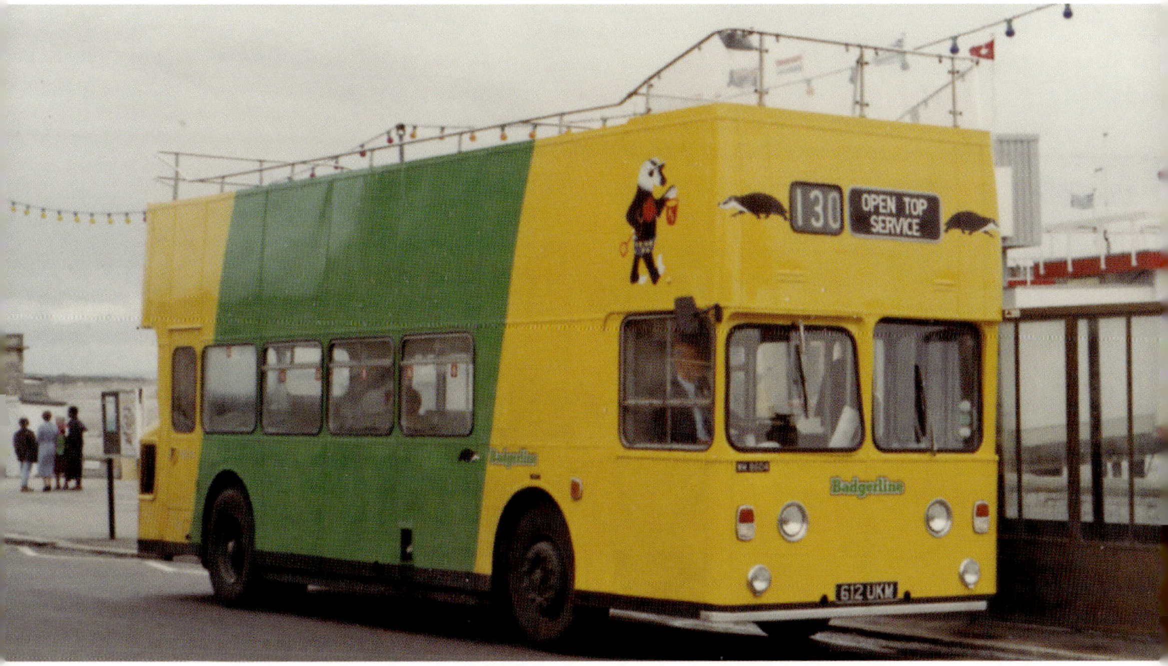

Like many seaside towns, Weston-super-Mare has open-top buses. In my childhood they were all-cream convertible open-top Bristol Lodekkas. On 4 July 1990, this former Maidstone & District Weymann-bodied Leyland Atlantean 8604, 612 UKM, dating from 1963, was on duty.

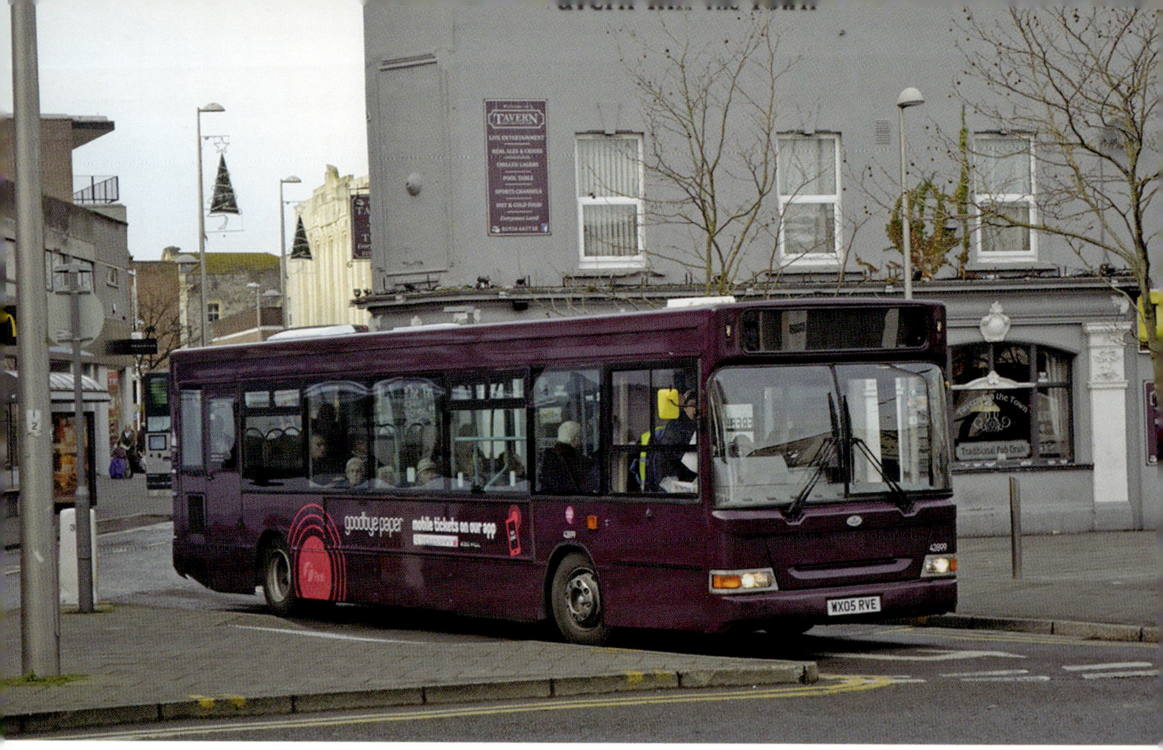

Plaxton Pointer-bodied Dennis Dart SLFs were still in use in the late 2010s, as shown here by Dart 42899, WX05 RVE, loading in Weston-super-Mare on 12 December 2017 for a trip to Burnham-on-Sea on service 20.

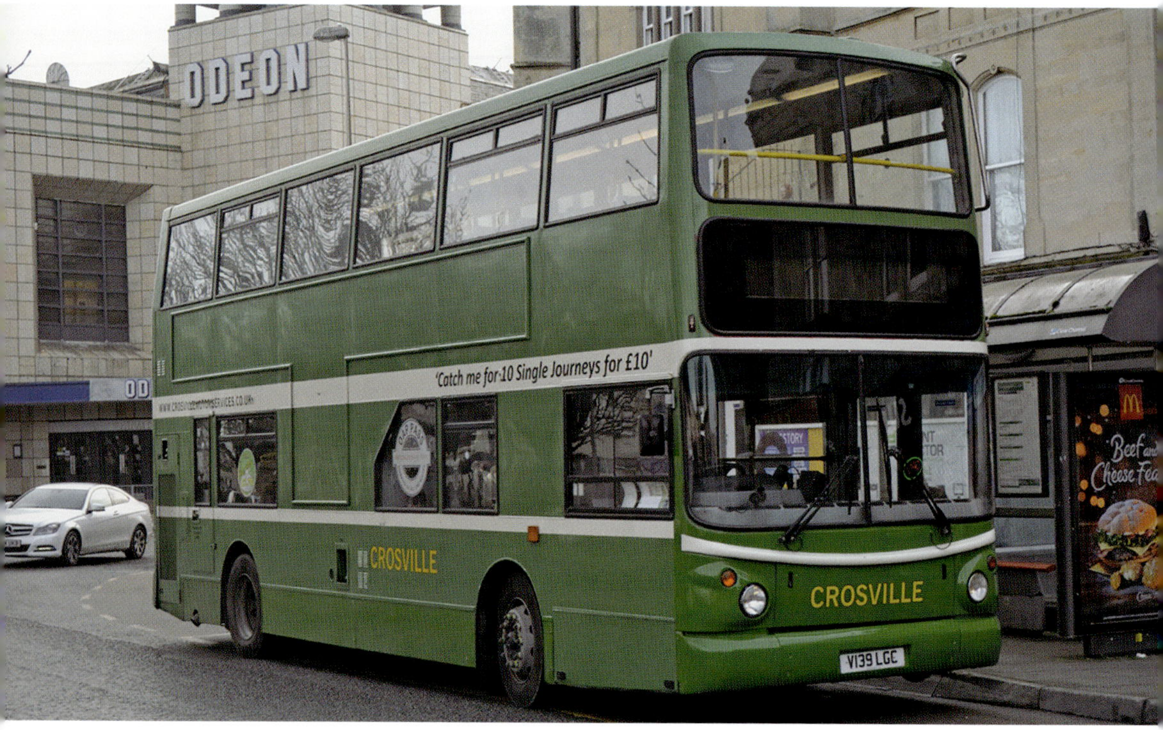

12 December 2017 also found Crosville's former London Central Alexander ALX400-bodied Volvo B7TL V139 LGC in use on a town service. This operator ceased entirely just a few months later.

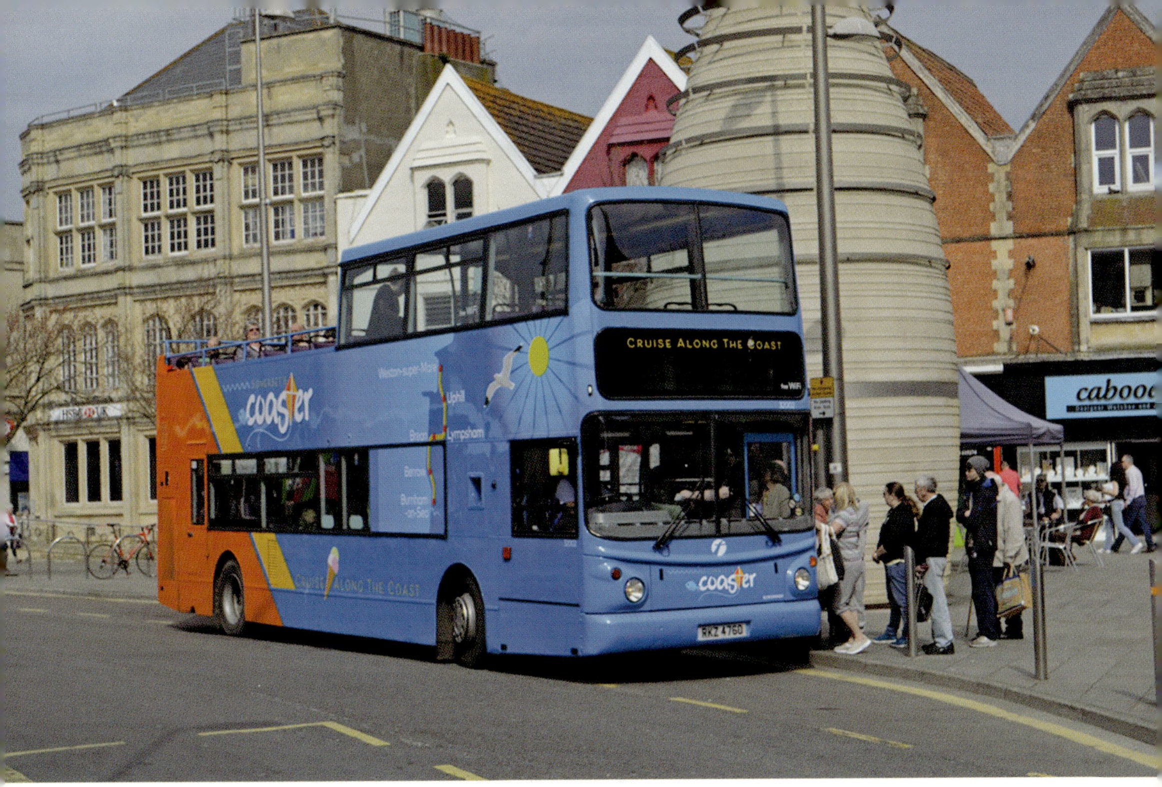

First West of England still operate open-toppers in Weston. Alexander ALX400-bodied Volvo B7TL 32002 is seen here loading for a trip to Burnham-on-Sea on 21 April 2018.

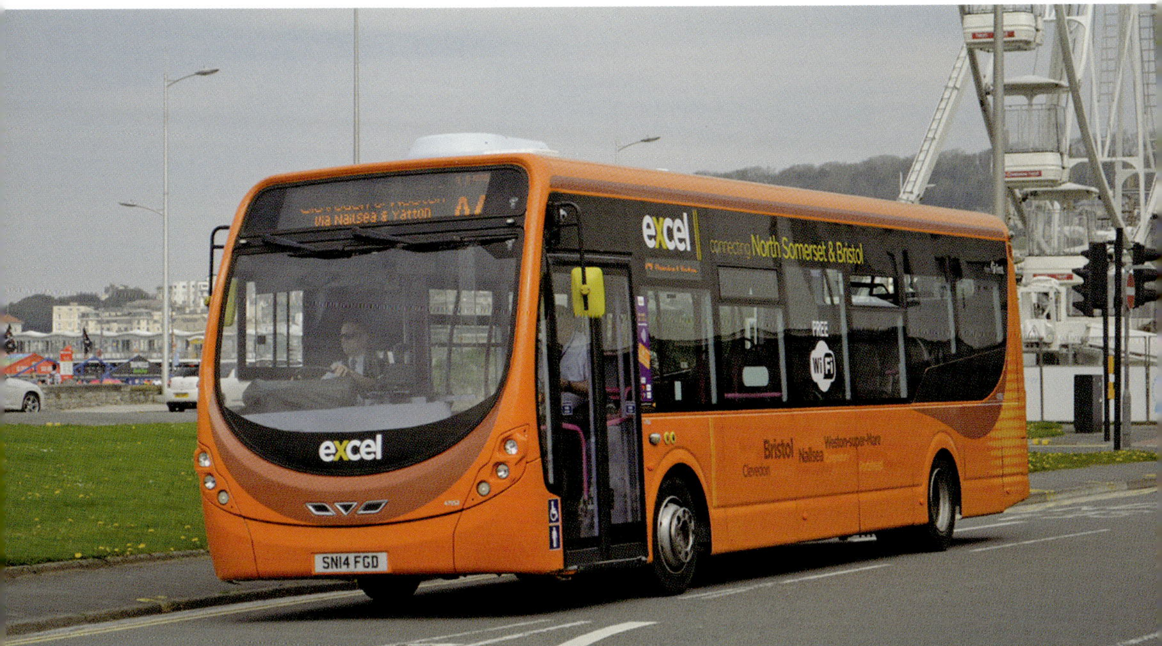

First West of England used the Excel brand name for services working into North Somerset to places such as Weston-super-Mare, Clevedon and Portishead. Excel-liveried Wright StreetLite DF 47552, SN14 FGD, is seen on the sea front on 21 April 2018 on an X7 service.

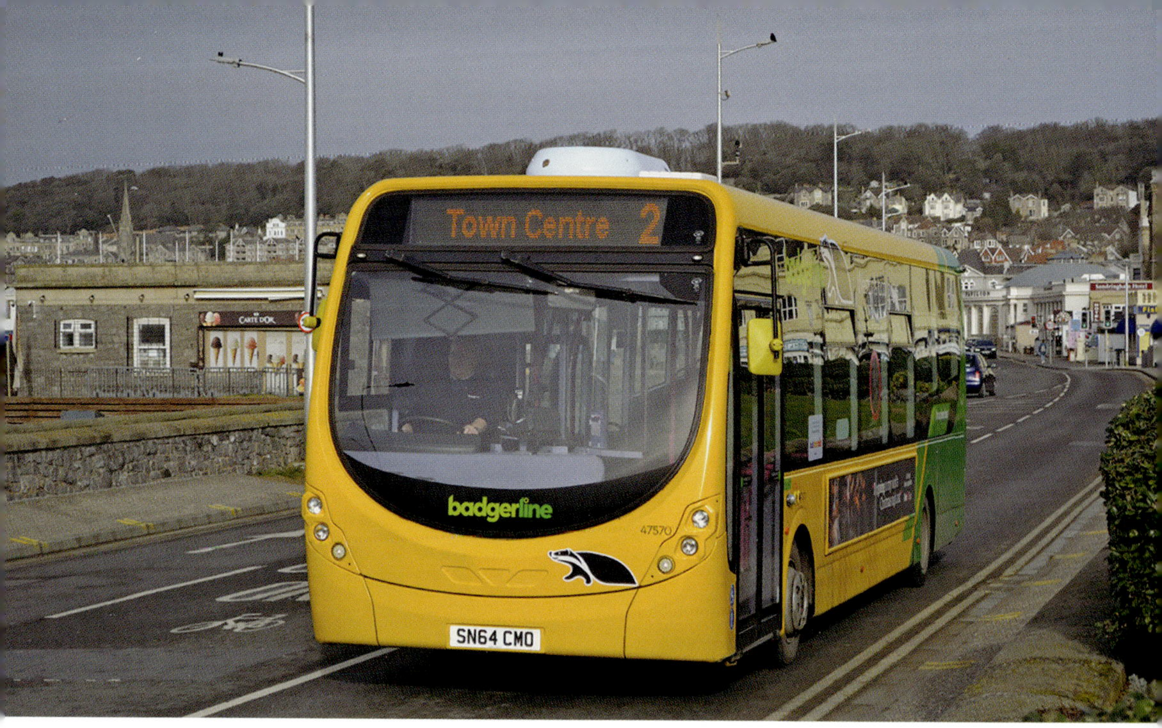

During 2018 First West of England's Weston operations were rebranded as Badgerline with vehicles receiving an updated version of the original green and yellow livery. Here we see Wright StreetLite DF 47570, SN64 CMO, passing along the seafront on a town service on 7 February 2022.

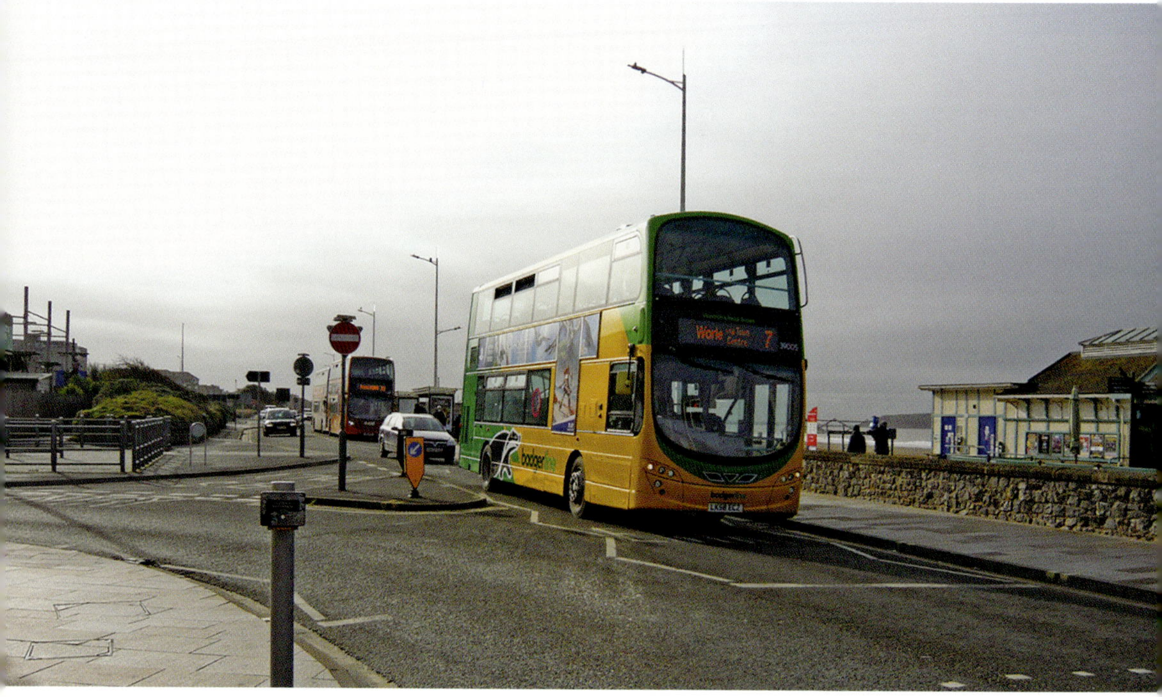

Badgerline-liveried Volvo B5TL 39005, LK58 ECZ, with Wright Eclipse Gemini 2 body, new to Centrewest and arriving in Weston from First York, is seen here, also on 7 February, passing along the seafront bound for Worle on service 7.

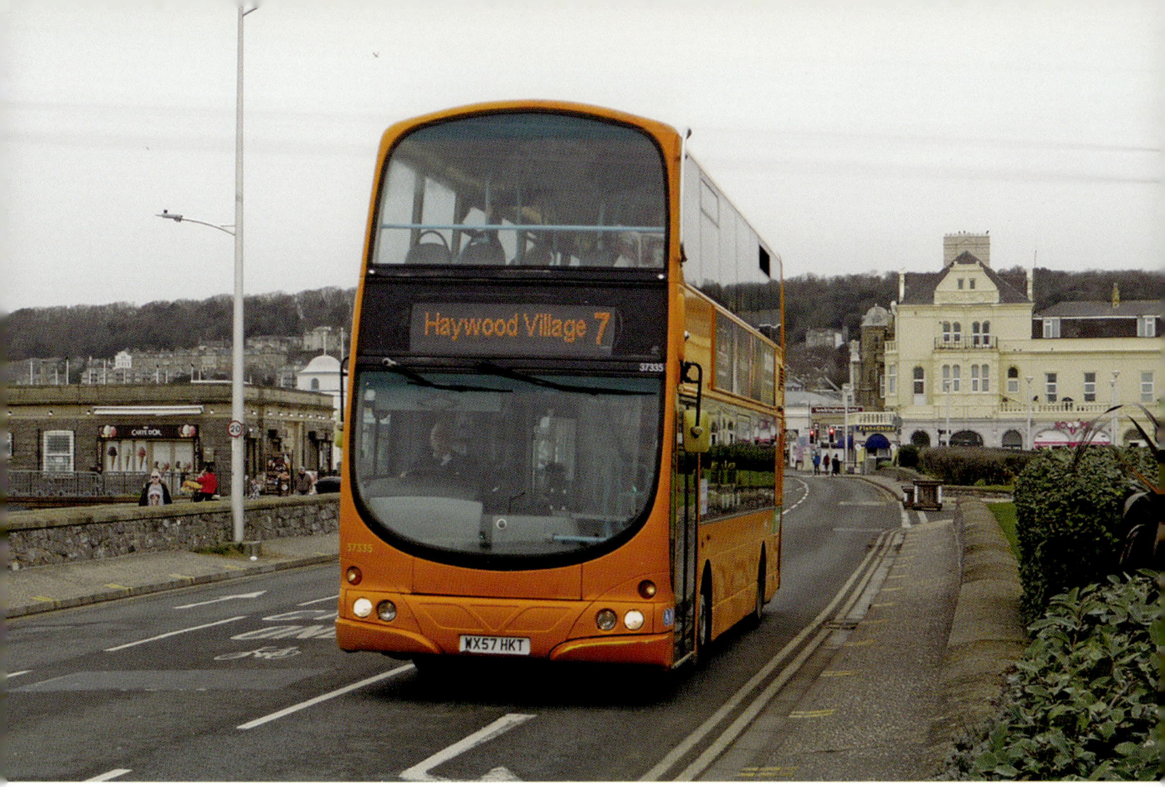

On 7 February 2022 I counted five different vehicles on service 7, each one in a different livery! Wright Eclipse Gemini-bodied Volvo B9TL 37335, WX57HKT, is seen here on the seafront.

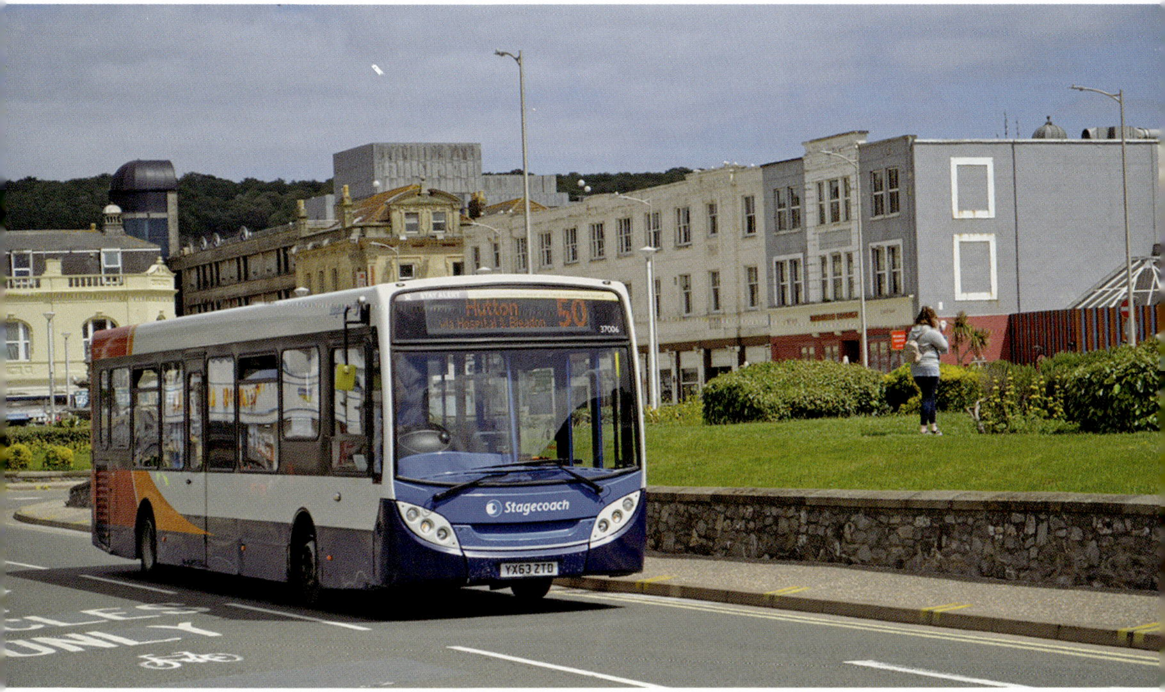

Stagecoach West now operate in Weston as well. Enviro200 37006, YX63ZTD, is seen here on 10 June 2022 on service 50 to Hutton.

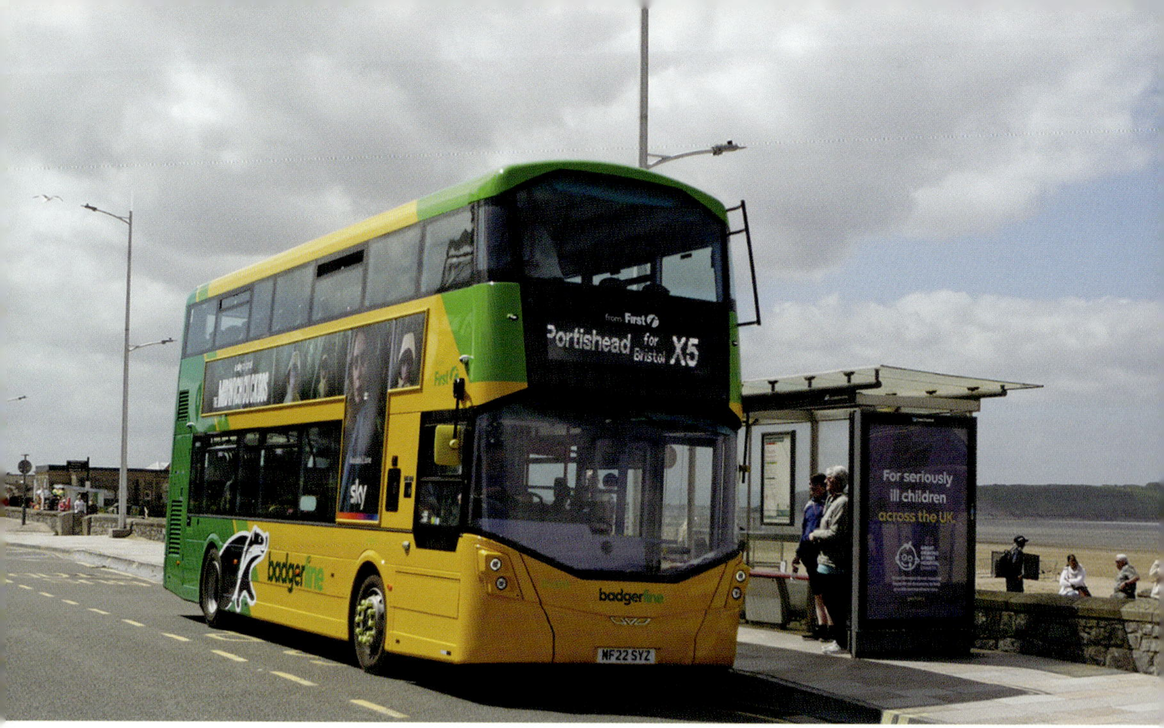

In 2022 Weston depot took delivery of a batch of 27 new Wright StreetDecks in Badgerline livery. Here, 35688, MF22 SYZ, is on Weston seafront on 10 June 2022, awaiting departure to Portishead on service X5. Their arrival has seen the phasing out of the Excel branding illustrated previously.

BRIDGWATER

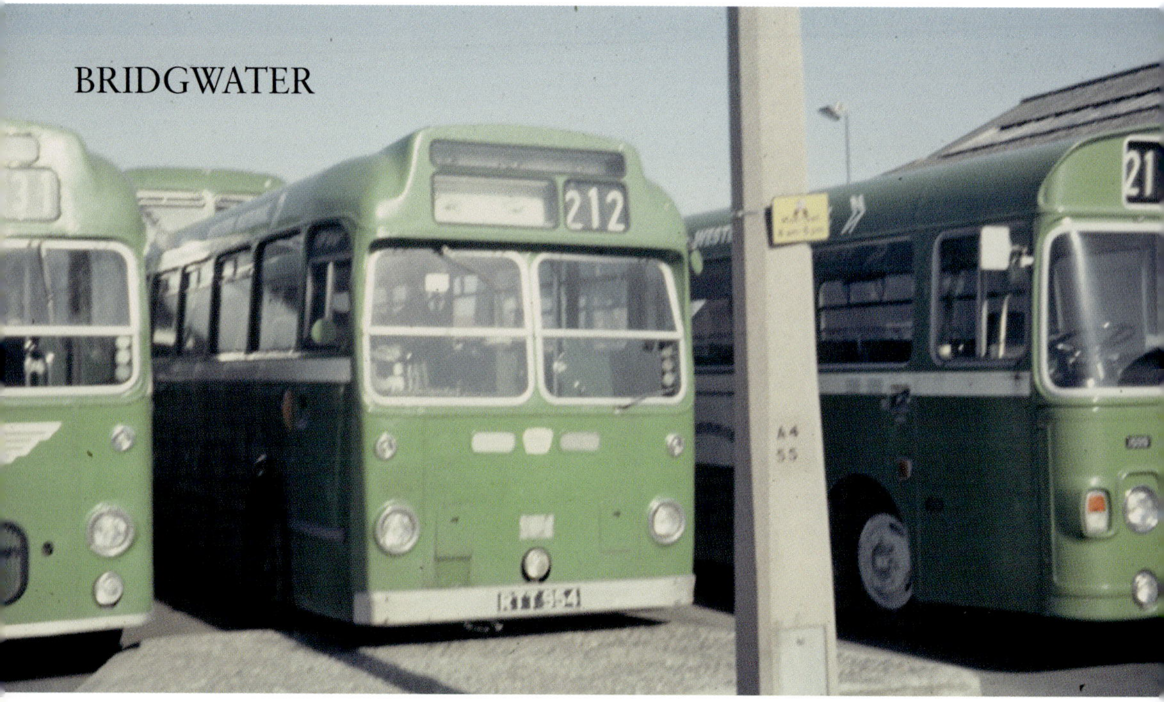

In this shot we see 1955 Bristol LS 1744, RTT 954, parked up in Bridgwater depot, fully repainted in NBC green and displaying route number 212. This was the run out to my home village of Burtle, where my father was the vicar. This vehicle was withdrawn in 1976.

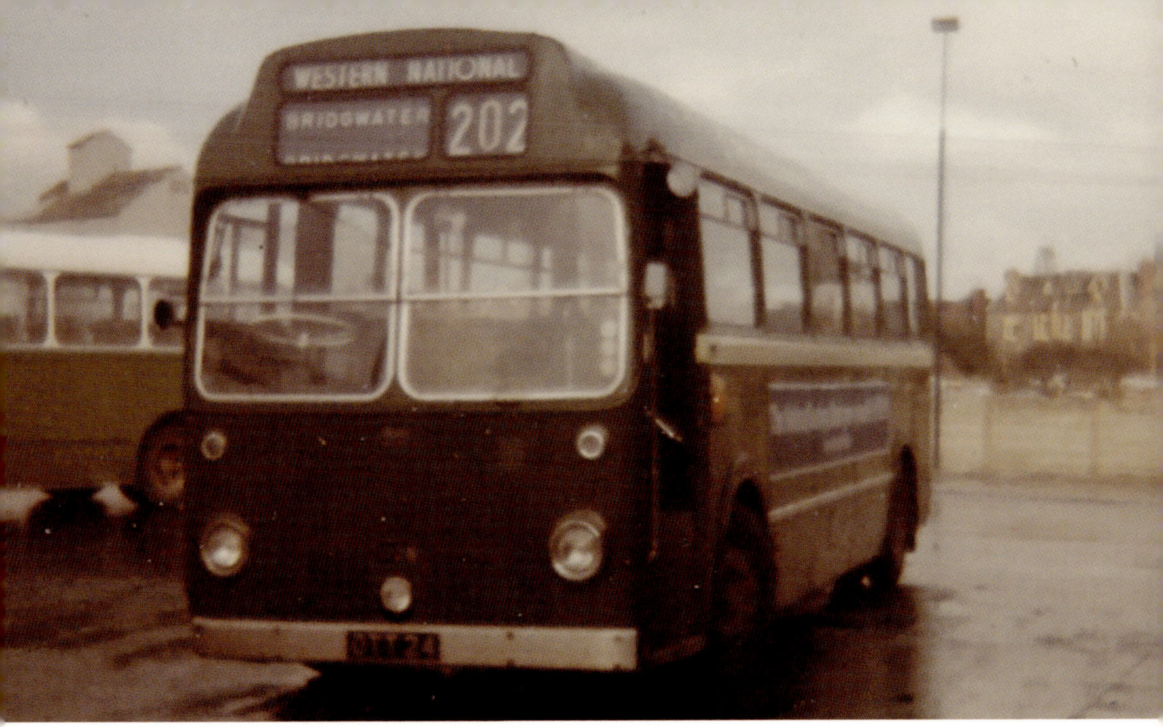

My home village outside Bridgwater was served three times a day by Bristol LS types like this one, 1728, OTT24, and dating from 1954. It still wears Tilling green but with NBC style fleet names in this picture, taken in late 1973. Between them, Western and Southern National operated around 200 of these vehicles in both bus and coach form, some of the latter in the Royal Blue fleet.

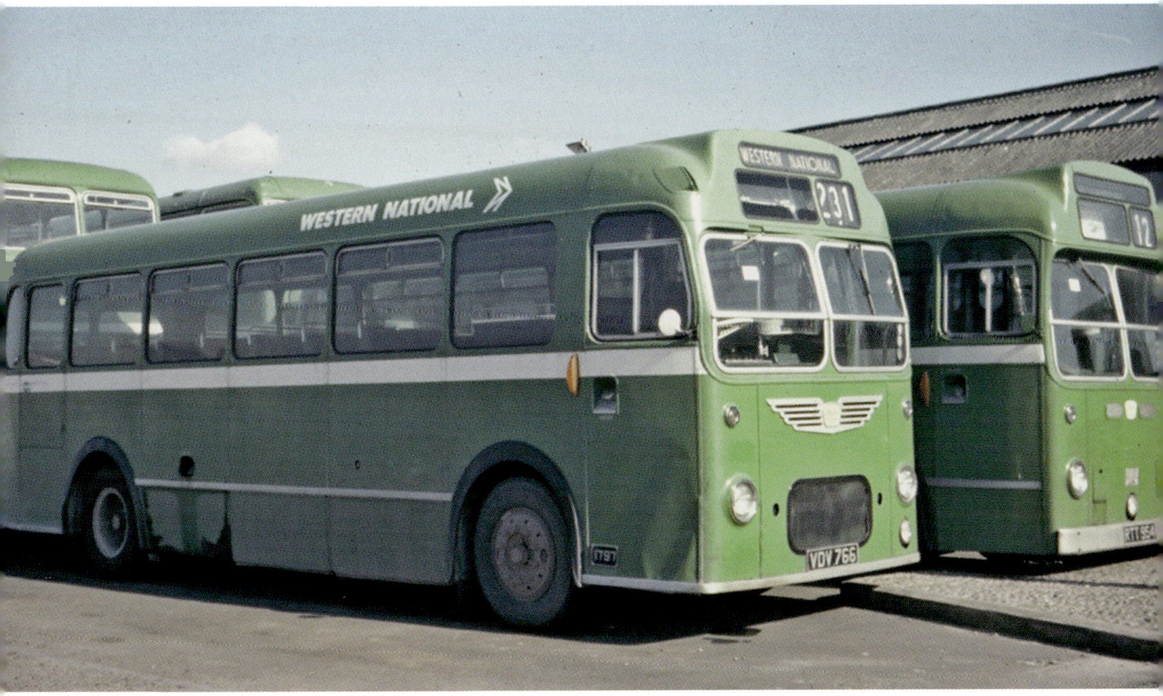

Parked next to 1766, and also now fully repainted into NBC leaf green, is Bristol MW5G 1797, VDV 766, a 1958 model that remained in the fleet until 1978. Parked behind, you can just see two Bristol FLFs.

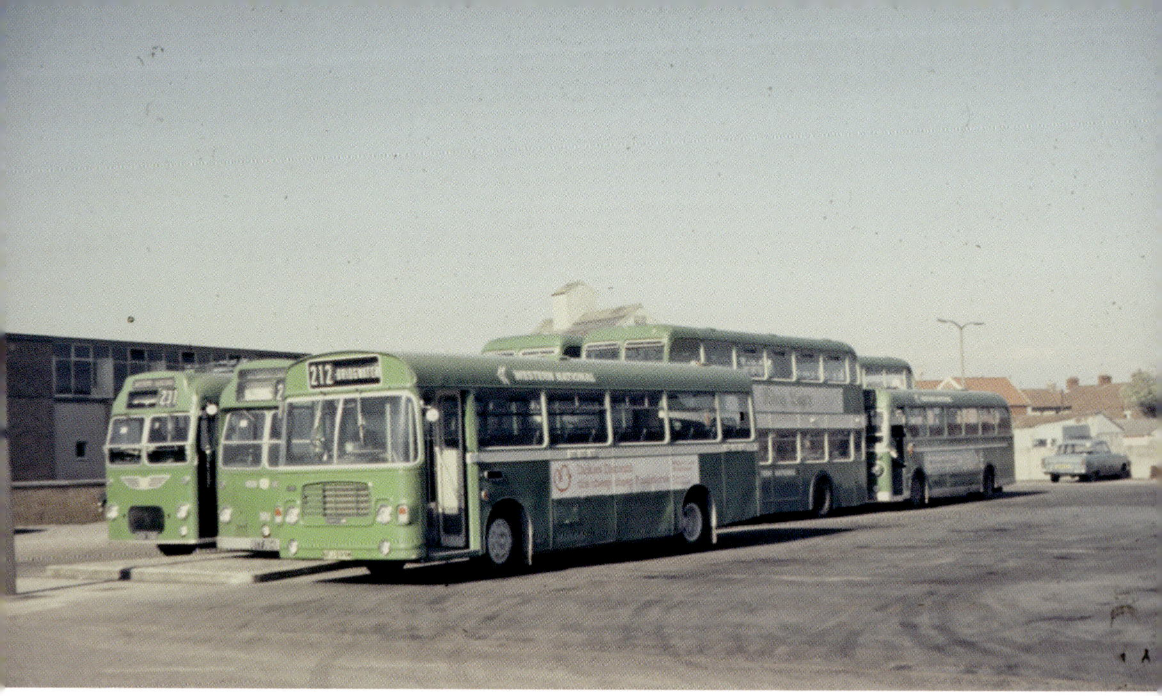

I remember this Bristol LH, 1599, NFJ 599M, being delivered to Bridgwater, and the duty inspector letting me look it over unattended, at age fourteen! That wouldn't happen now! The 212 served my home village. Also in this photo at Bridgwater depot, taken in late 1974, are a Bristol LS, an MW, an SU and three FLFs. The site where these buses are parked is now an ASDA supermarket.

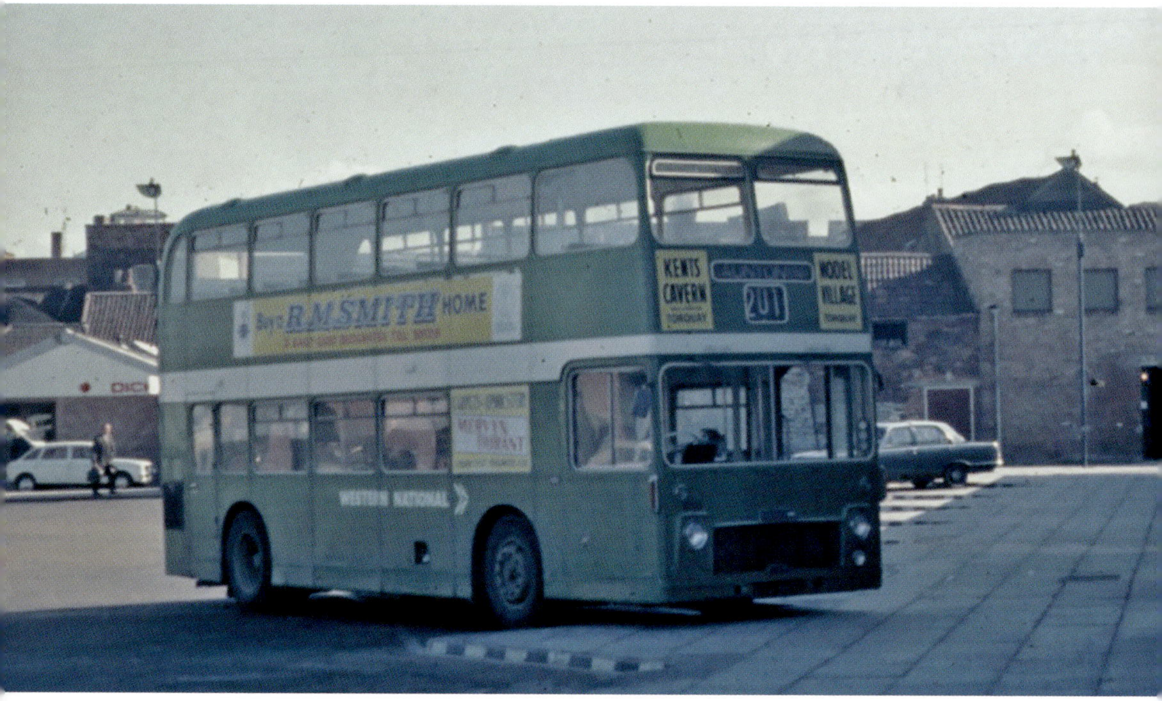

Bristol VRT 1053, OTA287G, seen in Bridgwater bus station in about 1973, bound for Taunton on service 201 from Burnham-on-Sea. This bus station was opened in 1967 and was used until 1981. There is now a filling station on the site of the bus station building. I seem to remember these VRs also working on Bridgwater town services.

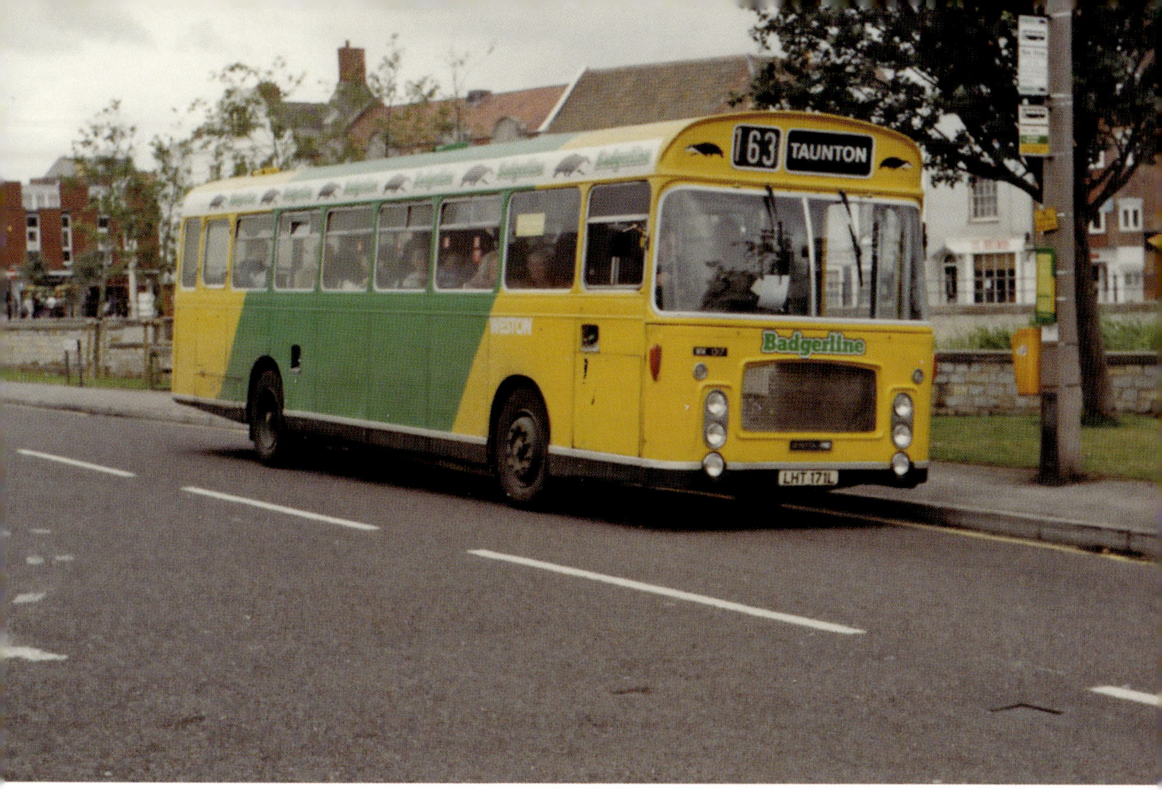

Badgerline worked through Bridgwater with its service 163 to Taunton from Wells between 1988 and 2005. Working the service on 5 July 1990 was Bristol RE 1317, LHT171L, illustrated earlier in Wells on a 376 working.

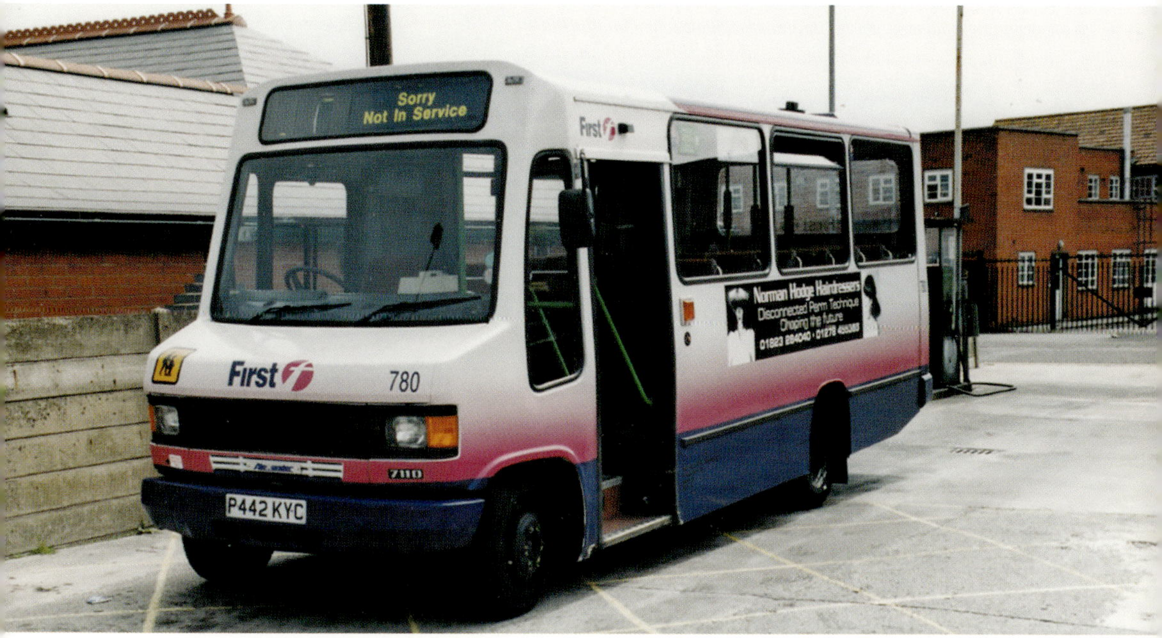

When Western National was divided up in 1983 prior to privatisation, Bridgwater came within the area of the reformed Southern National. It was sold to the management in 1988, and was in turn sold to First Group in 1999. Seen at the depot on 15 August 2002, wearing full First Group colours is Mercedes-Benz 709D 780, P442KYC, carrying an Alexander Belfast body.

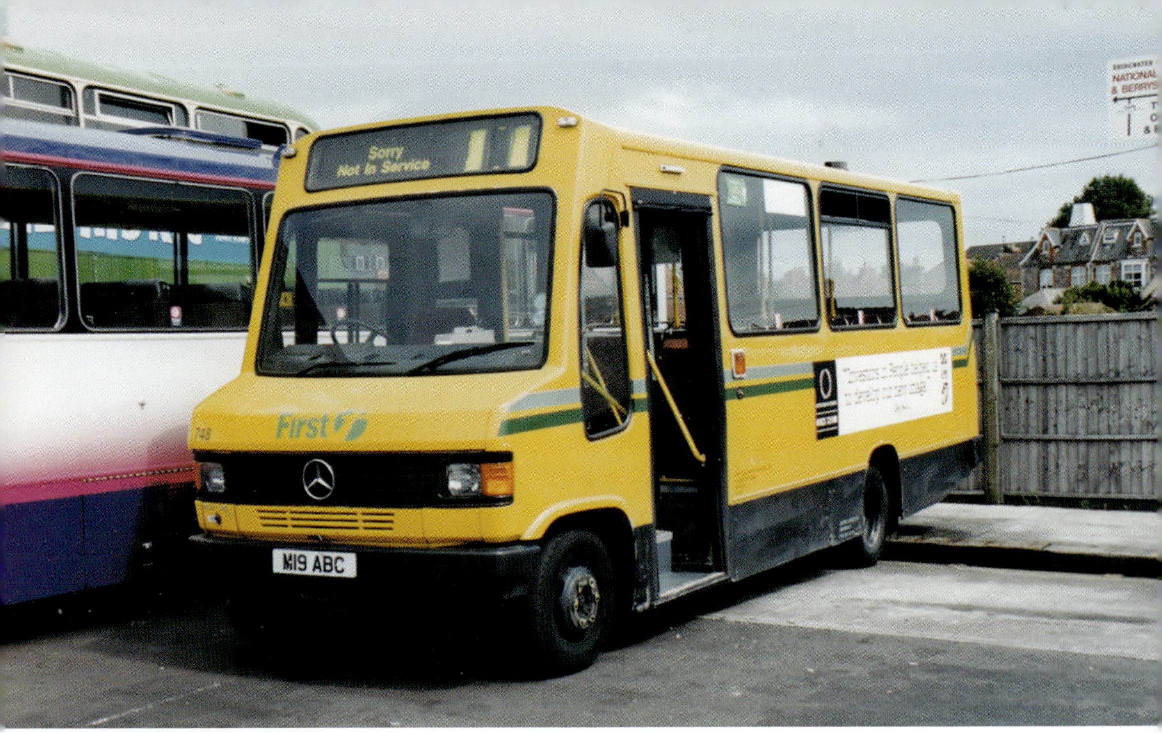

Southern National initially operated its minibuses in a rhubarb and custard colour scheme with the name 'Shuttle', as will be seen in a later picture. Later though, minibuses appeared in a yellow livery with a coloured flash, as shown here by Alexander-bodied Mercedes-Benz 709D 748, M19 ABC, seen here at Bridgwater depot on 15 August 2002, complete with First Group logos. This vehicle came from Patel of Leicester in 1997.

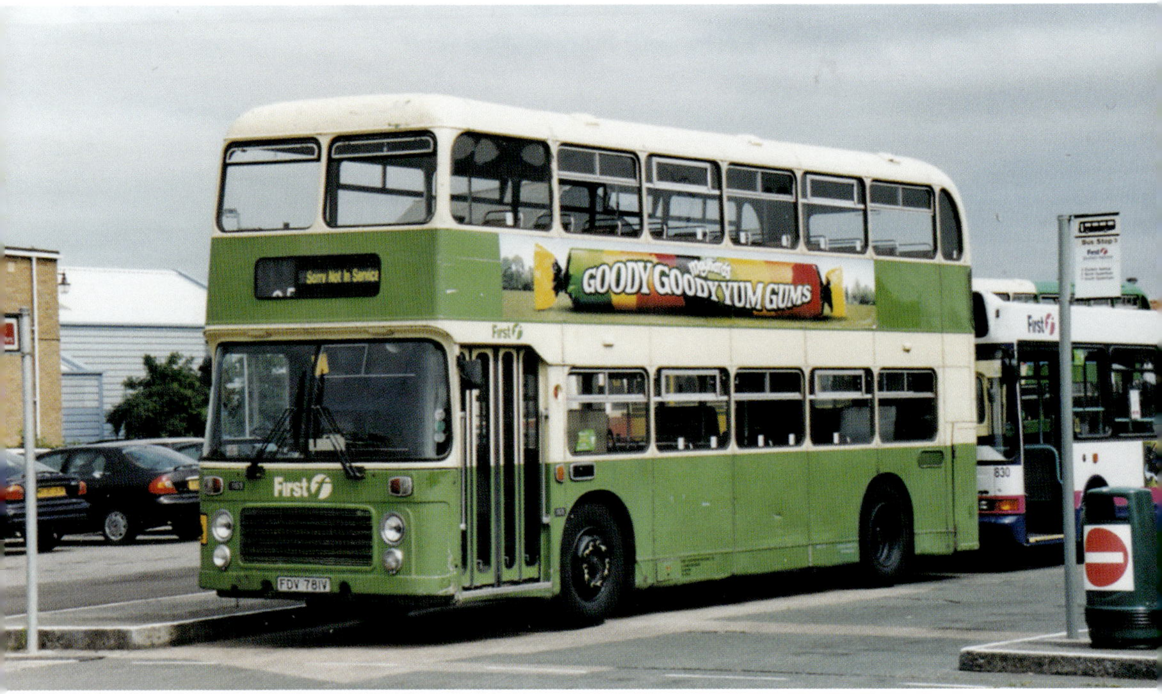

Seen resting in the bus depot on the same day, in Southern National livery but with First Group logo is Bristol VRT 1169, FDV 781V.

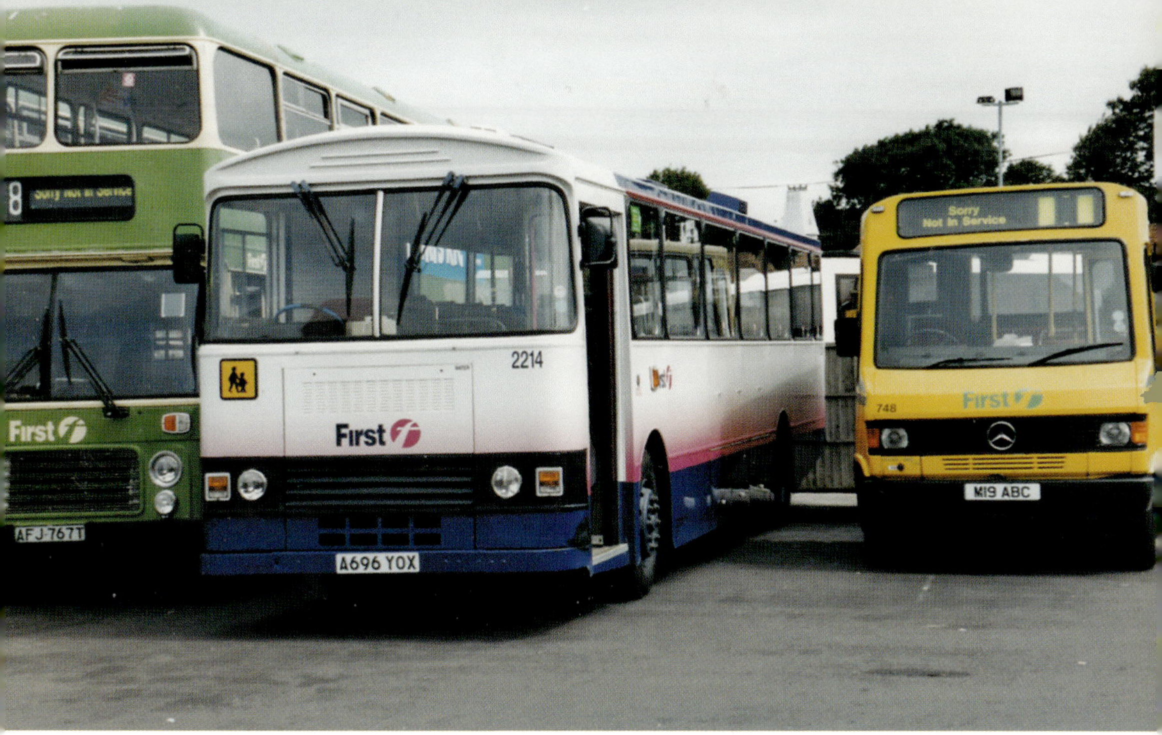

An interesting second-hand purchase allocated to Bridgwater was this former MoD Marshall-bodied Leyland Tiger 2214, A696 YOX, bought probably for school bus use. It is seen in Bridgwater depot on 15 August 2002 and survived with the company until 2004.

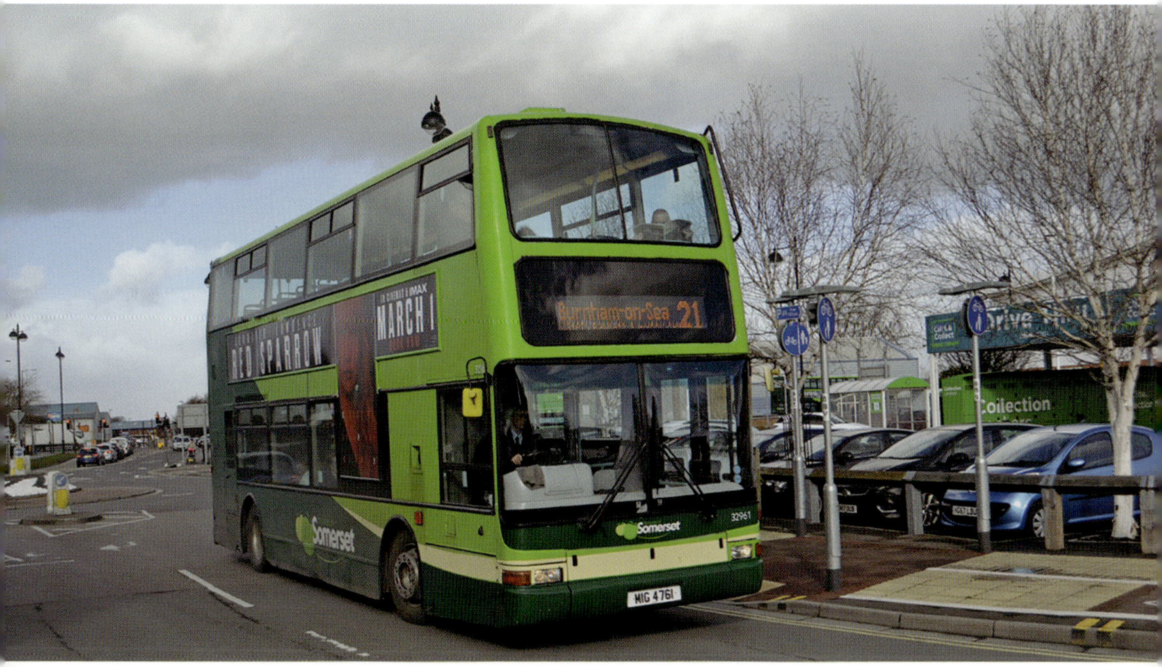

The successor to the 201 service from Taunton to Burnham-on-Sea that Bristol VRT 1053 was pictured on is Buses of Somerset 21. A contrast to the Bristol VRT is Plaxton President-bodied Dennis Trident 32961, MIG 4761, entering the bus station on 15 February 2018. This vehicle has since been withdrawn.

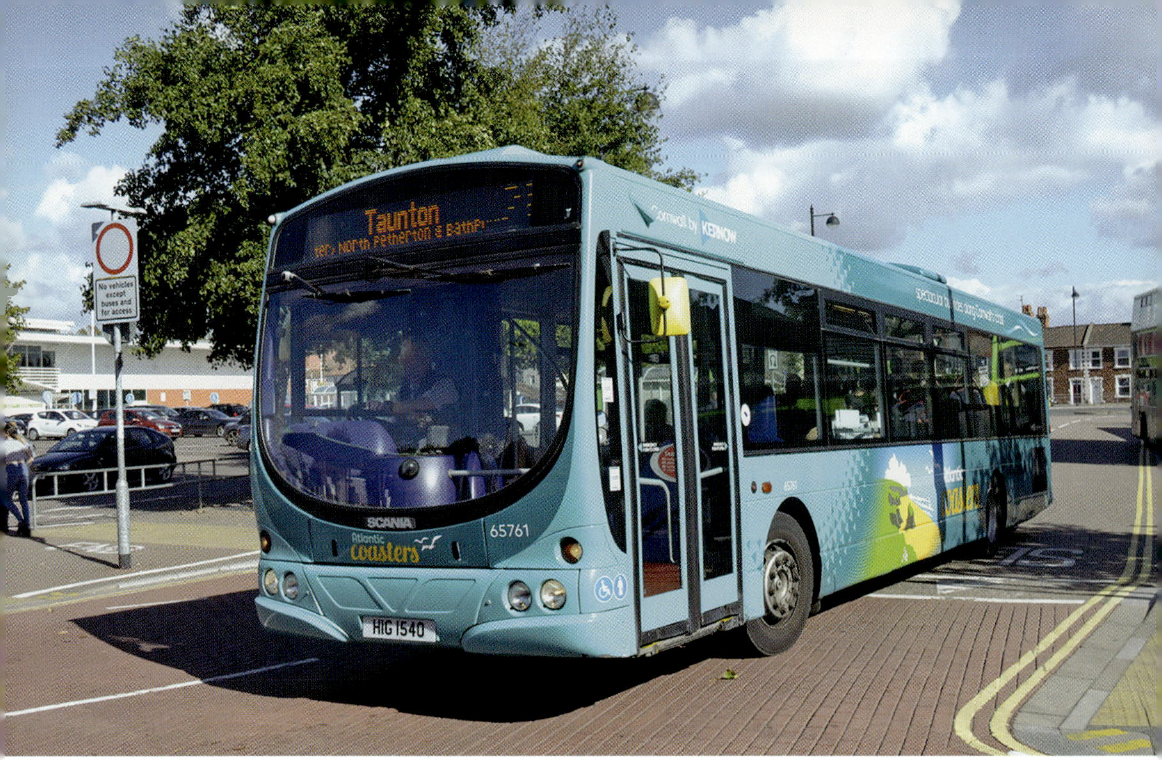

Buses of Somerset gave a number of Wright Eclipse Solar-bodied Scanias and Enviro300s a special dedicated livery for the Burnham service, based on the Coaster liveries in Cornwall that the Scanias initially worked on. Here Scania 65761, YN06 NXP, is leaving the bus station for Taunton on 19 April 2021.

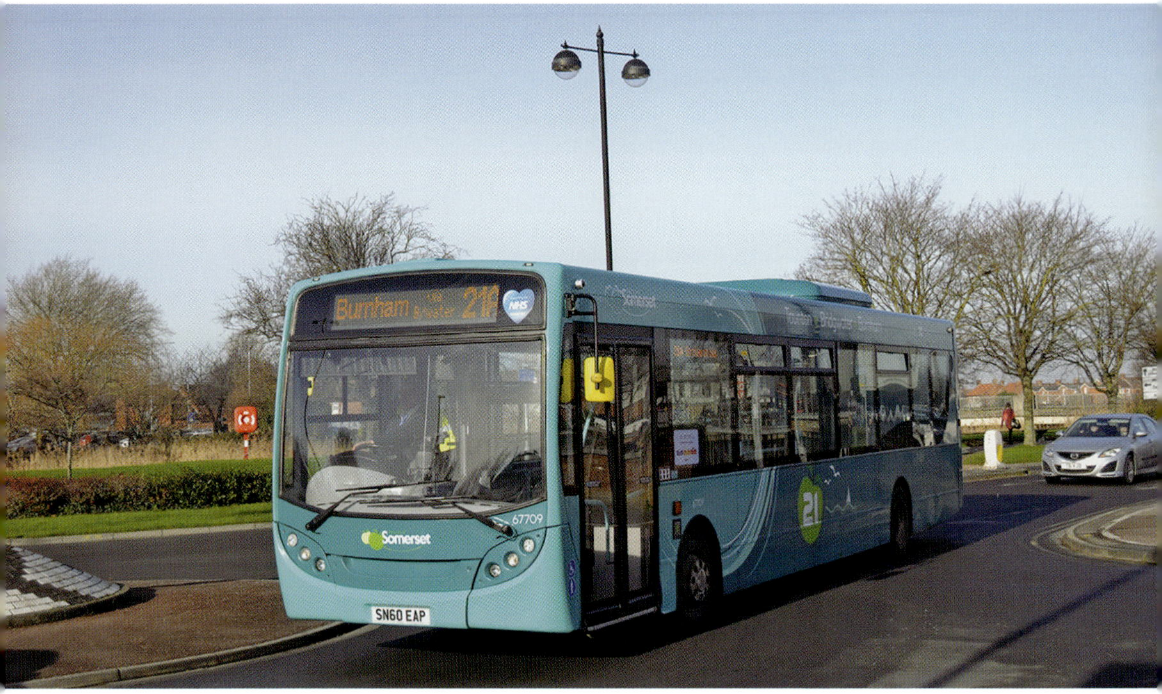

An example of the service 21 route-dedicated Enviro300 is 67709, SN60 EAP, heading the opposite way on 28 January 2022. The 21A variant of this route serves Taunton's Musgrove Park Hospital.

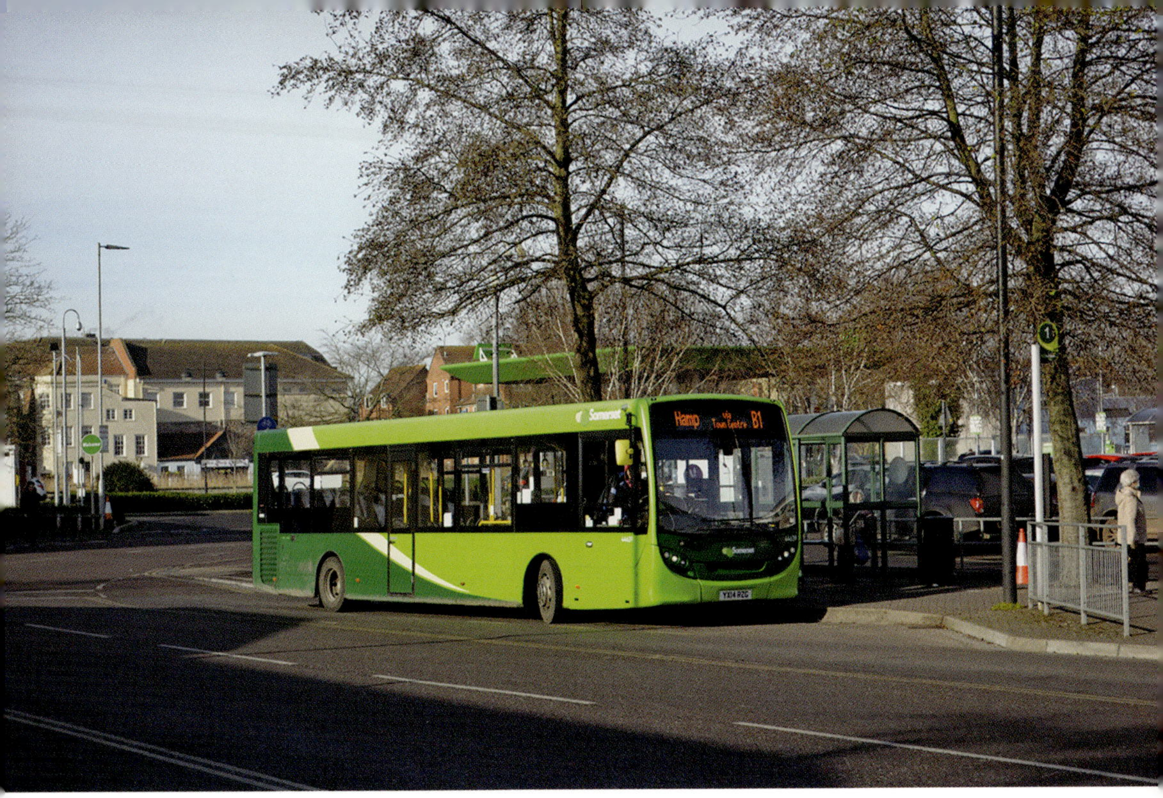

The green livery of Buses of Somerset was the first time First Group had really moved away from their corporate identity. Enviro200 44639, YX14 RZG, is seen in the bus station on 28 January 2022, working a town service.

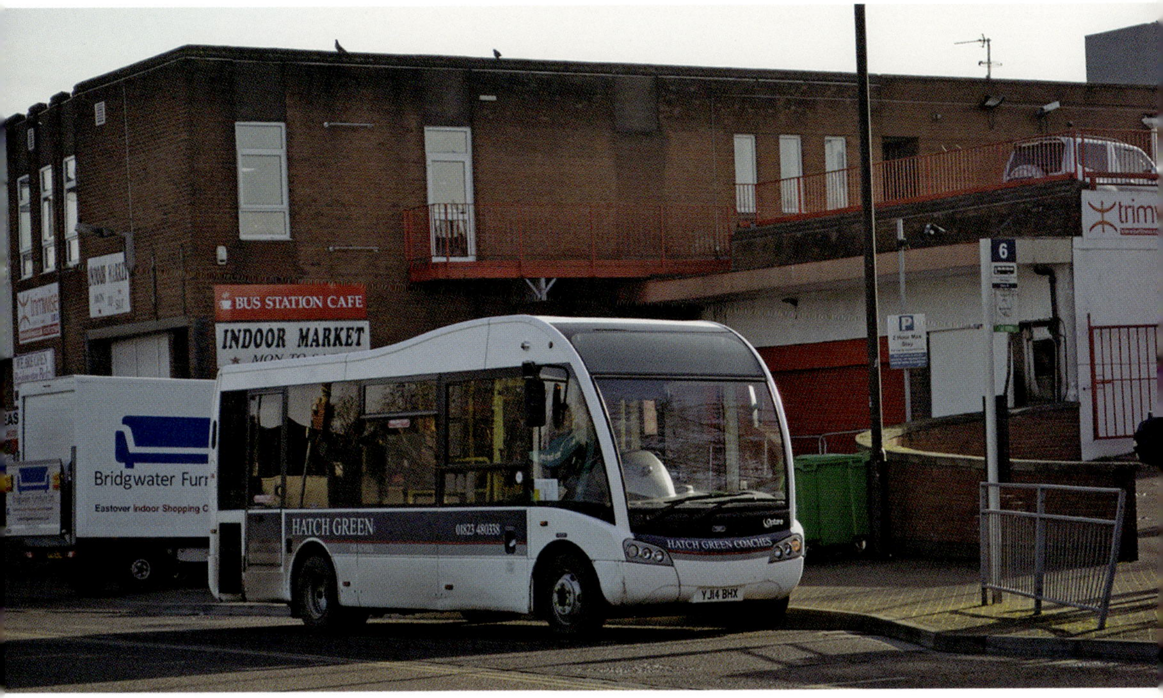

A couple of Bridgwater area services are worked by the Optare Solos of Hatch Green Coaches of Hatch Beauchamp. Solo SR YJ14 BHX is seen laying over in the bus station on 28 January 2022.

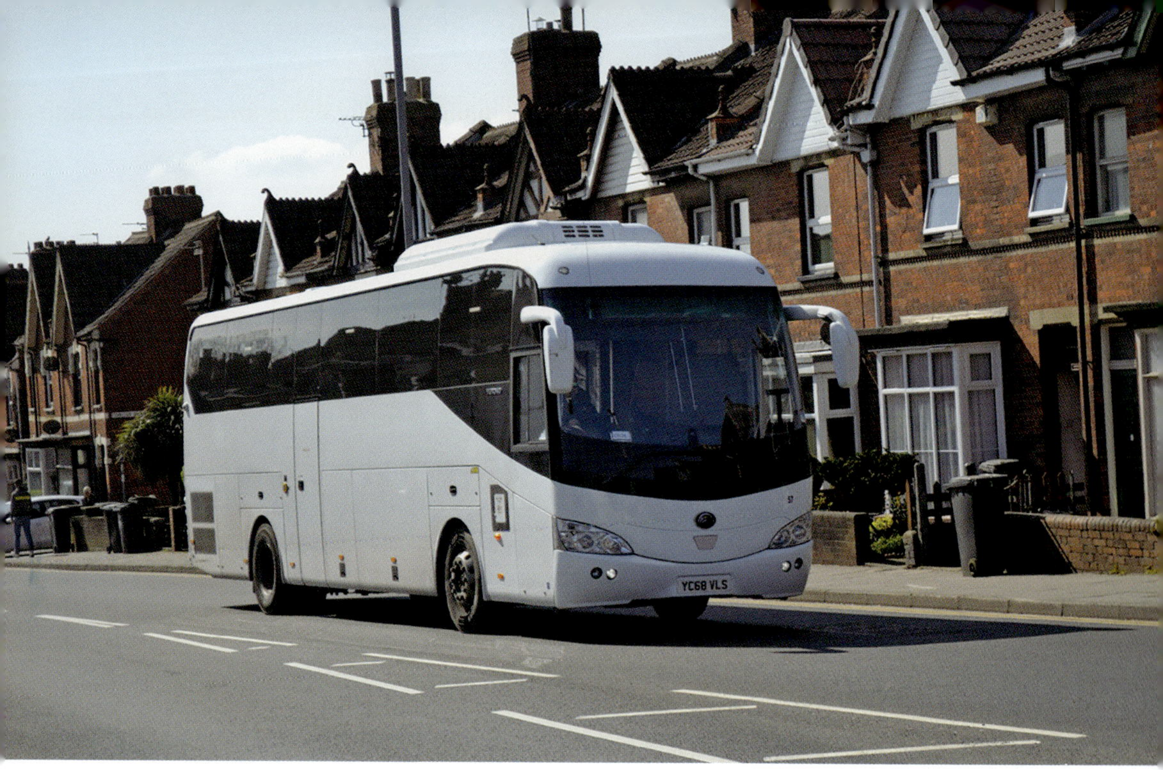

A new operator in the area is Somerset Passenger Solutions, a company formed to provide transport to and from the construction site for the Hinkley Point nuclear power station. It is now wholly owned by Buses of Somerset. Seen on Taunton Road on 19 April 2021 is Chinese-built Yutong coach YC68 VLS.

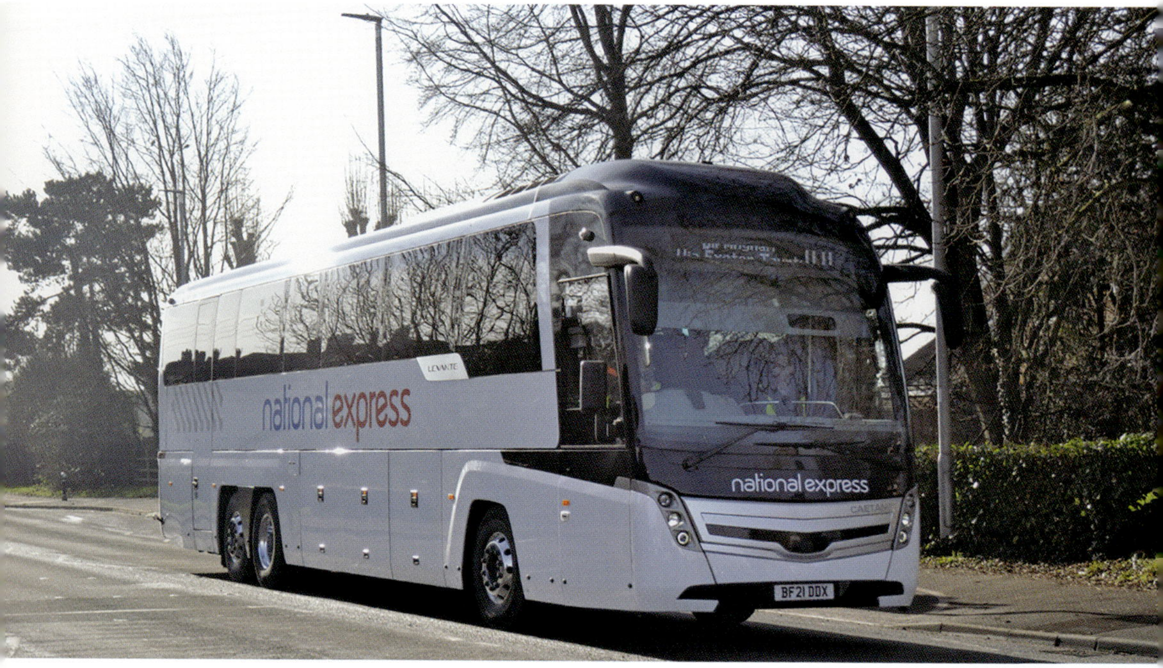

National Express work through Bridgwater with various services. Seen on 28 January 2022 is Volvo B11RT BF21 DDX, with Caetano Levante 3 body from the Park's of Hamilton fleet, working to Plymouth from Birmingham on service 101.

TAUNTON

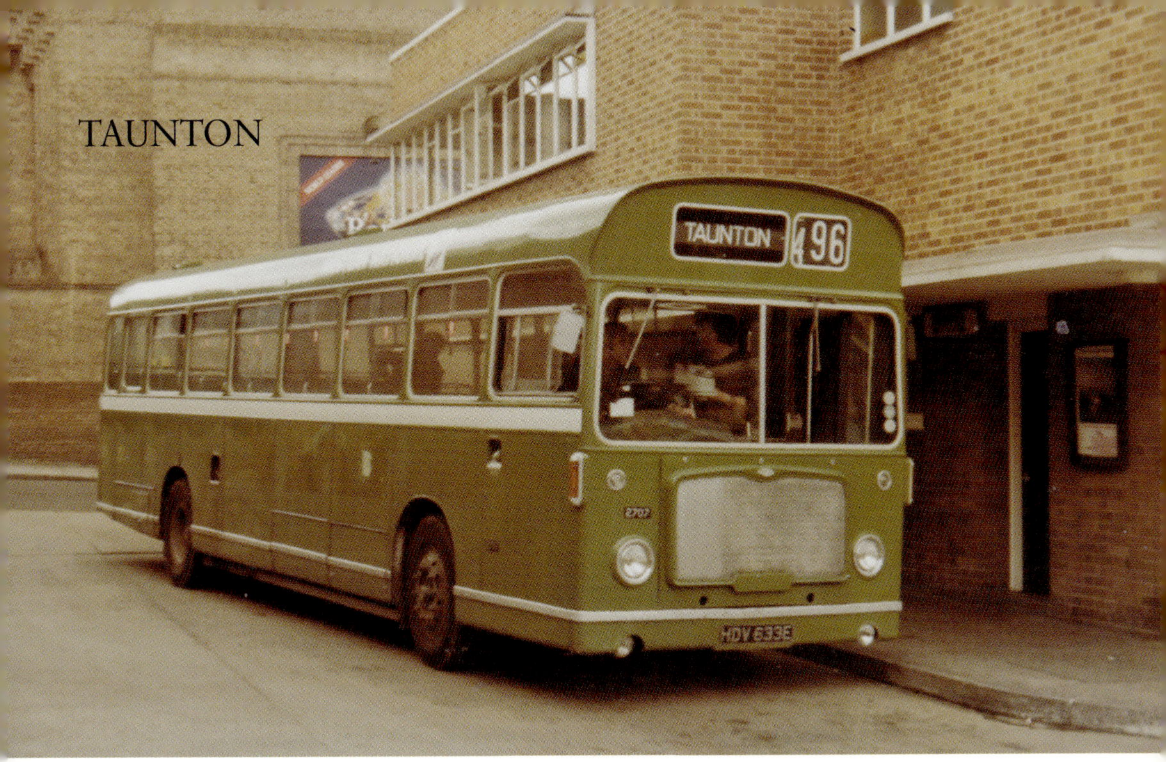

Loading in Taunton bus station in about 1980 is Bristol RELL 2707, HDV 633E. This bus station closed in 2020, with vehicles now loading at various stops around the town centre.

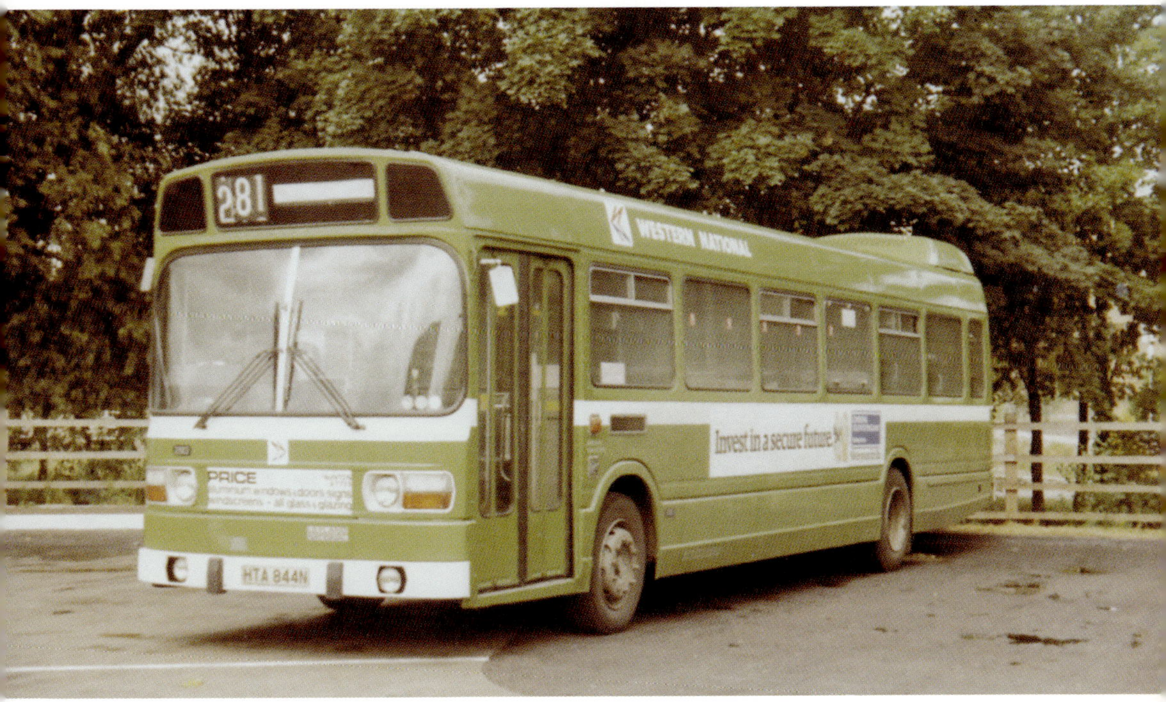

Standing in the parking area at the back of the bus station is Leyland National 2813, HTA 844N. After subsequent service with North Devon Red Bus and First Western National, this vehicle has now been superbly preserved in the NBC livery it carried when new.

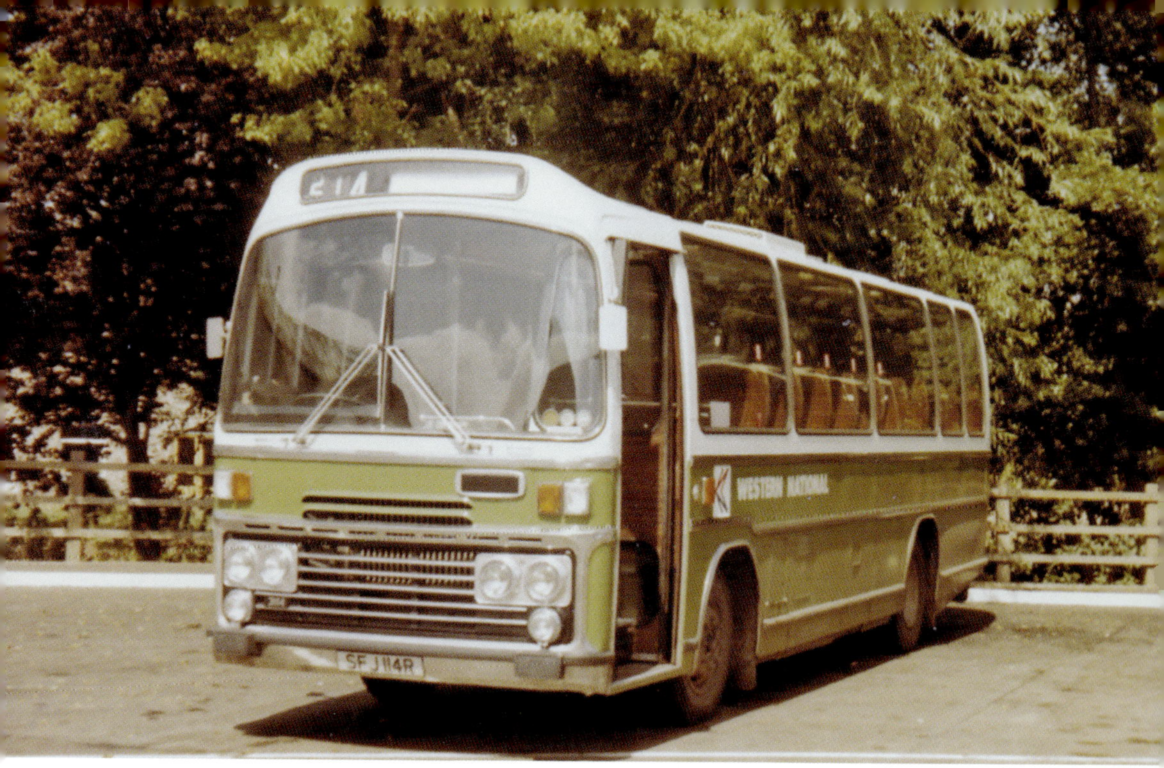

During the late 1970s Western National built up a fleet of Plaxton Supreme Express-bodied Bristol LHs for use as dual purpose vehicles. Some of them were built to 7-foot 6-inch width for use round smaller roads so common in the west country. 3114, SFJ 114R, is seen parked at the rear of the bus station in about 1980.

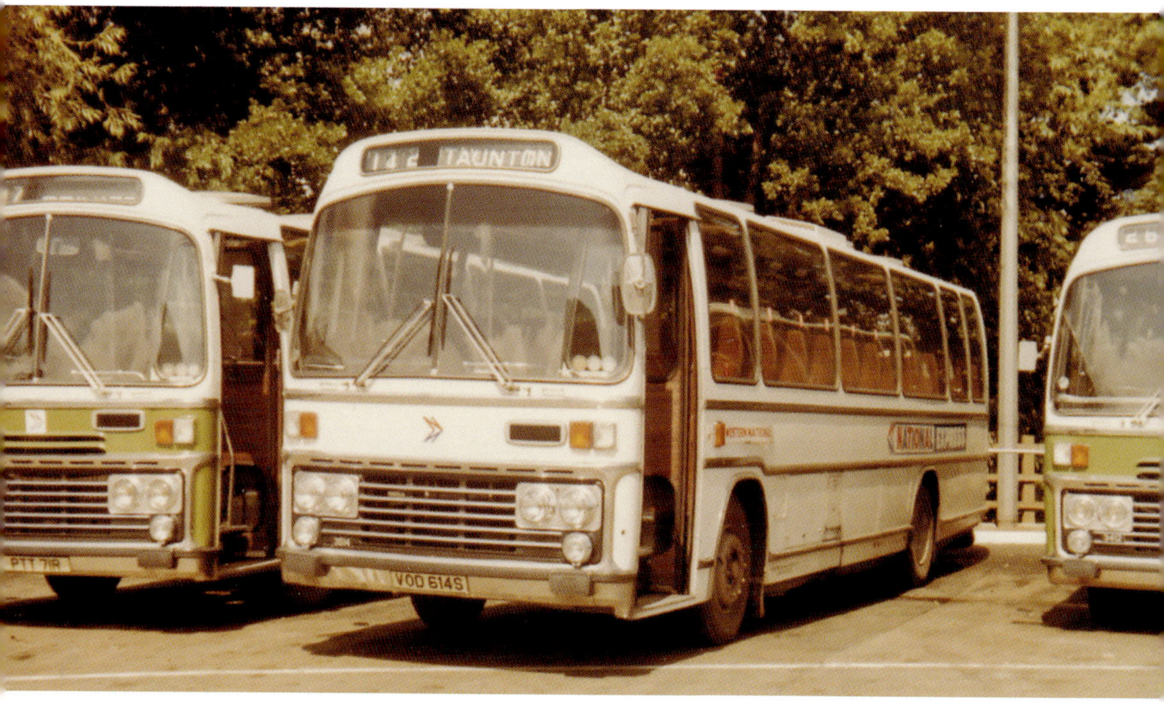

Parked between two Plaxton-bodied Bristol LHs in Taunton bus station, Western National 3514, VOD 614S is a Leyland Leopard with Plaxton Supreme Express body, resting after arriving on National Express work.

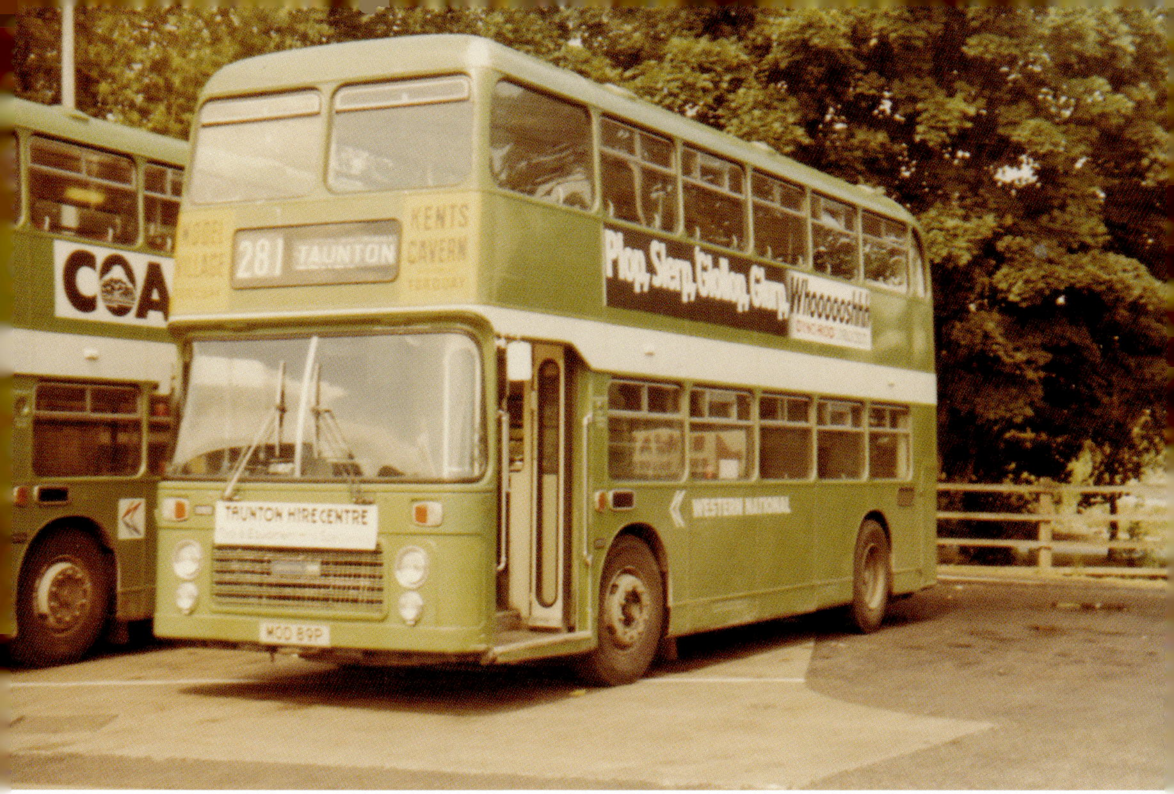

Also parked at the rear of the bus station is Bristol VRT 1089, MOD 89P. The original Western National operation built up a sizeable fleet of Bristol VRs.

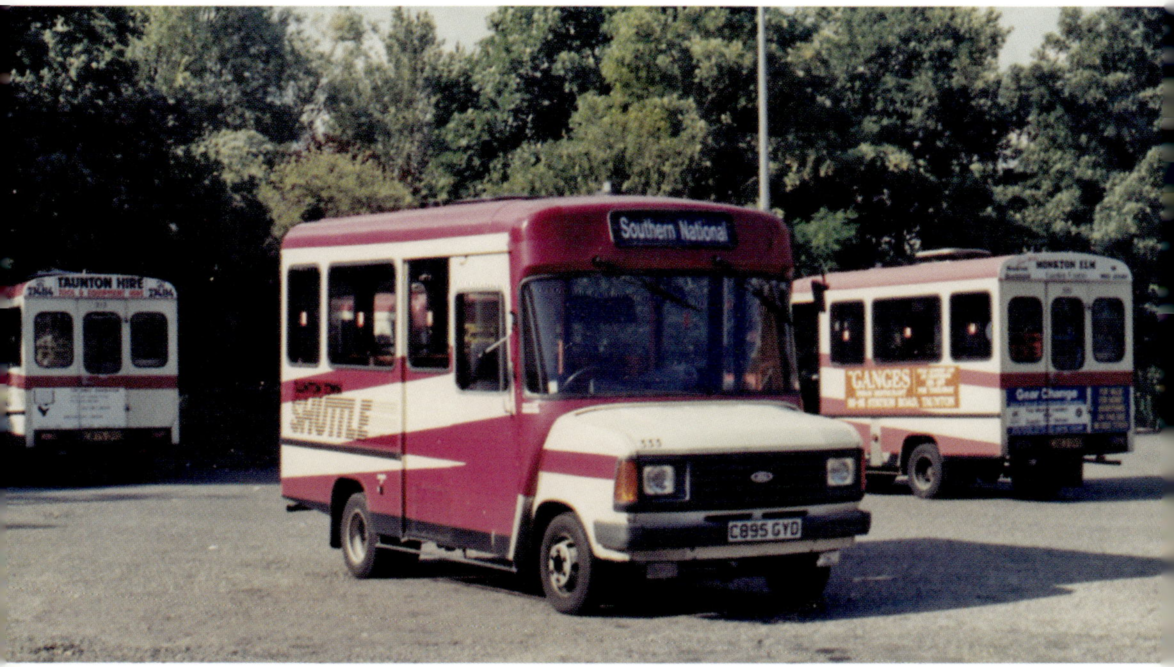

Minibuses joined the Southern National fleet after privatisation with the appearance of vehicles such as Robin Hood-bodied Ford Transit 333, C895 GYD, caught in the bus station on 18 August 1989. In Taunton they wore the rhubarb and custard livery mentioned earlier and carried the fleetname 'Taunton Town Shuttle'.

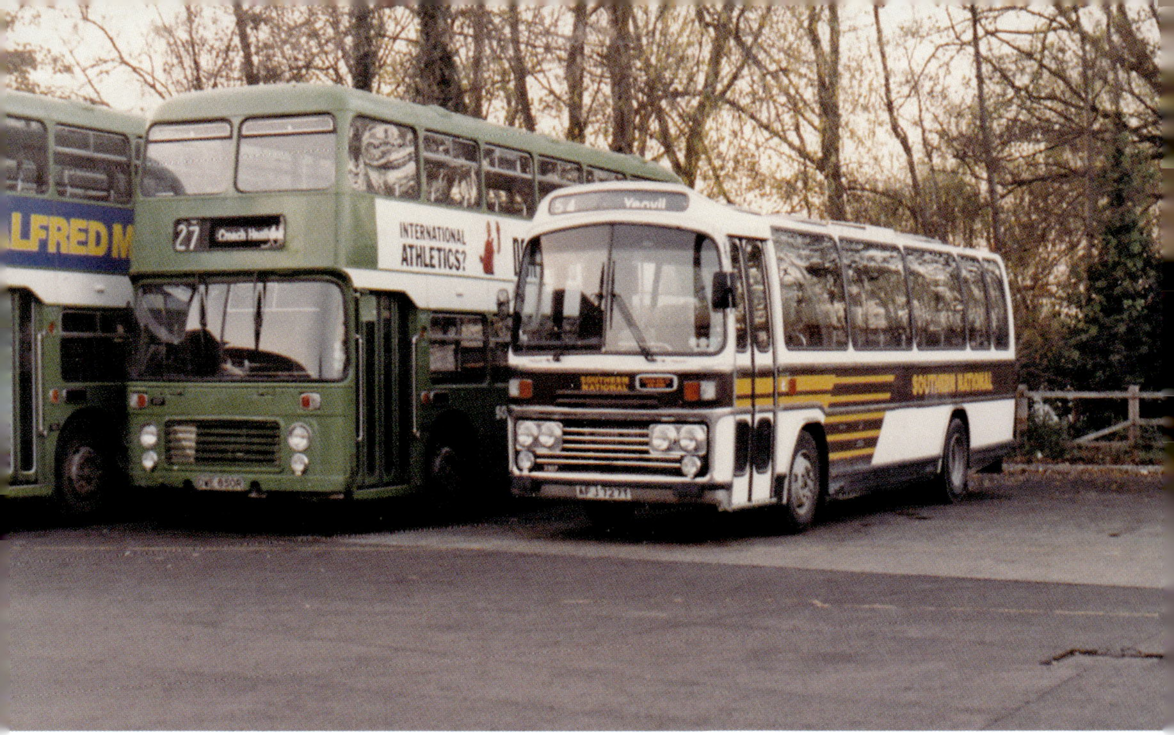

Seen at the back of the bus station on 24 November 1989 is one of the 7-foot 6-inch wide Plaxton-bodied Bristol LHs, 3307, AFJ 727T, wearing a brown and yellow livery introduced for coaches. This vehicle went on to carry out driver trainer duties and is now preserved. Next to it is former Yorkshire Traction Bristol VRT 607, OWE 850R, which moved to the west country in 1982.

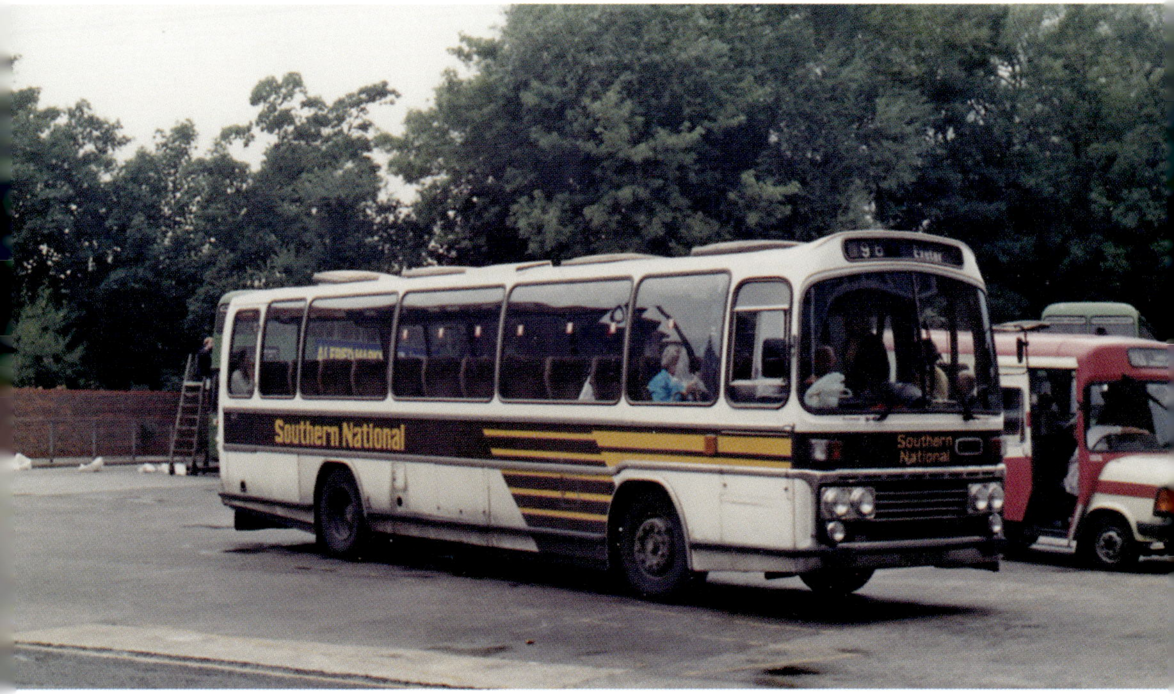

Wearing the same livery as the Bristol LH in the previous picture is Plaxton Supreme-bodied Leyland Leopard 3515, VOD 615S, in the bus station on 14 August 1989 working the long X96 service to Exeter from Bristol.

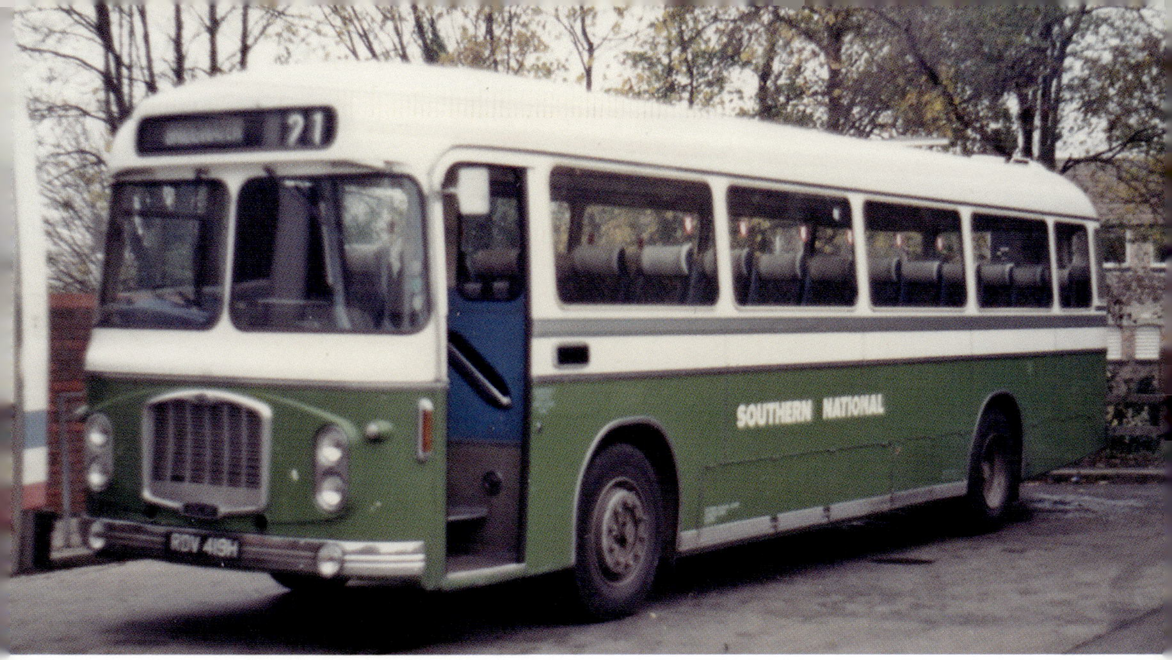

This former Royal Blue Bristol RELH, 1468, RDV 419H, was caught in the bus station on 14 August 1989 still in NBC dual-purpose colours.

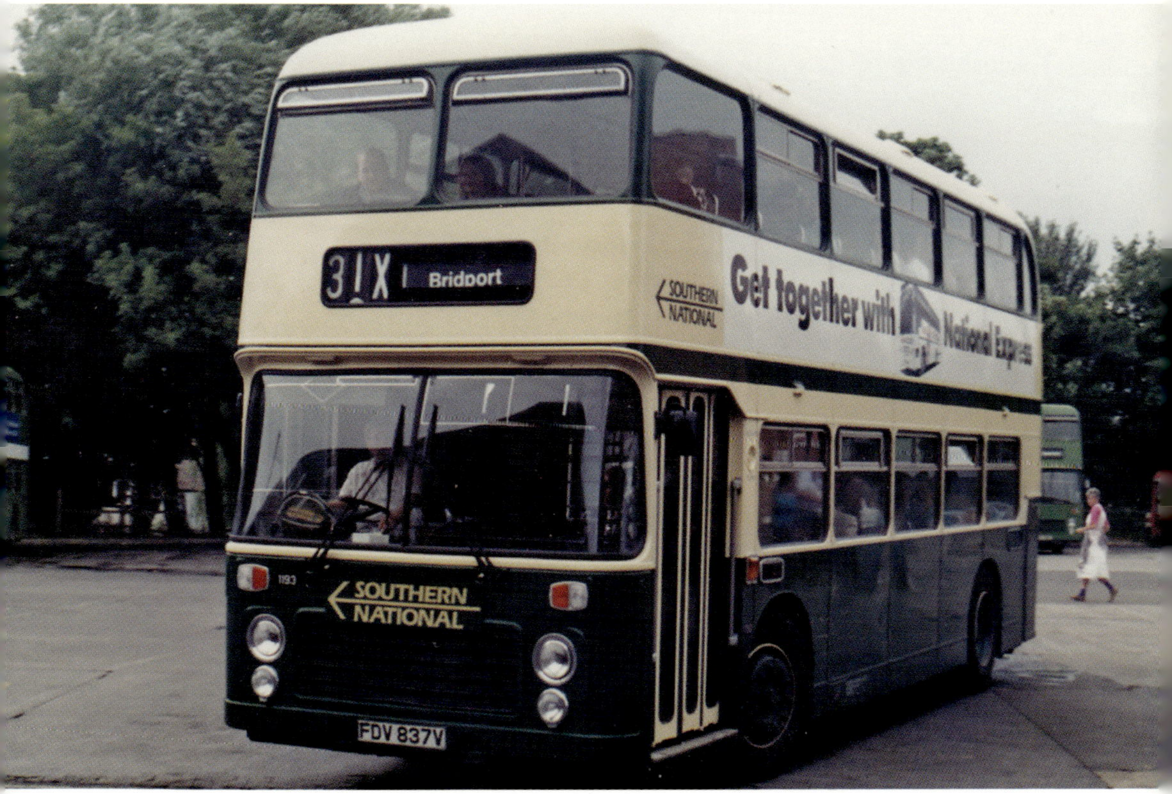

Bristol VRT 1193, FDV 837V, was painted in this experimental livery. As far as I know it was the only vehicle thus painted, which I think is a shame as I thought it was very smart. It's seen on 14 August 1989 leaving the bus station for Bridport.

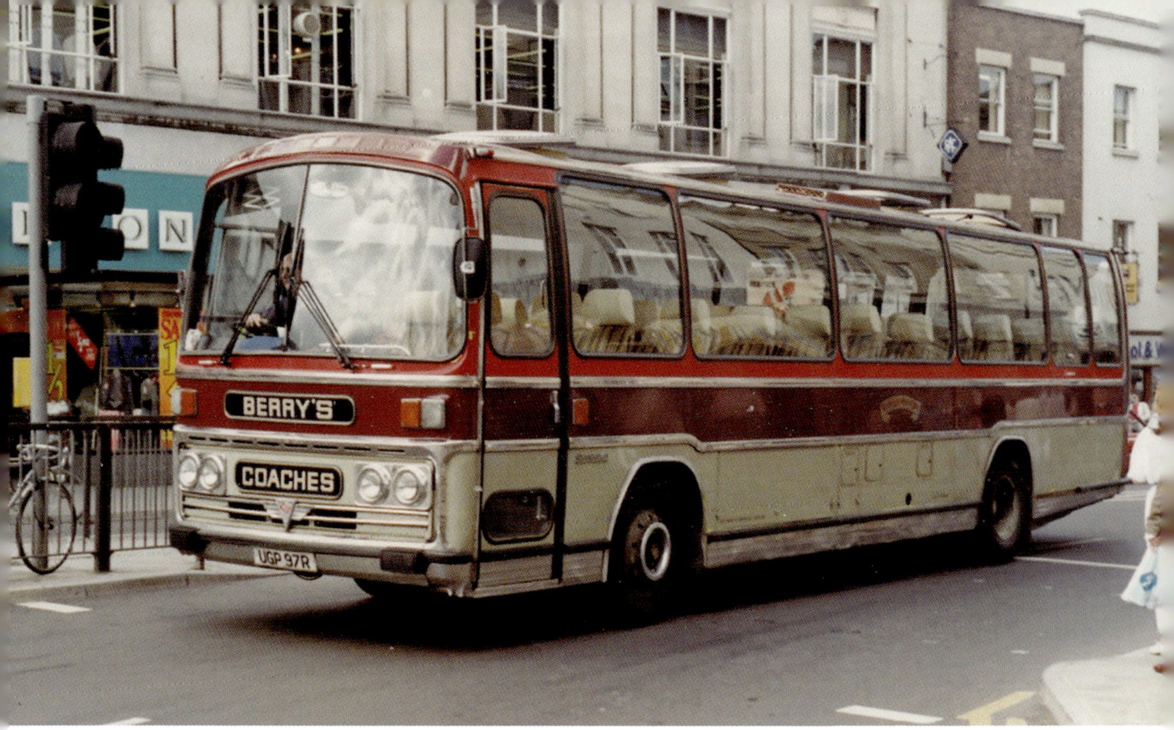

We shouldn't forget Taunton's best known independent operator, Berry's, a firm dating from the 1920s and one that I remember well from my childhood in Taunton in the early 1960s. A keen user of AEC vehicles, Plaxton Supreme-bodied AEC Reliance UGP 97R was bought from Surrey Motors of Sutton in 1980. It is seen at The Parade, Taunton, on 2 July 1990.

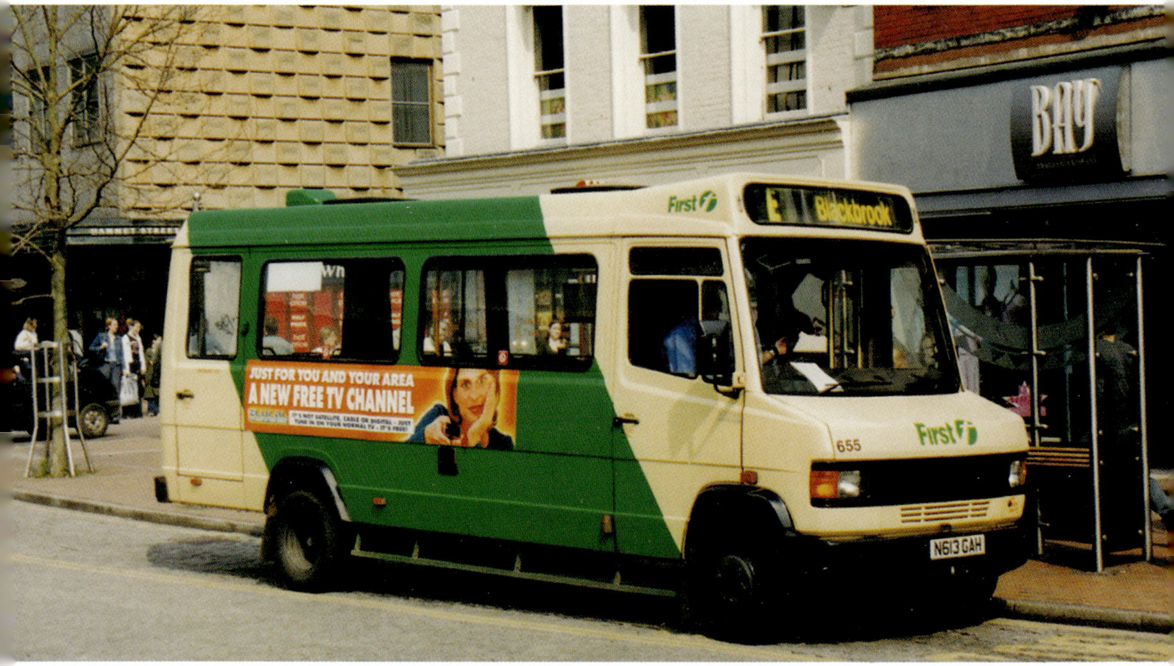

Southern National joined the First Group in 1999. Mercedes-Benz 609D 655, N613 GAH, was one of a number transferred from First Eastern Counties in 2000, where it was numbered MG113, to replace the original Ford Transits. Carrying bodywork by Frank Guy, 655 is seen at The Parade, Taunton, on 5 April 2002.

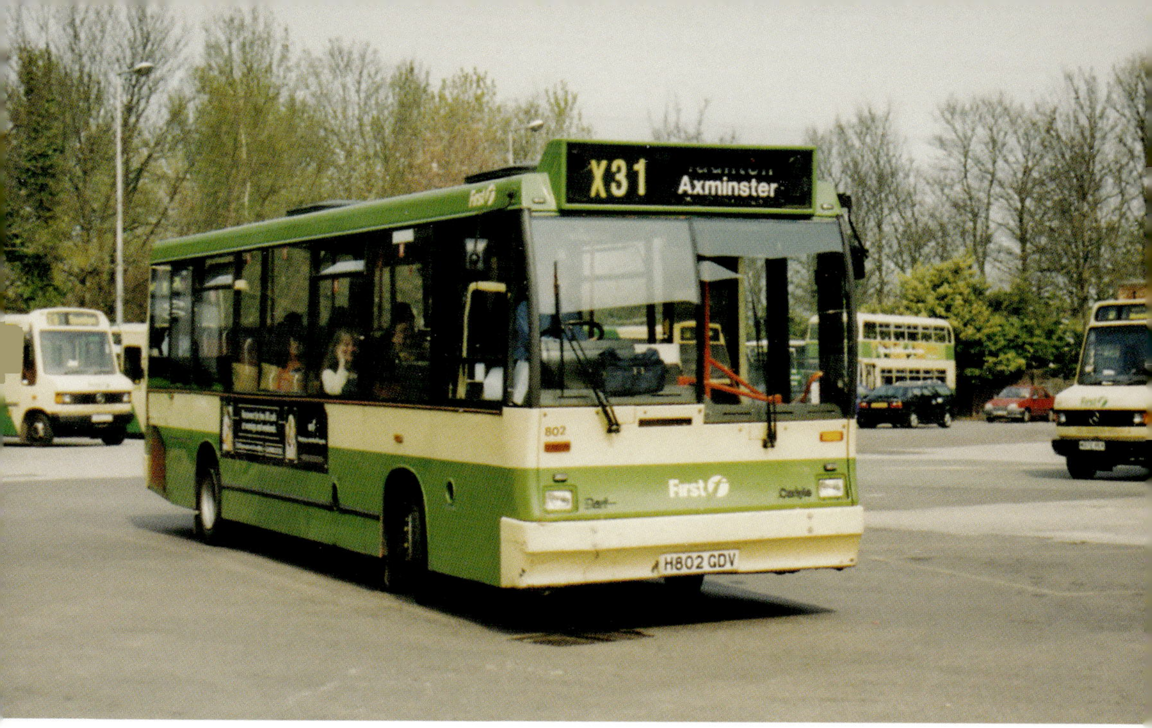

The First Southern National fleet was quite varied at this time, and it is only really possible to give a flavour of what was around. This Carlyle-bodied Dennis Dart, numbered 802, H802 GDV, is leaving the bus station for Axminster on 5 April 2002 and was transferred from North Devon Red Bus in 1998.

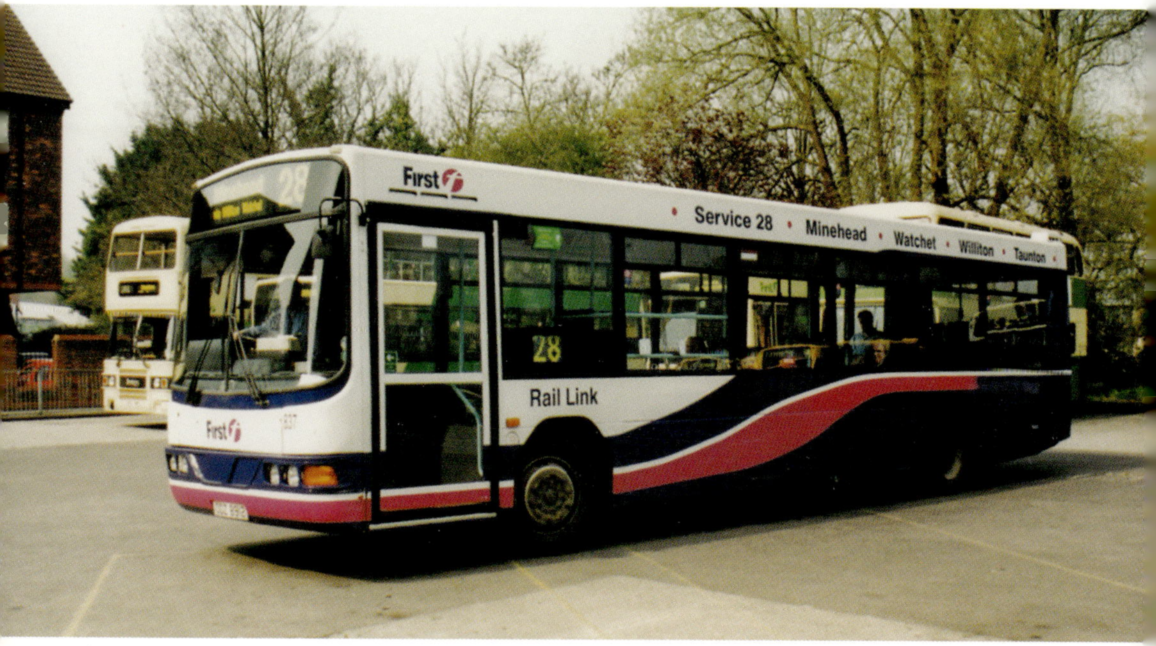

One of the first marques of low-floor easy-access vehicles was the Dennis Lance SLF with Wright Pathfinder body. A handful were delivered to Centrewest in London in 1994 and eventually migrated to the West Country. 837, ODZ 8912, is leaving the bus station on 5 April 2002, bound for Minehead on service 28. This route is branded 'Rail Link' as it connects with the wonderful West Somerset Railway, England's longest heritage railway, at Bishops Lydeard and then more or less follows its route to Minehead. 837 carries full First Group corporate livery.

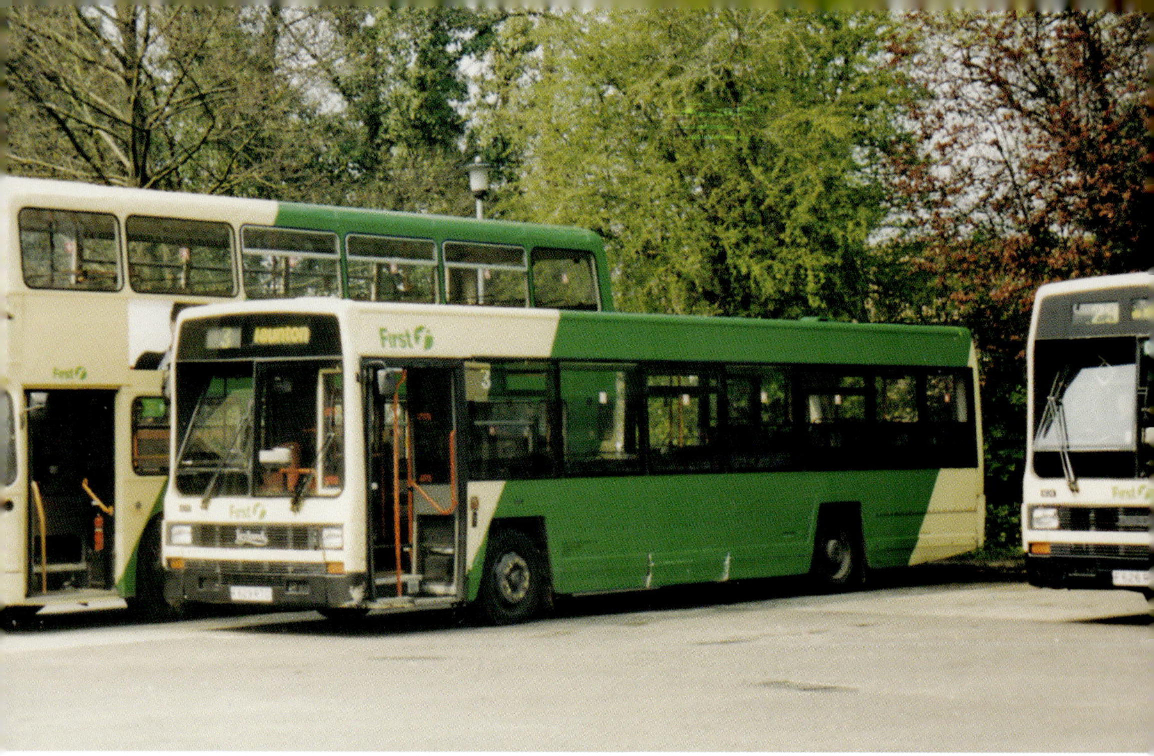

A number of Leyland Lynxes were transferred to Southern National from Bristol Cityline during 2000. 1629 F629RTC is seen in the bus station on 5 April 2002, next to 1626.

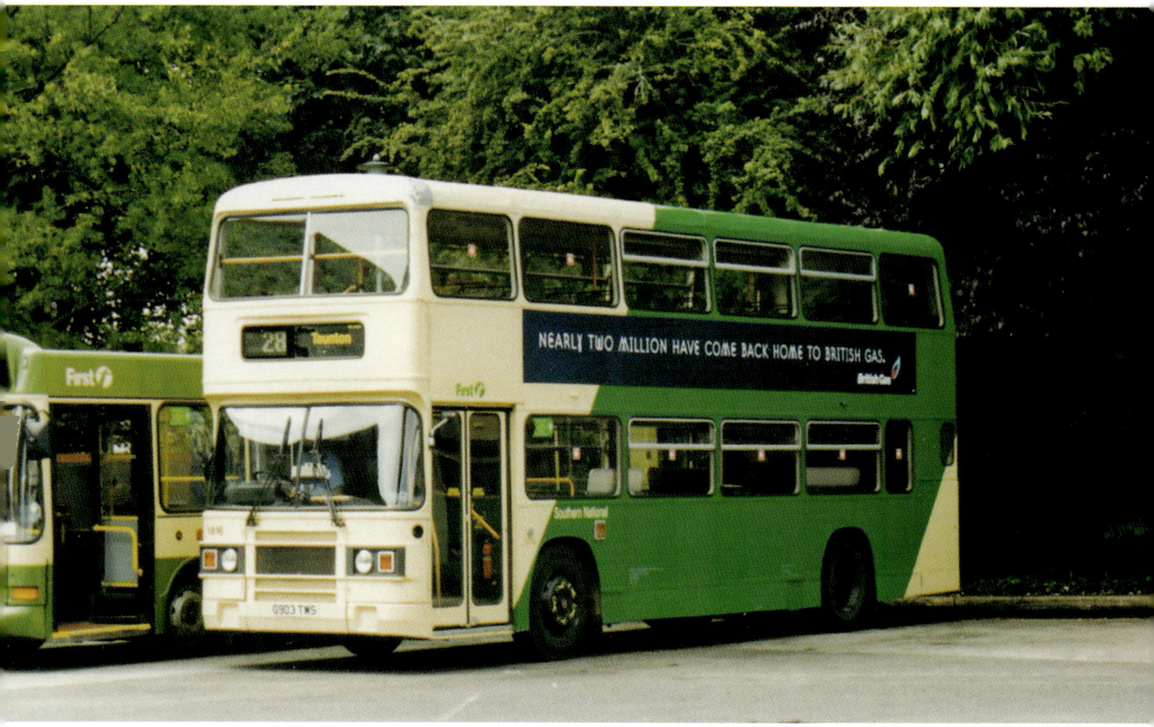

Leyland Olympian 1816, G903TWS, was new to Badgerline in 1989 and moved to First Southern National in 2000. Seen here in the bus station on 17 August 2001, it is displaying route number 28 for the service from Minehead.

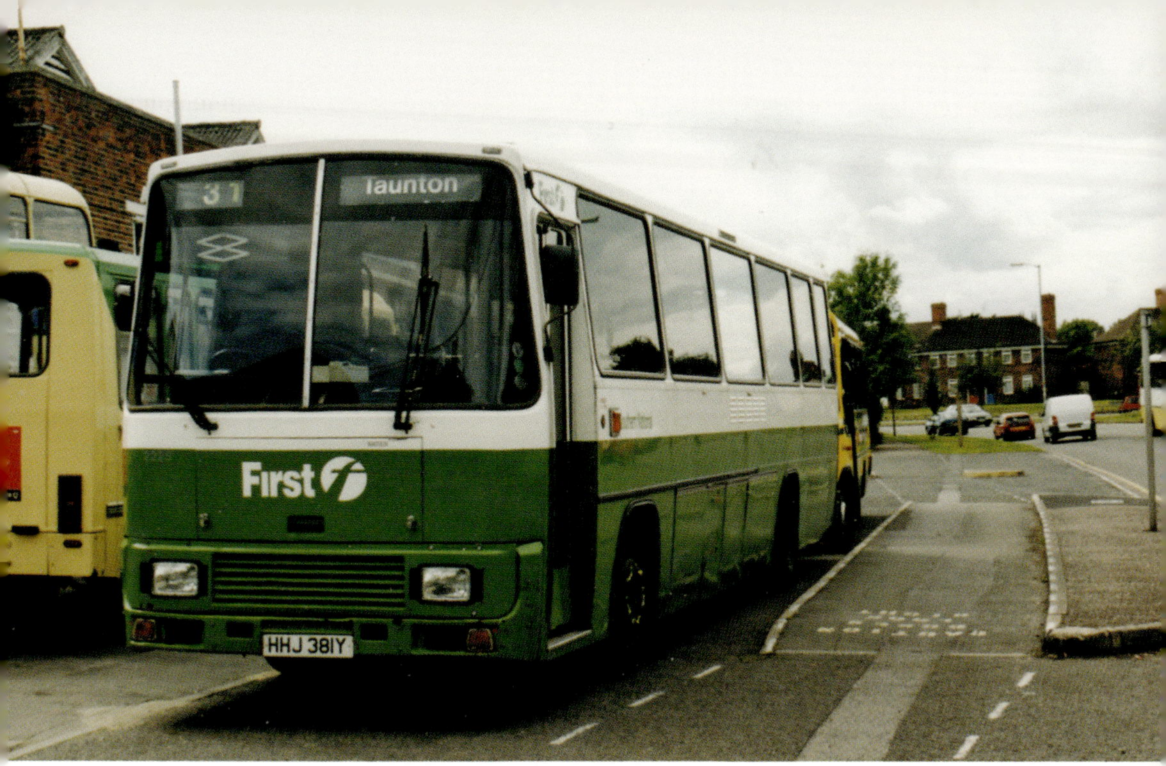

In 1933, Western National acquired Dunn's Services of Taunton, and with it their garage in Hamilton Road. The garage is now used by Buses of Somerset. However this view, taken on 17 August 2001, is of First Southern National's former Eastern National Alexander TE-bodied Leyland Tiger 2225, HHJ 381Y, as it rests outside between duties.

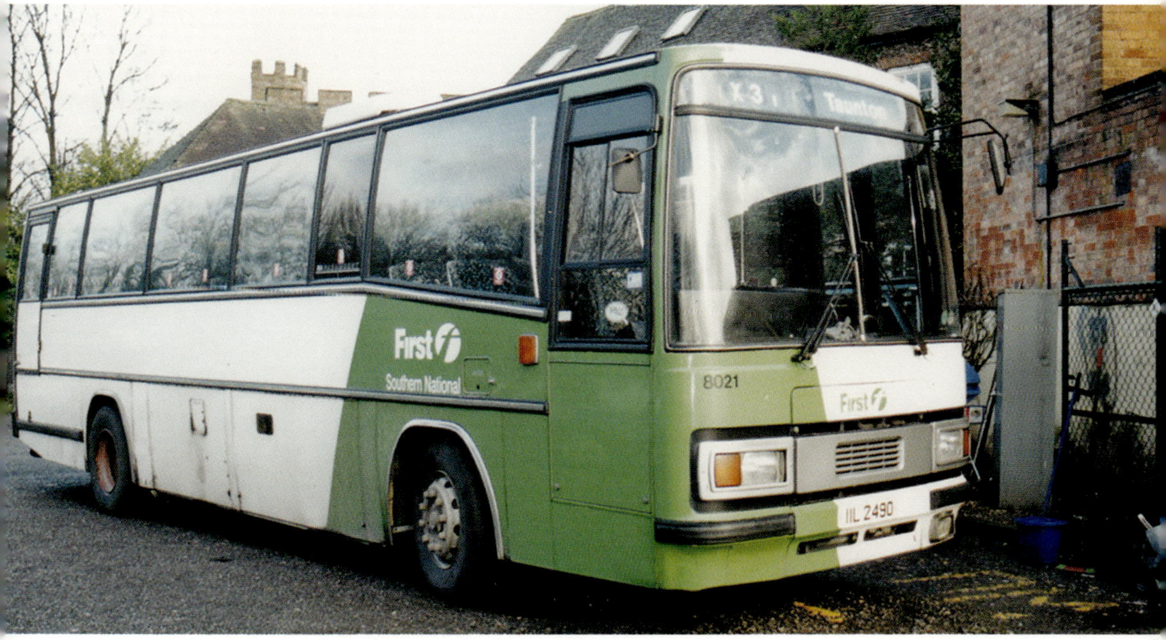

First Southern National 8021, IIL2490, came into the fleet by way of Southern National's acquisition of the fleet of Pearce, Darch & Wilcox of Martock, a firm with the rather lovely trading name of 'Comfy-Lux'. New to Lancaster City Council as C90 MHG, it is a Leyland Tiger TRCTL11/2RH with a Plaxton Paramount 3200 body, and is seen parked in the bus station on 2 January 2001.

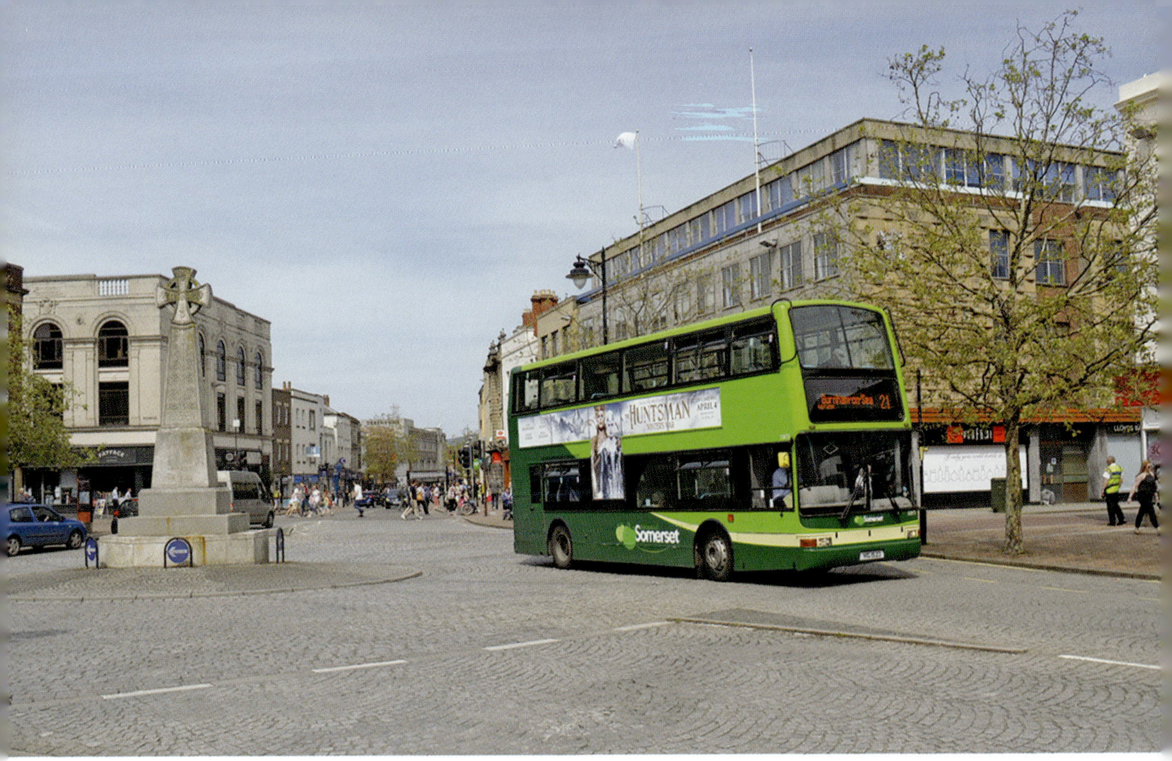

Plaxton President-bodied Dennis Trident 32873, HIG 1523, new to Capital Citybus with the registration T873 KLF, is seen here in The Parade at the start of its journey to Burnham-on-Sea on 8 May 2016.

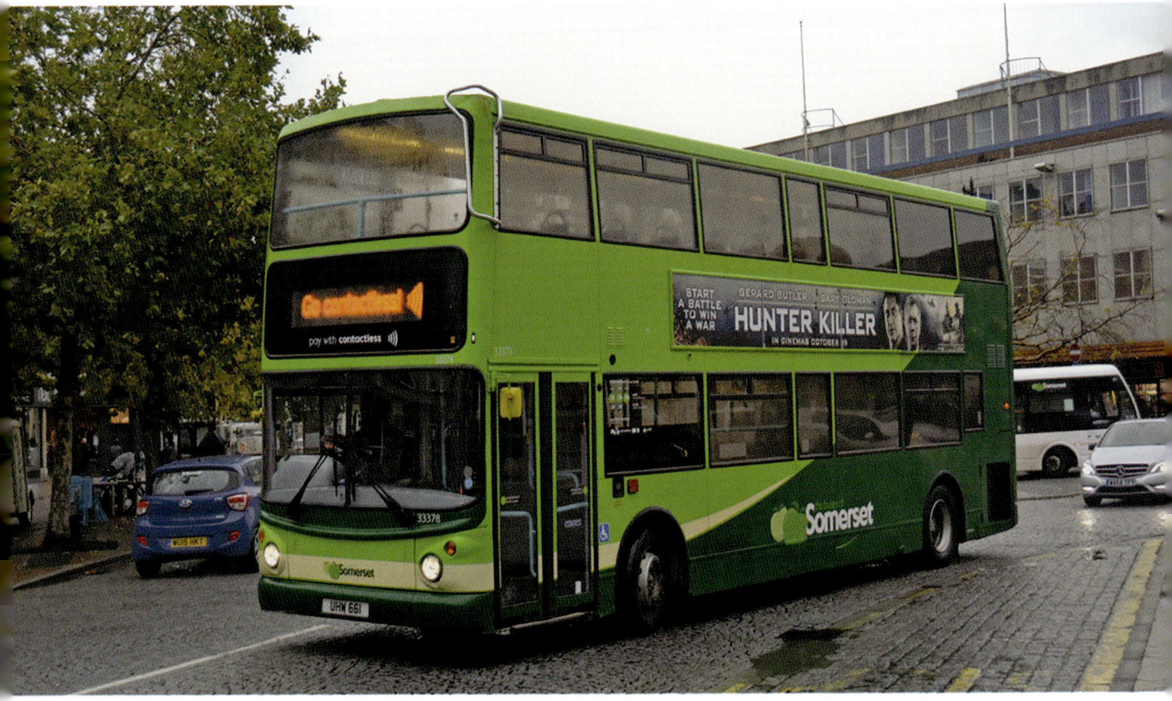

First Buses of Somerset came into being in 2014, bringing with it a smart two-tone green livery. Brightening up a dull wet 15 October in 2018, former Centrewest Transbus Trident 33378, UHW 661, fitted with Transbus ALX400 body, is seen in Corporation Street. It originally carried the registration mark LK53 LYX.

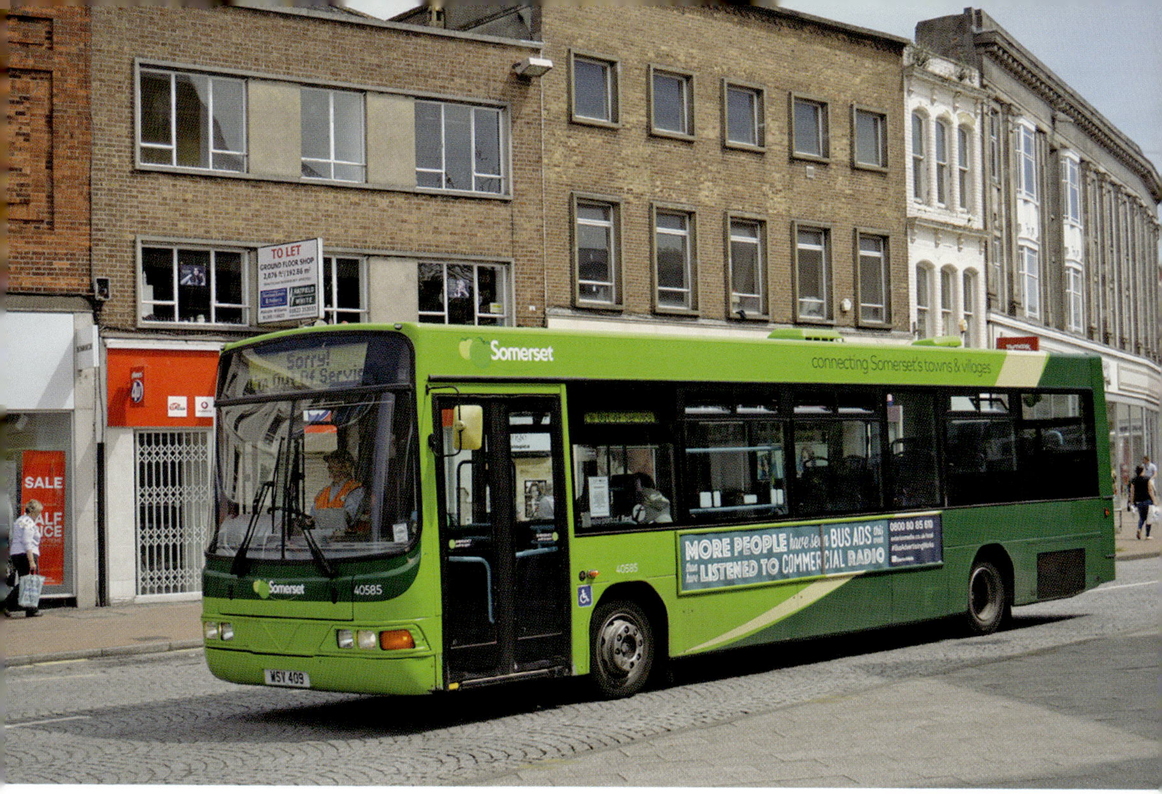

In 2016, The Buses of Somerset had a number of Wright Crusader-bodied Volvo B6BLEs on their books. Running back to the bus station from the depot on 8 May is 40585, WSV 409, new to Rider York as YJ51 RJV.

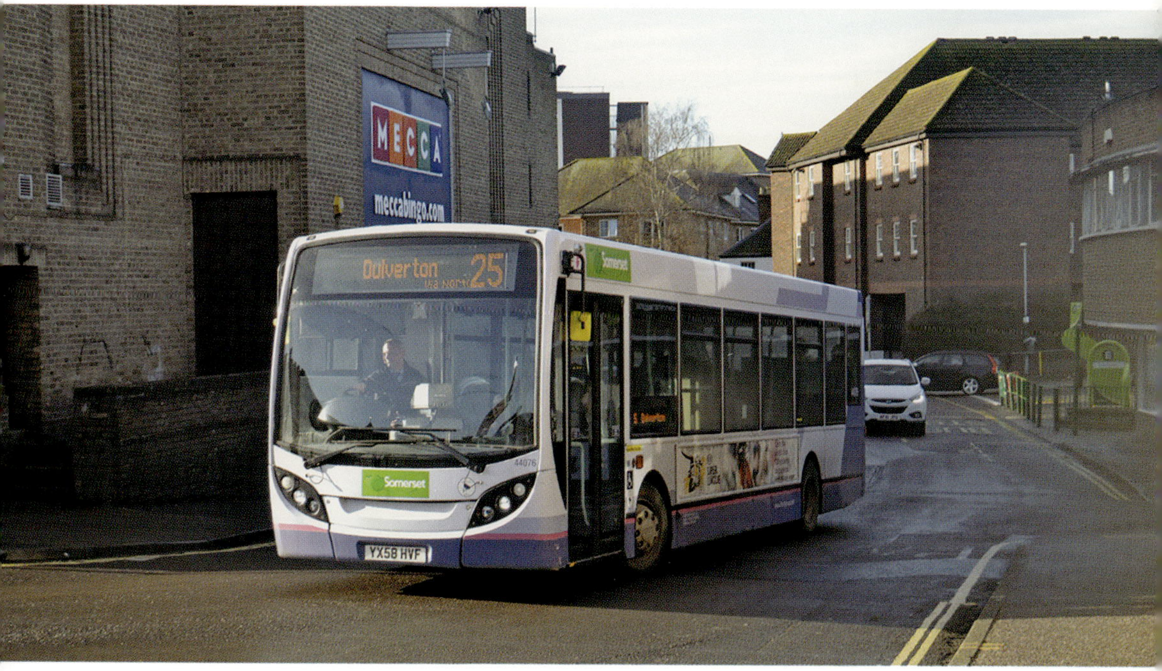

Even in 2018, not all vehicles carried the green Buses of Somerset livery. Enviro200 44076, YX58 HVF, seen here on 10 January 2018 leaving Taunton for Dulverton, a lovely little town on Exmoor, was transferred from First Essex in 2017.

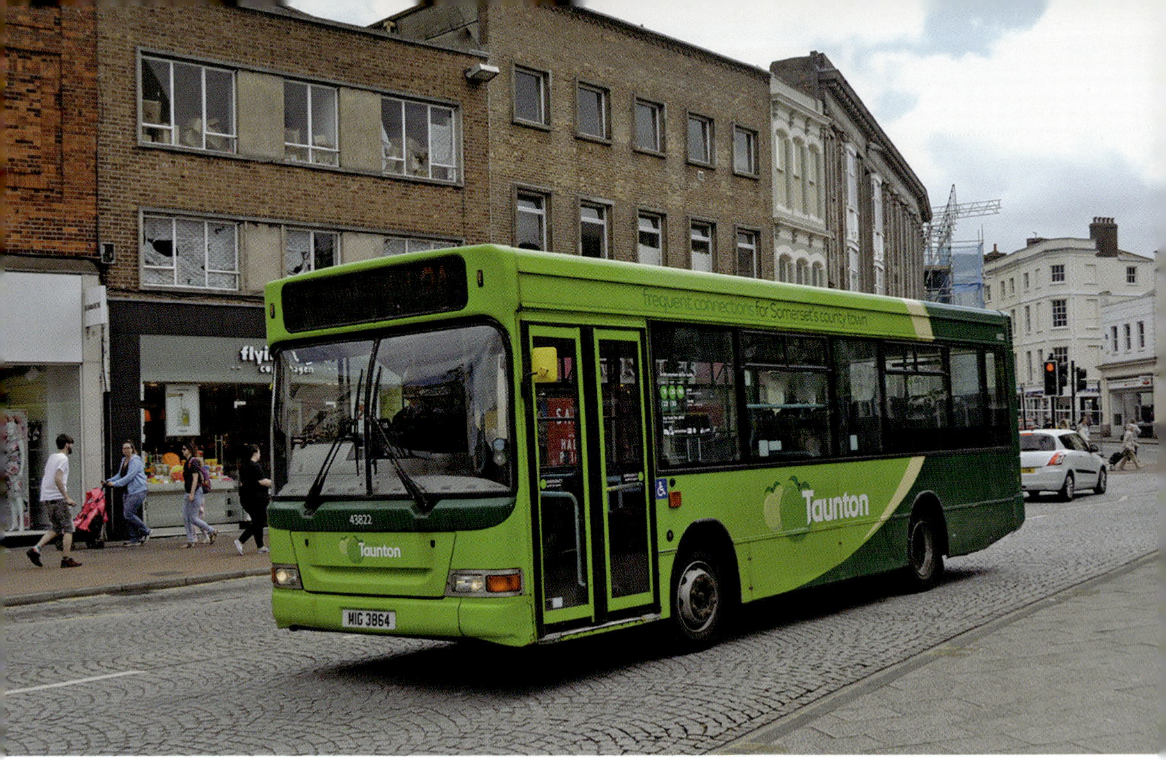

Vehicles working on Taunton's town services carried the fleetname Taunton, as shown here on 43822, MIG 3864, a Plaxton Pointer 2-bodied Dennis Dart SLF, seen on 14 June 2018 working a 2A service to Monkton Heathfield.

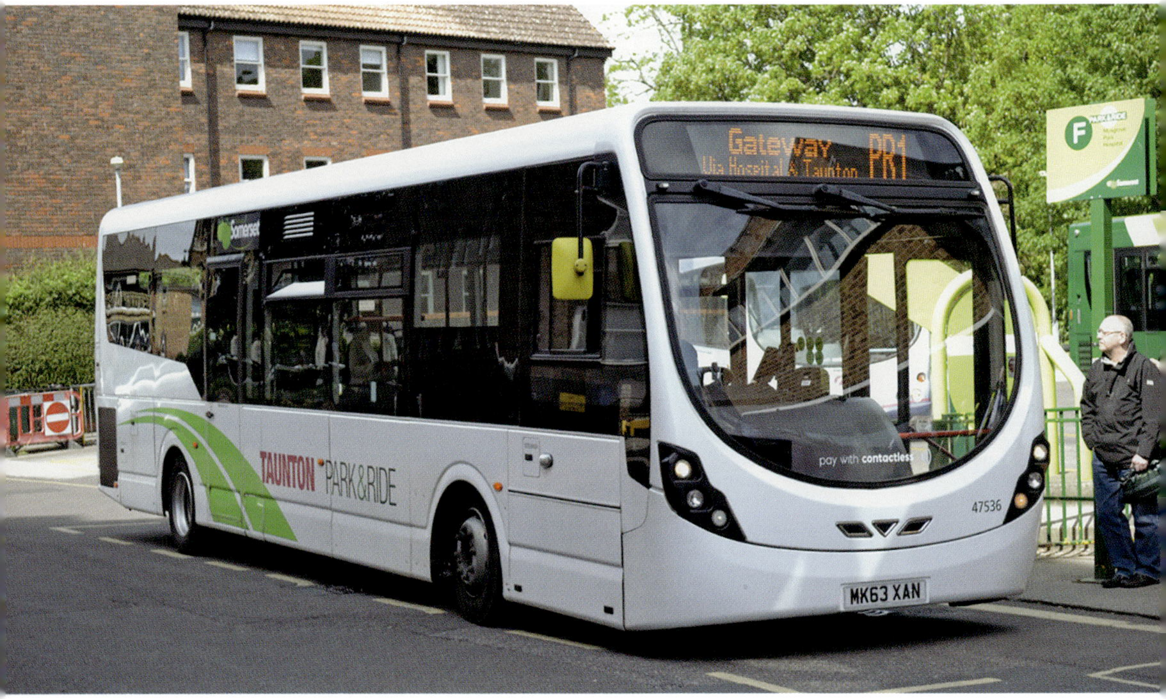

Taunton's Park and Ride services are in the hands of a number of Wright StreetLite DFs. Seen at the bus station on 17 May 2018, 47536, MK63 XAN, came to Taunton from South Wales Transport after first seeing service at Guernsey Airport.

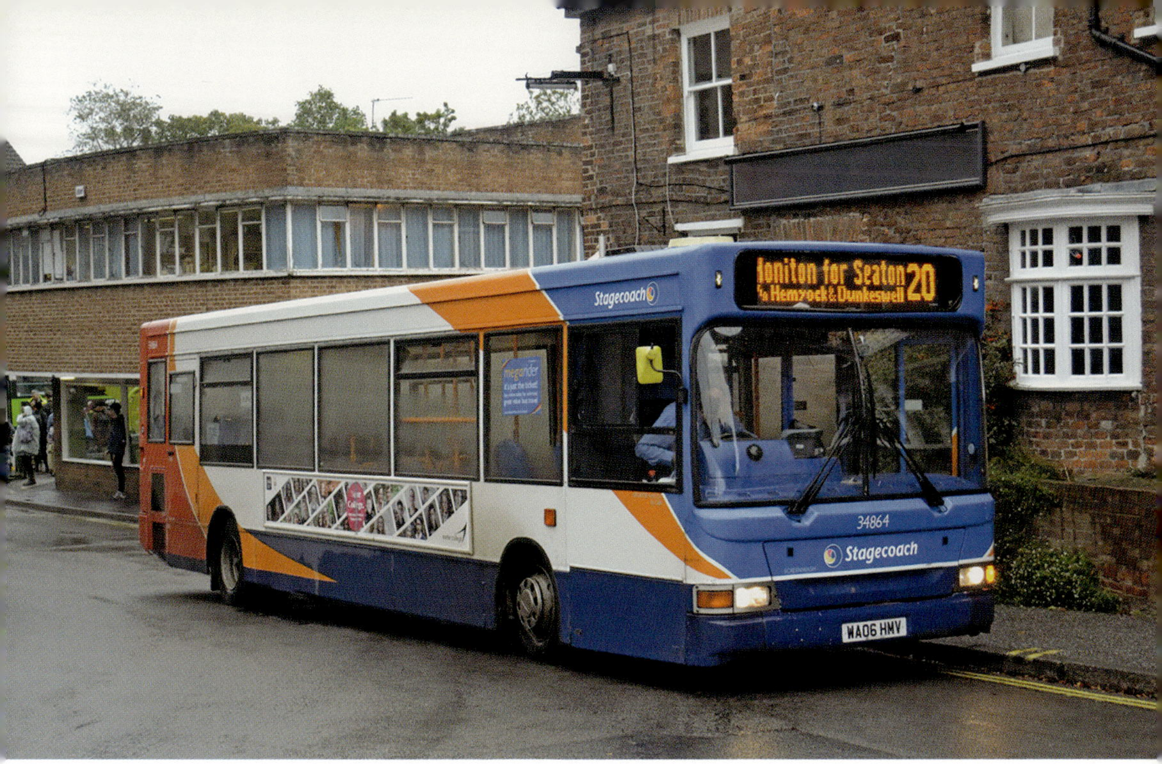

Stagecoach Devon began working into Taunton when they took over Cook's Coaches of Wellington. 15 October 2018, Alexander-Dennis Dart 34864 WA06 HMV, with a Pointer 2 body was operating former Cook's service 20 to Honiton.

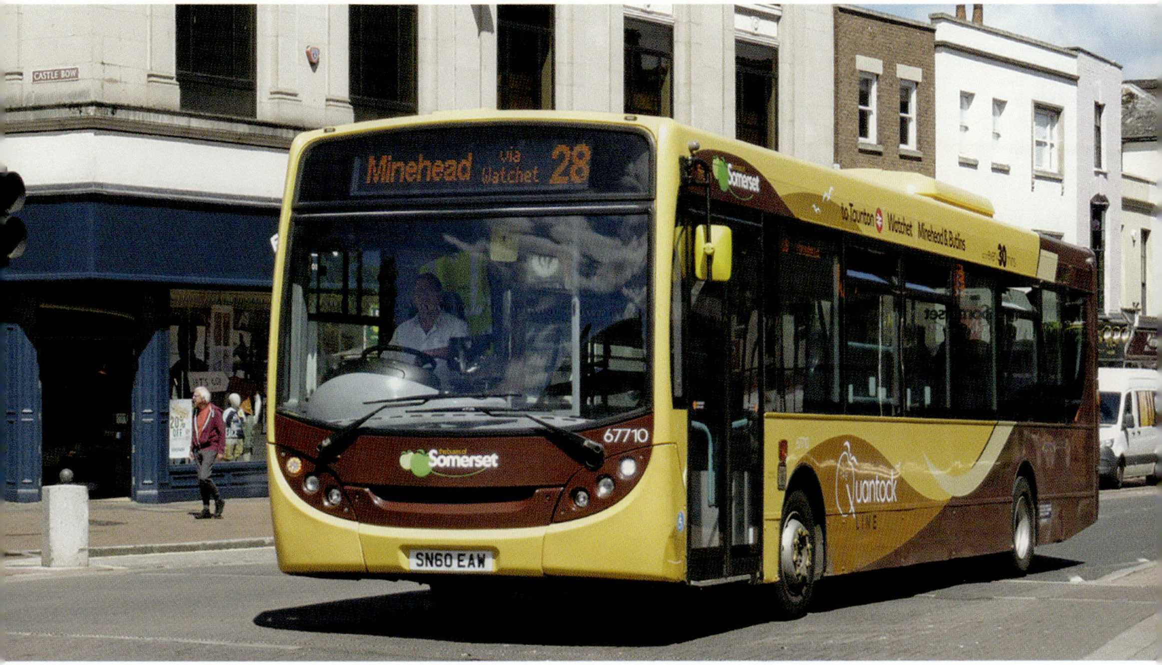

In contrast to the Dennis Lance on service 28 Rail Link to Minehead, pictured earlier, is The Buses of Somerset Enviro300 67710, SN60 EAW, seen leaving Taunton on 20 June 2022. The service was rebranded as 'The Quantock Line' and a number of Enviro300s received this smart brown and cream livery.

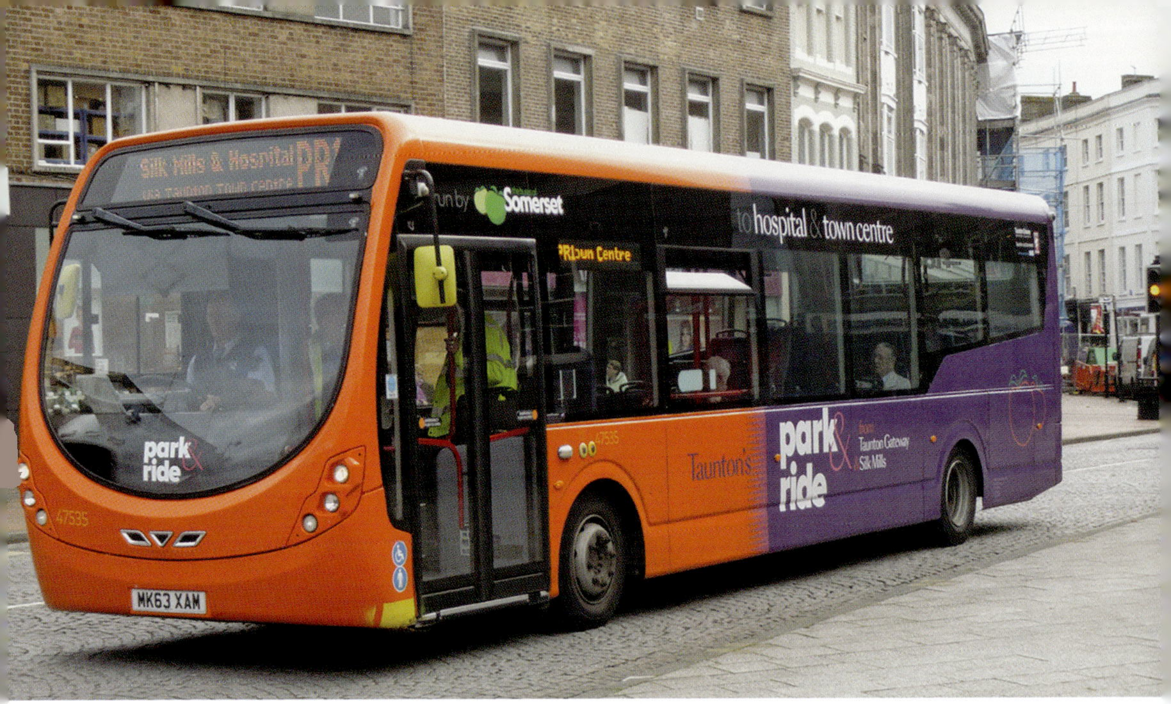

At the same time as the rebranding of the Minehead service, Taunton's Park & Ride also received a make-over, including this new orange and purple livery, modelled by Wright StreetLite DF 47535, MK63 XAM. This vehicle reached The Buses of Somerset from SGI Community Transport of Thornhill and is bound for Silk Mills, to which I remember being taken for walks when a small child in Taunton, where my father served as a curate in the early 1960s, and seeing such delights as Castle Class 4-6-0s pass-by... Happy days!

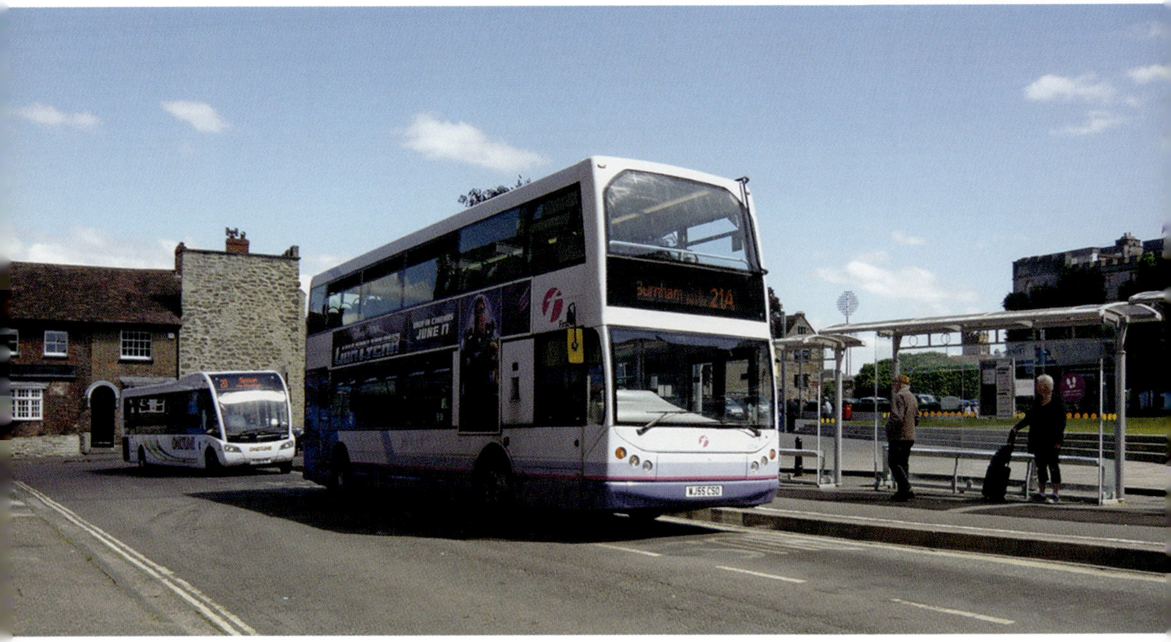

It seems that the only double-deckers in The Buses of Somerset fleet to carry the green livery are the older ALX400s like 33378 pictured earlier. Otherwise they carry the standard First Group livery, as seen on 32764, WJ55 CSO, a Dennis Trident with East Lancs Myllennium Lolyne body, seen on 20 June 2022 awaiting departure for Burnham-on-Sea.

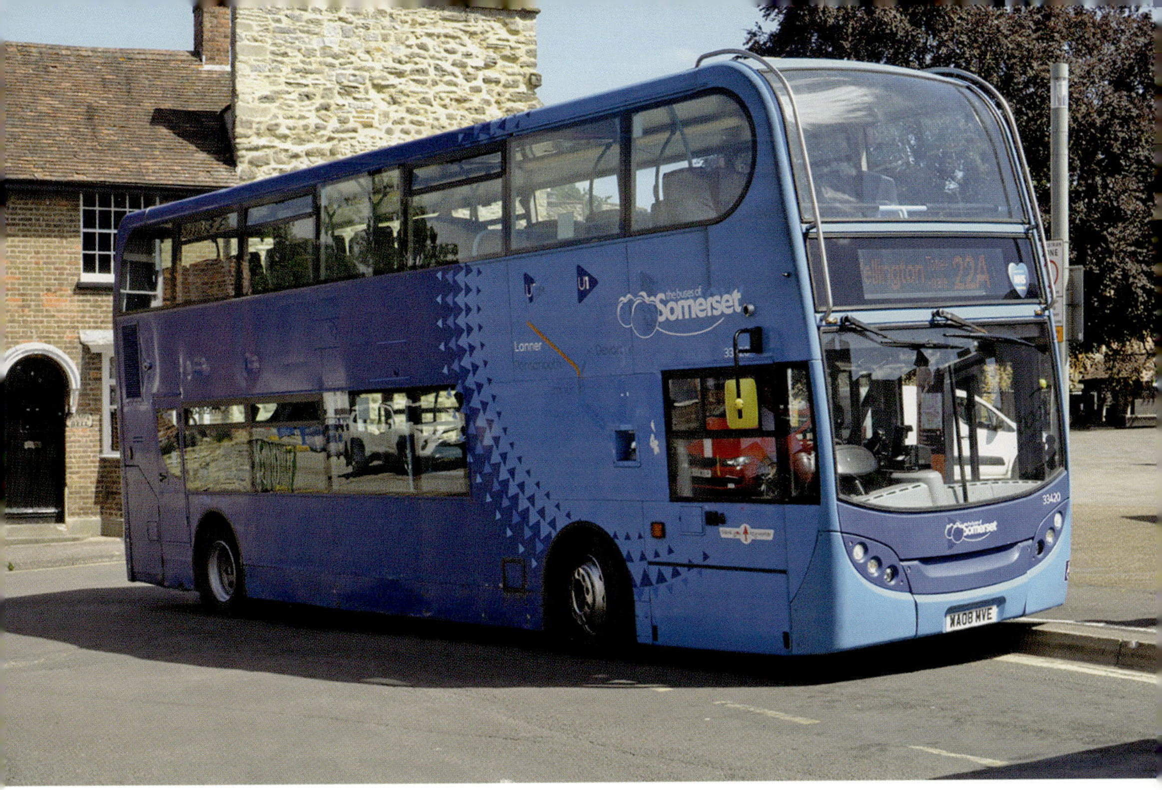

Carrying The Buses of Somerset names, Enviro400 33420, WA0 8MVE shows signs of a previous life in Cornwall as it awaits departure for Wellington on 20 June 2022.

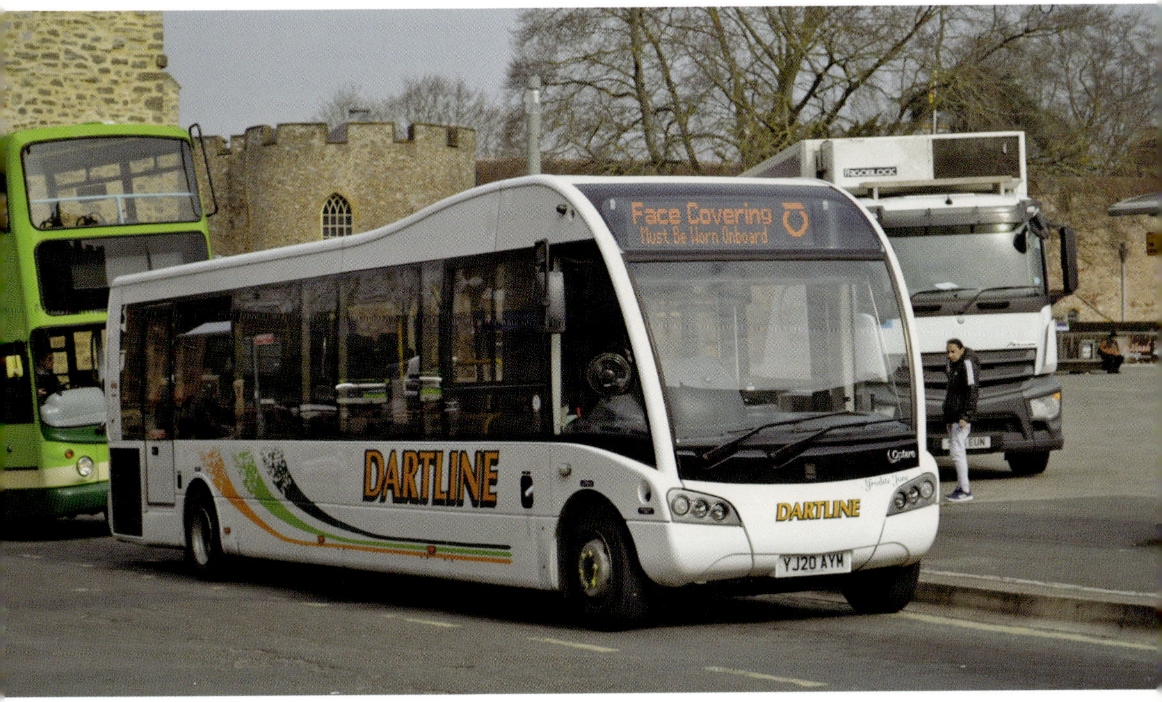

Contrasting with the Stagecoach Dart seen earlier on service 20 to Honiton, this route is now in the hands of Dartline, whose Optare Solo SR YJ20 AYM is waiting to leave for Seaton on 20 June 2022.

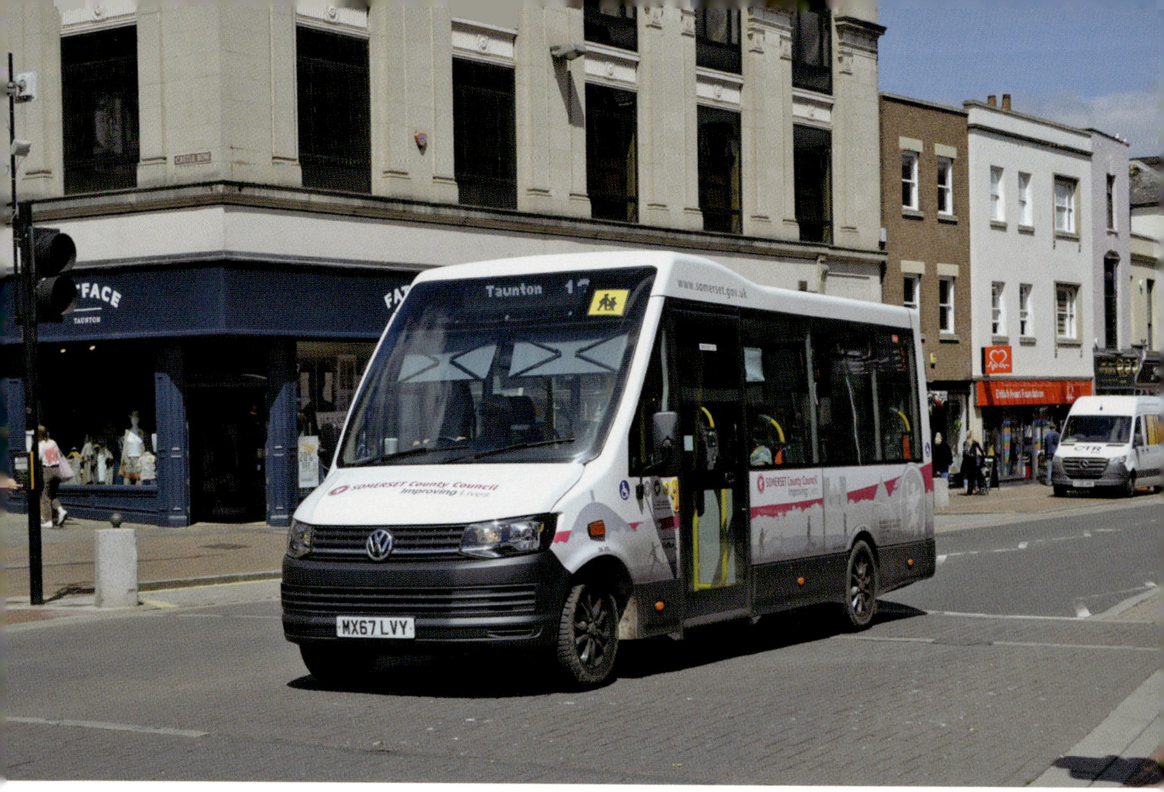

Some services in Taunton are now operated by Somerset County Council. Mellor-bodied Volkswagen MX67LVY is seen at The Parade on 20 June 2022 bound for Monkton Heathfield on service 12.

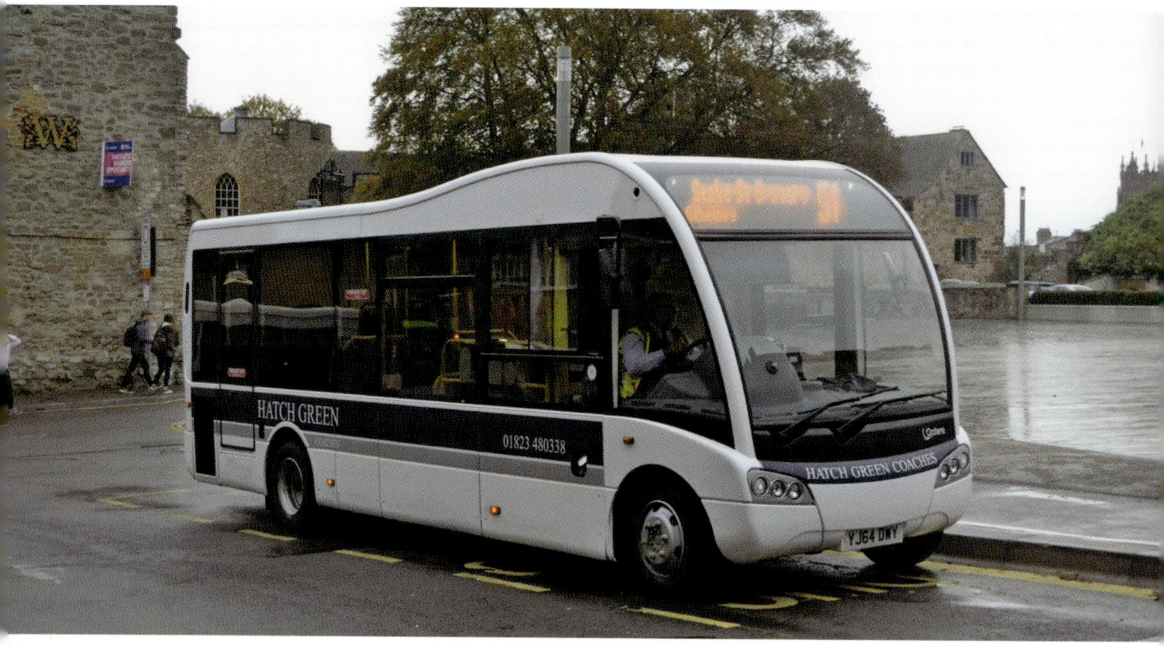

The Optare Solo SRs Hatch Green Coaches of Hatch Beauchamp have a presence in Taunton, as seen here by YJ64 DWY on a wet 15 October 2018 in Castle Way, awaiting departure for Stoke St Gregory. Hatch Beauchamp is the burial place of Colonel John Chard of the Royal Engineers who, as a Lieutenant, commanded the defence of Rorke's Drift in South Africa, for which he received the Victoria Cross.

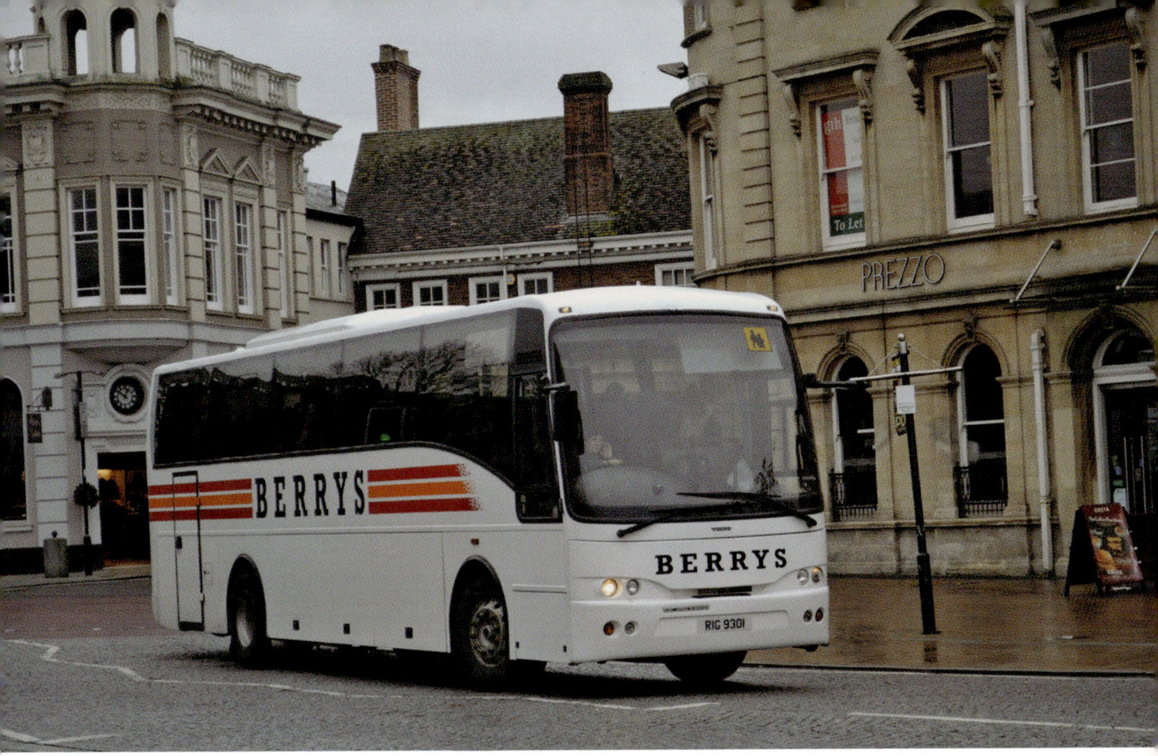

Berry's of Taunton is now one of the largest coach operators in the south-west. Contrasting with the AEC seen earlier is Jonckheere Mistral-bodied Volvo B10M RIG9301, new to Shearings as R938 YNF. It is seen in Corporation Street on 15 October 2018.

MINEHEAD

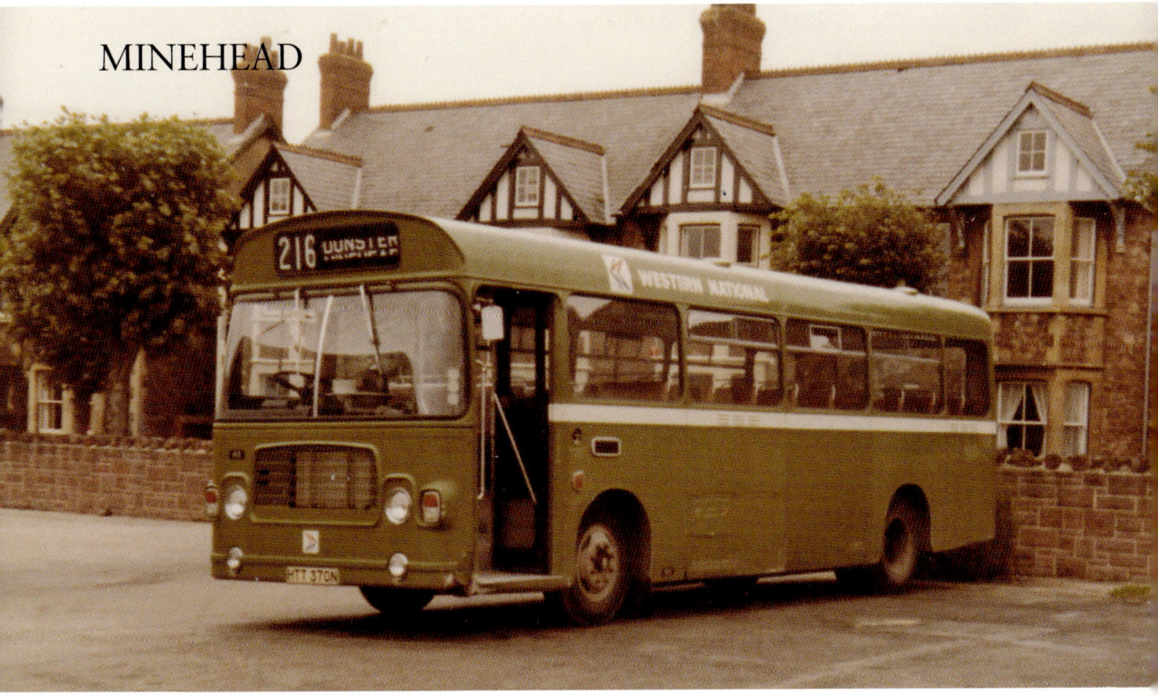

In the late seventies Minehead still had a bus station. Seen resting before heading off on the short journey to Dunster is Bristol LH6L 1615, HTT 370N.

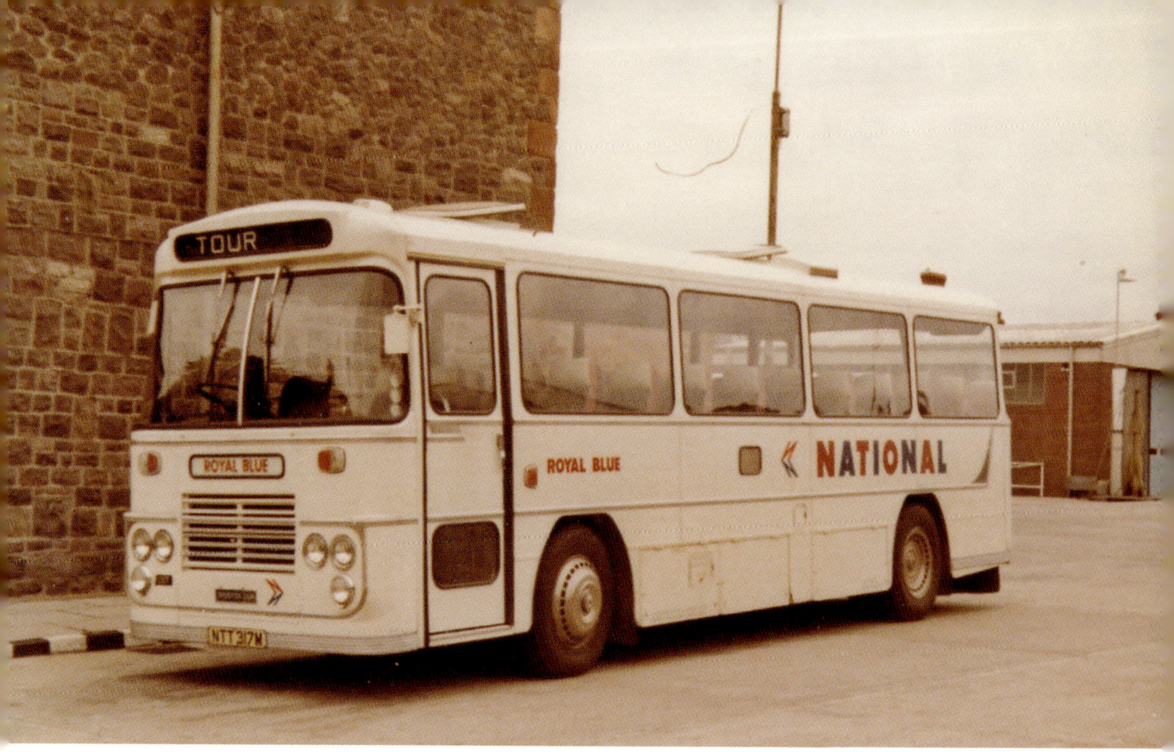

With the depot in the background is Marshall-bodied Bristol LH6L 1317, NTT 317M, carrying Royal Blue fleetnames. These were, as far as I know, the only Marshall-bodied LH coaches built.

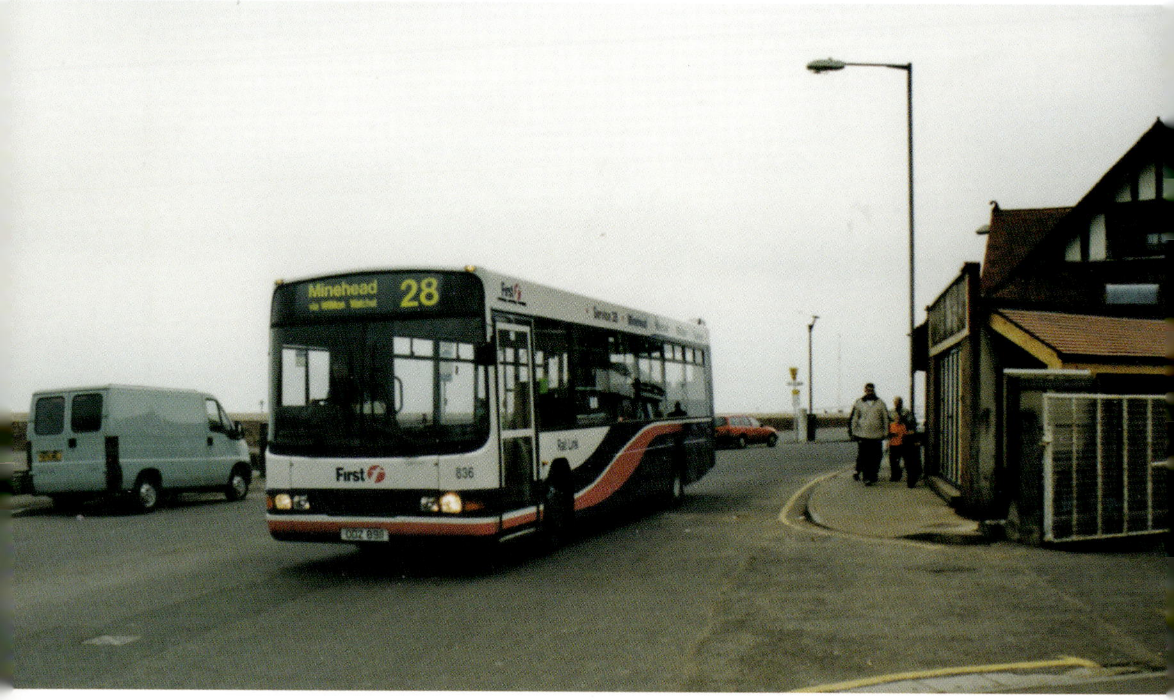

Seen on a rather miserable 23 March 2002 at Minehead Station, First Southern National were operating route dedicated Dennis Lances with Wright Pathfinder bodies, new to Centrewest in London during 1993, such as 836, ODZ 8911, on service 28 from Taunton.

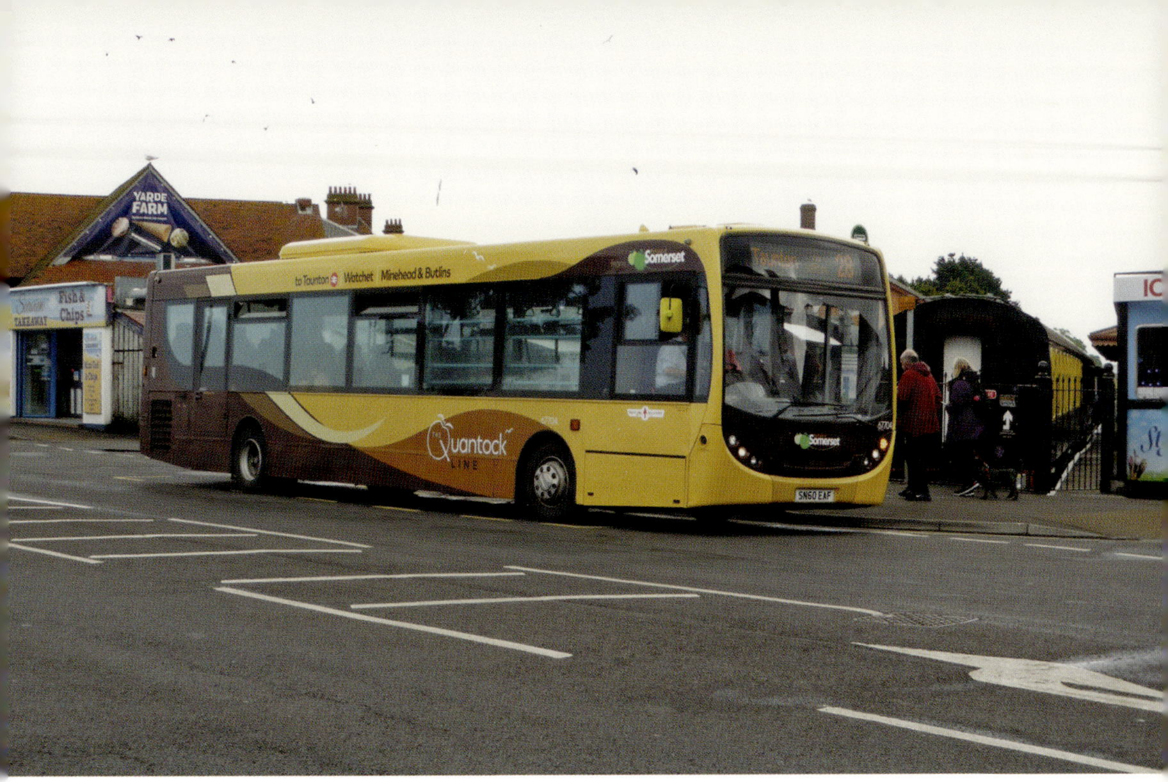

7 July 2021, and service 28 is now marketed as The Quantock Line and operated by The Buses of Somerset, whose Enviro300 67704 is seen at Minehead Station.

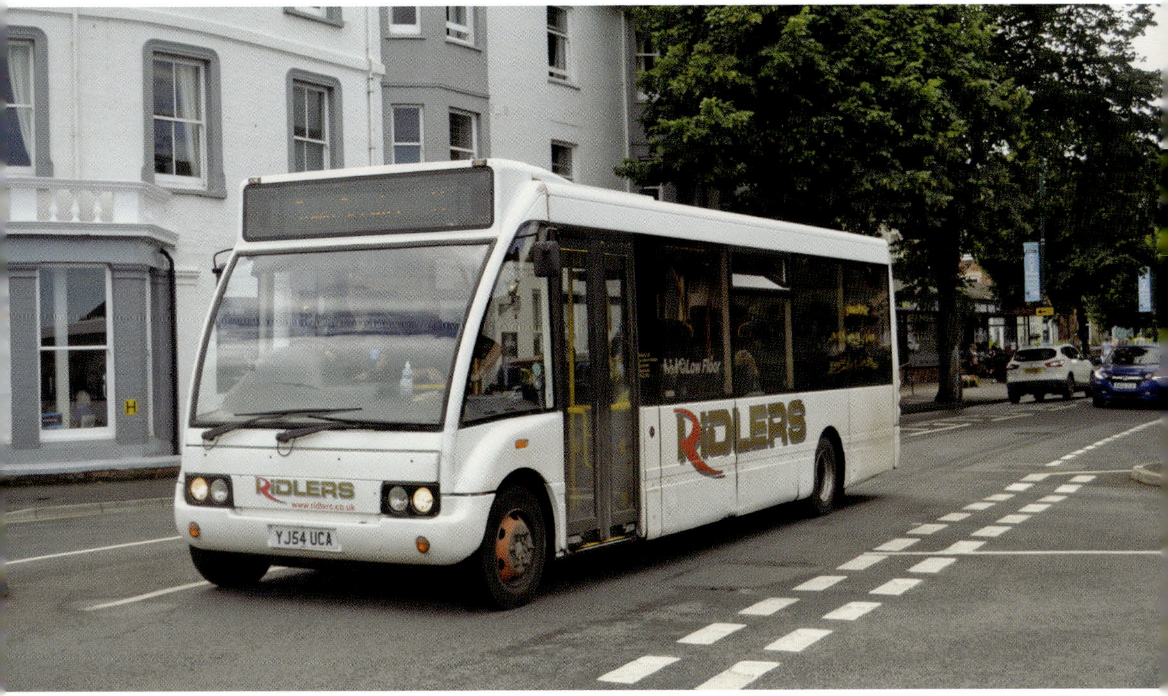

The town service in Minehead is provided by Ridlers of Dulverton. Their Optare Solo YJ54 UCA, bought from Dartline in 2017, is seen here on 7 July 2021.

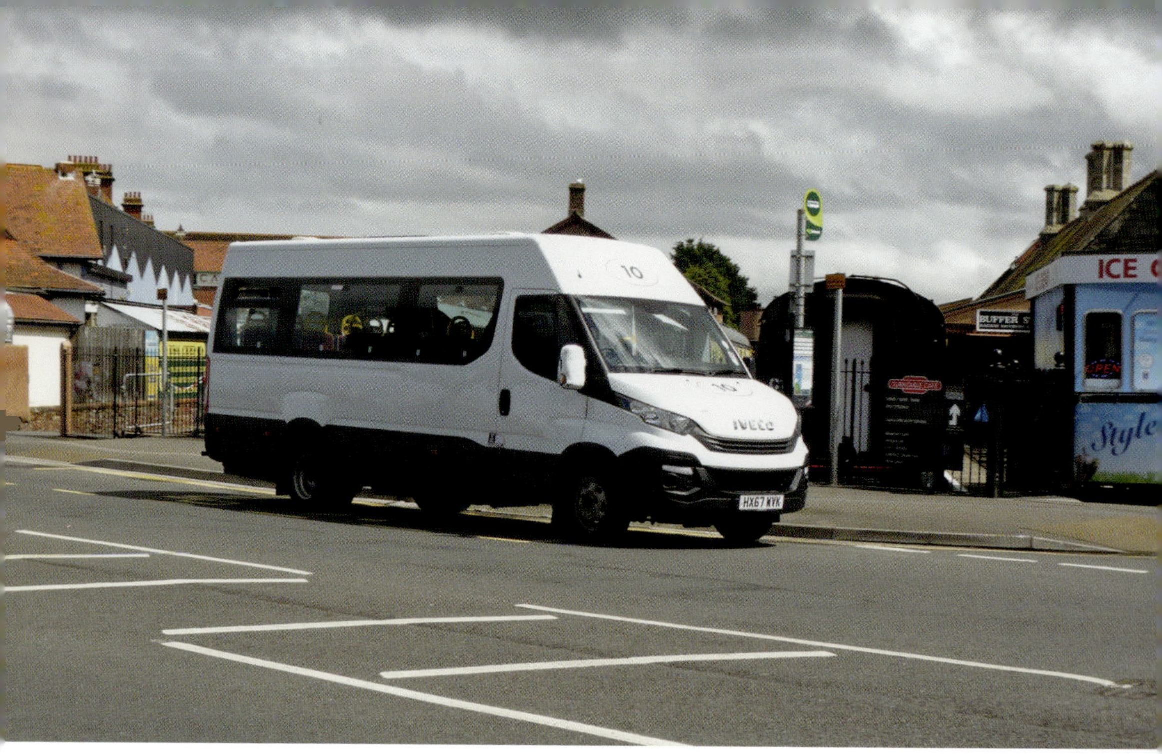

Atwest is a registered charity providing accessible transport across West Somerset They operate this Iveco minibus, HX67 WVK, on a service from Minehead to Porlock Weir. It is seen here on 7 July 2021.

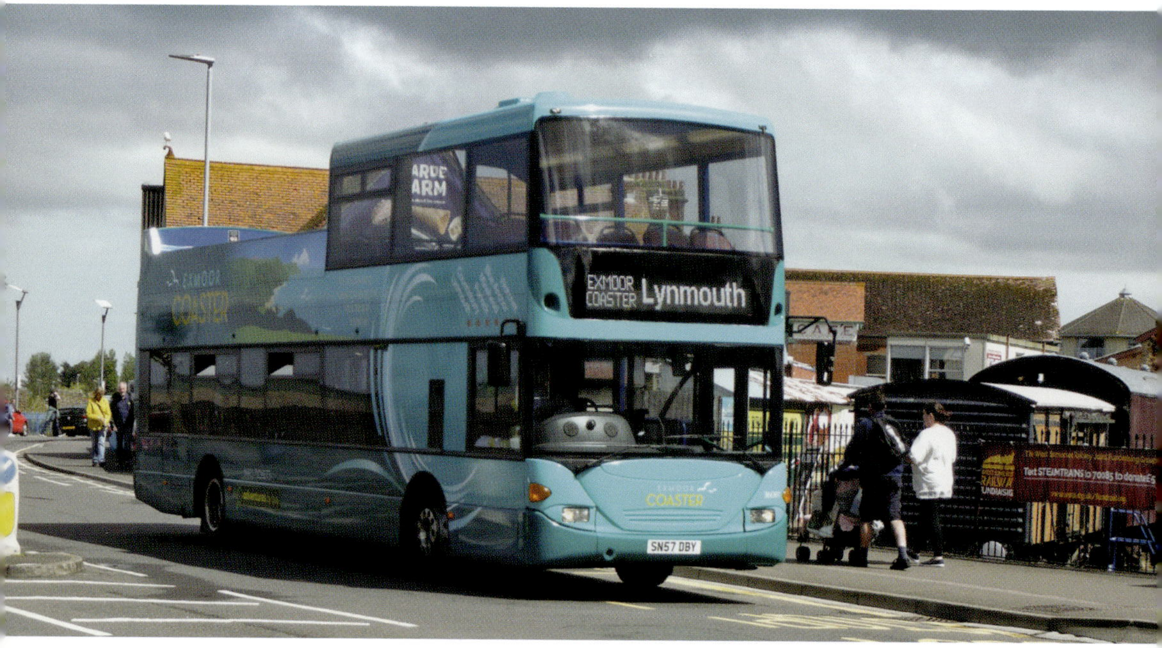

Double-deck operation returned to Minehead in 2021 with the start of the Exmoor Coaster service from Lynmouth. This must be one of the most spectacular bus journeys in the country, going over the top of Exmoor with views over the Bristol Channel – plus the 1:4 gradients of Countisbury Hill and Porlock Hill. The route is worked by two open-top Scania OmniCity vehicles purchased from the East Coast Buses operation of Lothian Transport. 36081, SN57 DBY, is seen at Minehead Station on 7 July 2021.

YEOVIL

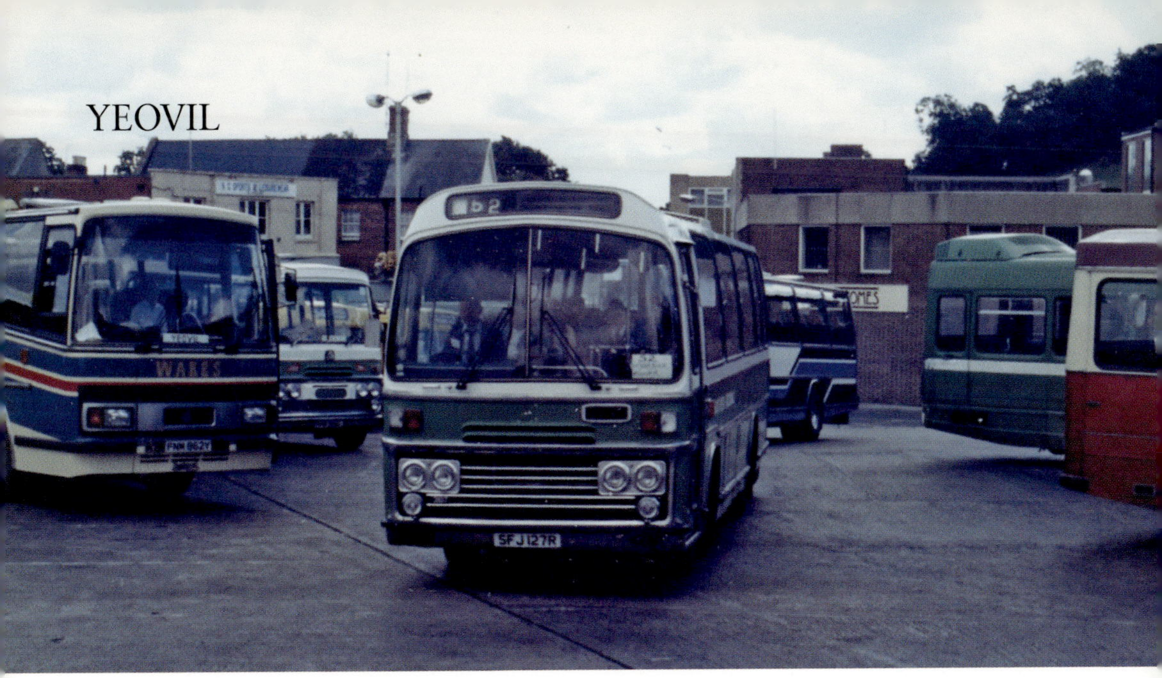

Yeovil Bus Station on 14 August 1989, and Southern National 3107, SFJ 127R is seen leaving on service 52. A Bristol LH6L with Plaxton Supreme Express body, it still wears its old NBC green and white dual-purpose livery, while the Leyland National on the right similarly carries NBC green. Also visible are vehicles of Wake's of Sparkford and Pearce Darch & Wilcox of Martock, who operated as Comfy-Lux and Safeway of South Petherton. In the days of the Tilling Group, Yeovil was served by Southern National, whose operations were transferred to Western National shortly after the formation of the National Bus Company in 1969.

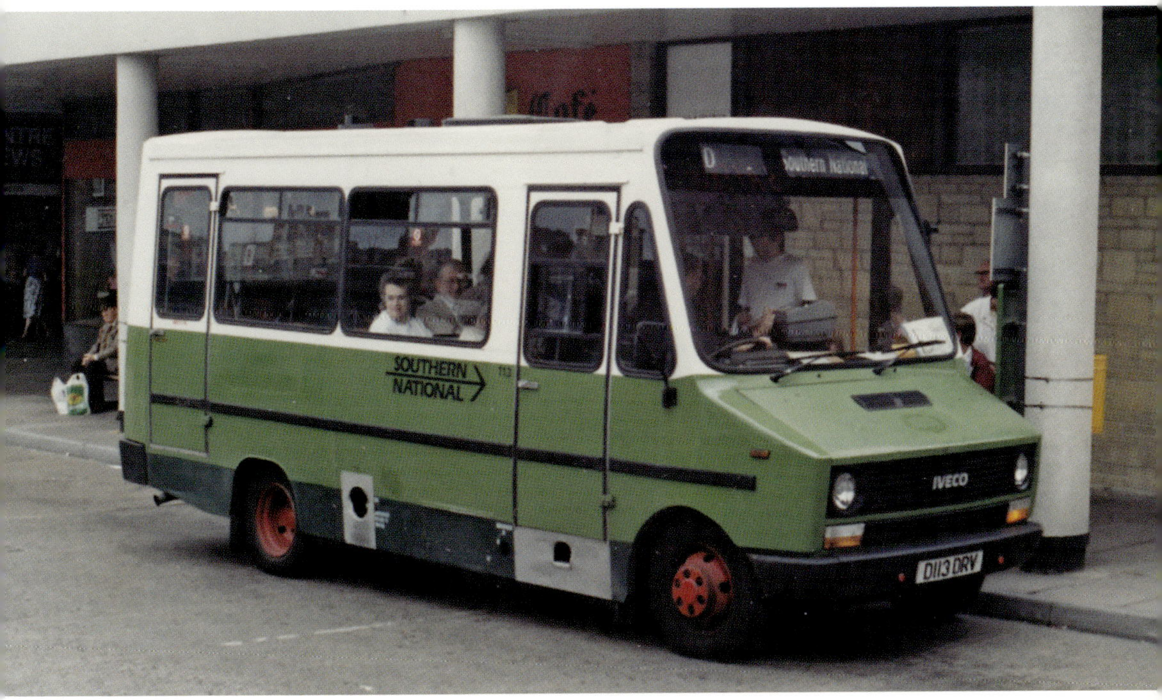

Seen in the bus station on 14 August 1989, Southern National 113, D113 DRV, is a Robin Hood-bodied Iveco Daily 49.10 that was bought from Provincial just a couple of months earlier.

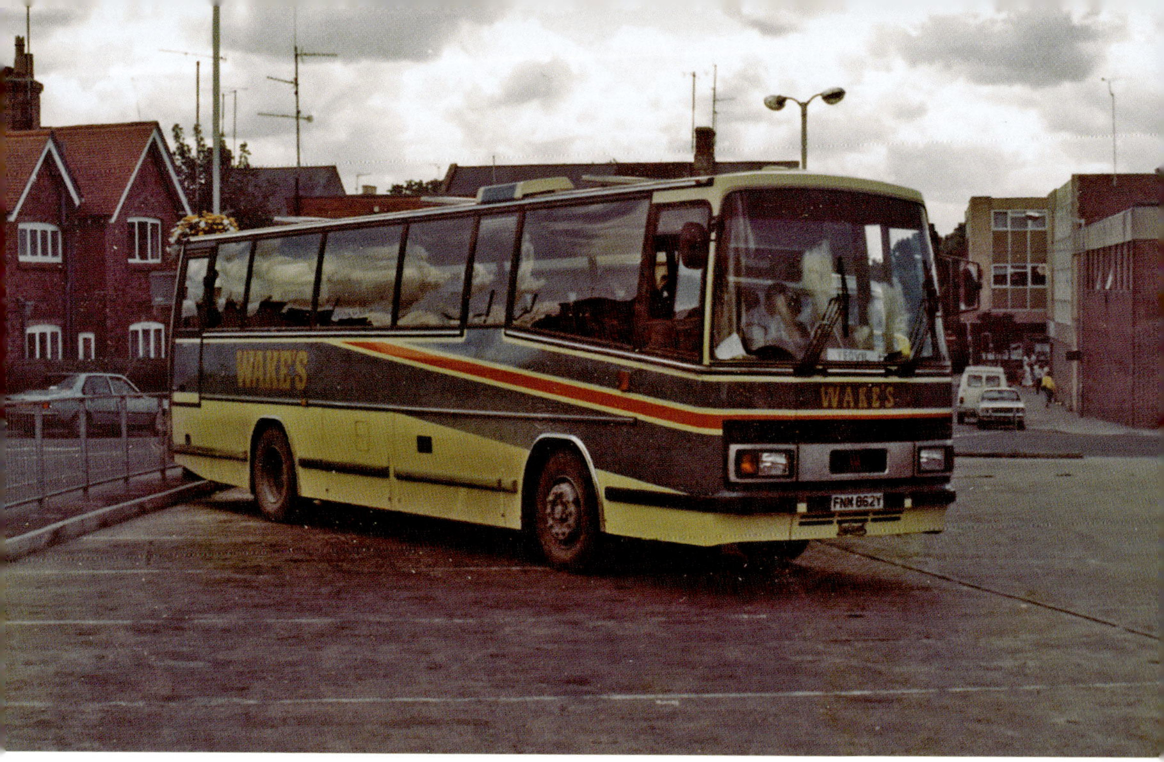

Wake's of Sparkford was one of several independent operators that served the Yeovil area for many years. Seen in the bus station on 14 August 1989, a month or so after purchase from Lodge of High Easter, FNM 862Y is a Leyland Tiger with Plaxton Paramount 3200 body.

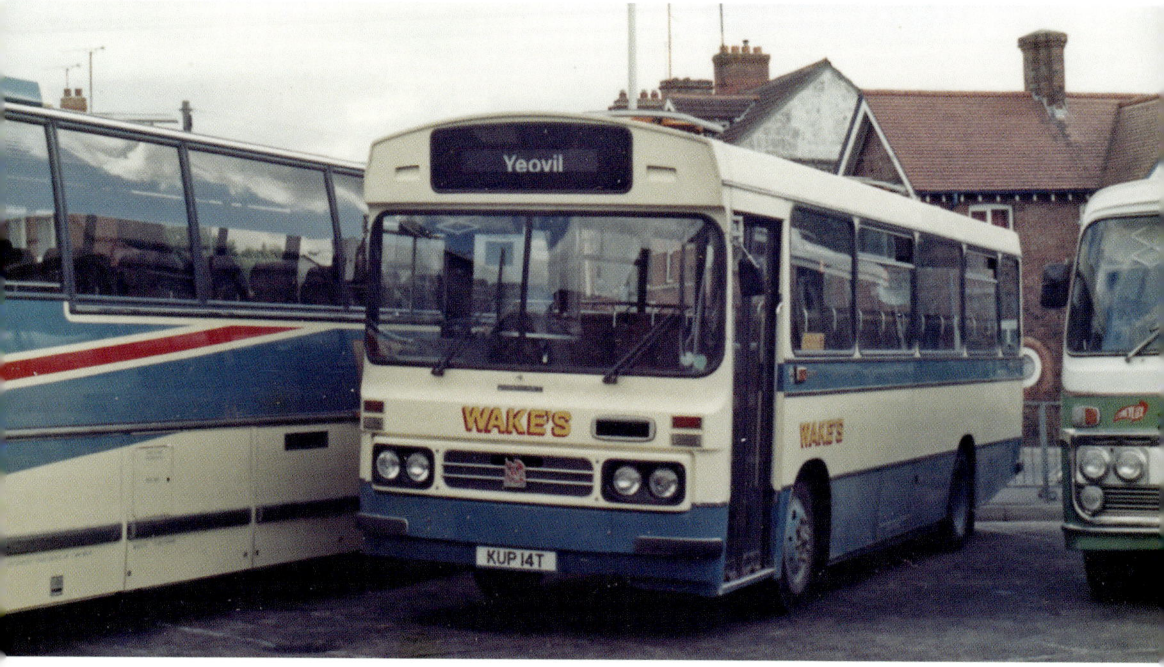

Seen in the bus station four days later on 18 August 1989, Duple Dominant-bodied Bedford YLQ KUP 14T came to the Wake's fleet when they took over the operations of Osmond, Curry Rivel. It was new to Gypsy Queen of Langley Park, County Durham. Sadly this vehicle was stolen by joyriders and burnt out.

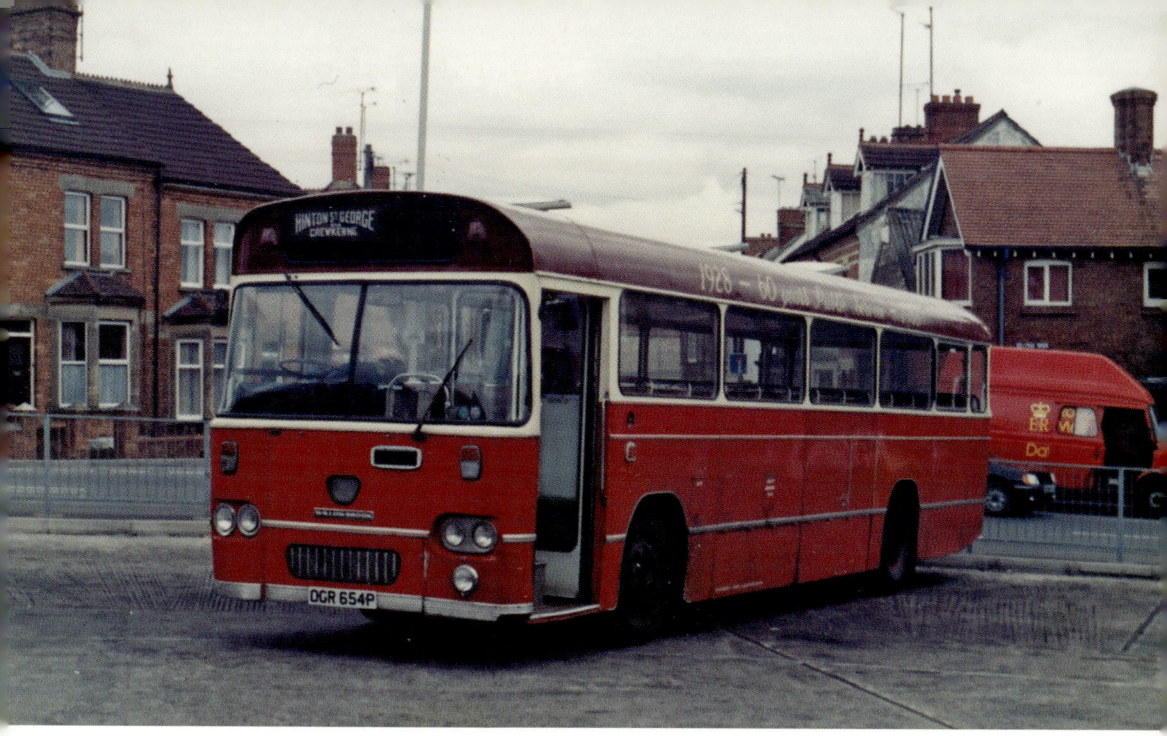

Another well-known operator around Yeovil was Safeway of South Petherton, who had a fondness for Leyland Leopards, buying several, both new and second-hand, with both bus and coach bodies. This Willowbrook-bodied example, OGR 654P, came from Trimdon Motor Services and is seen in the bus station, again on 14 August 1989, prior to departure for Hinton St George.

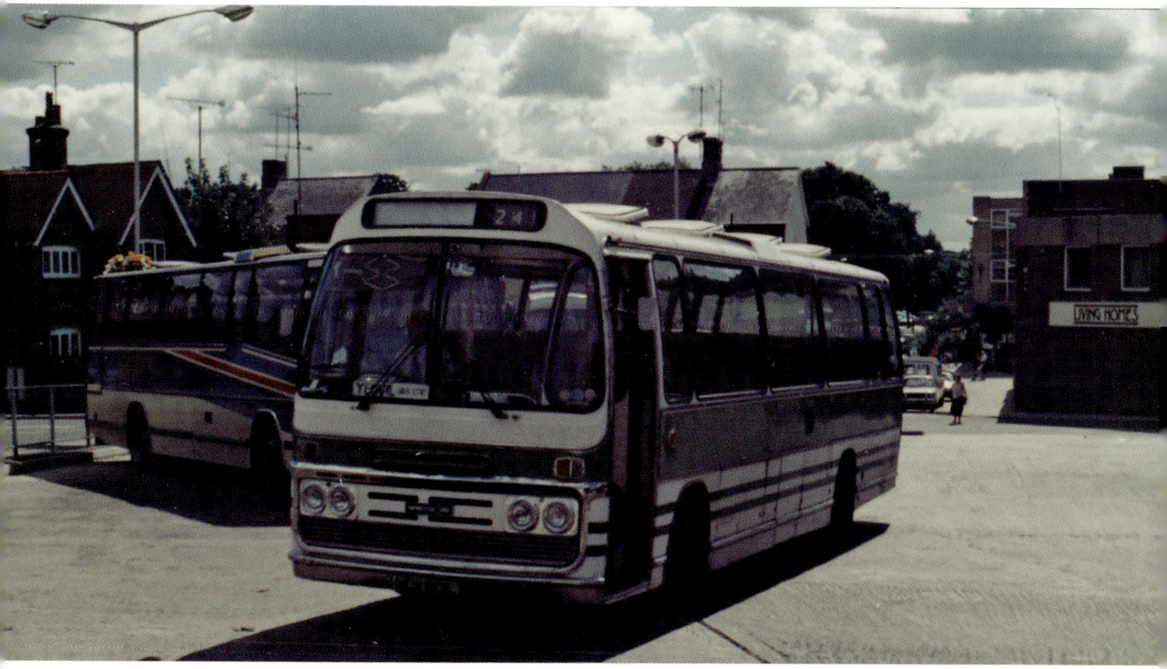

Ray Cuff, working into Yeovil from the delightfully named Dorset village of Piddlehinton, developed an enthusiasm for Bristol REs, operating several over the years. Seen leaving the bus station on 18 August 1989, NCN 813L is former Northern General RELH6G with Plaxton Elite Express III body.

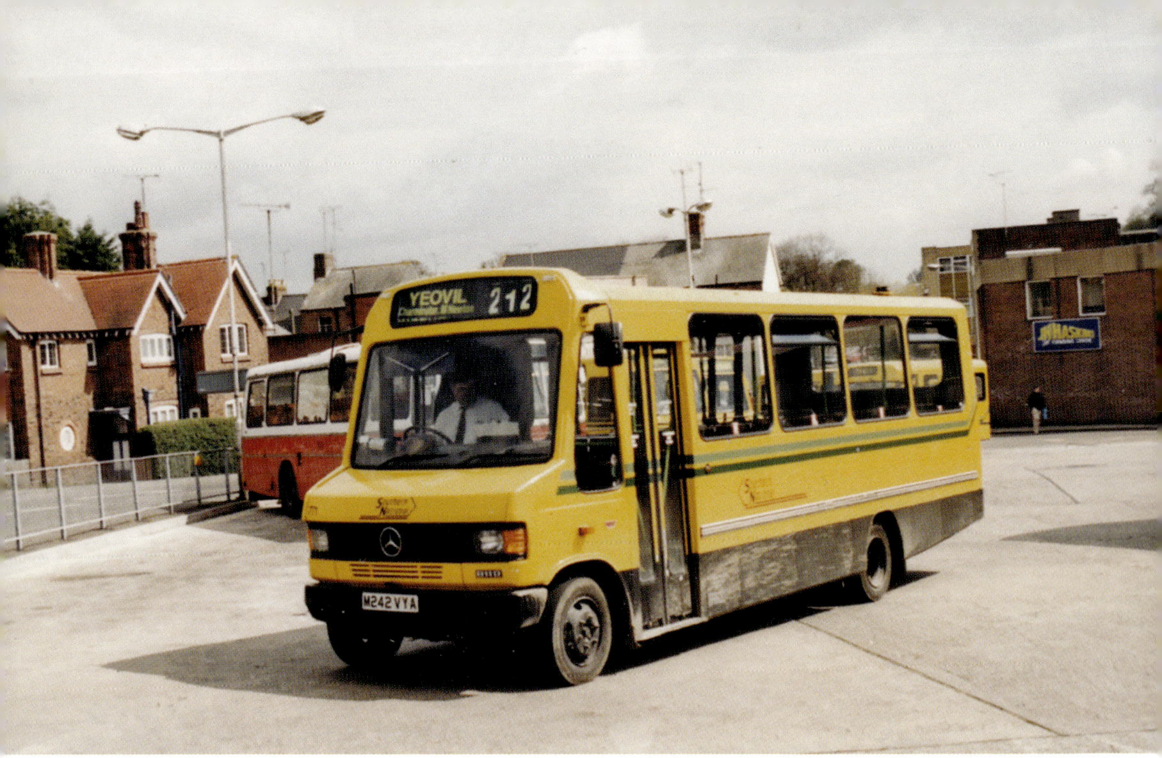

Seen in the mid-nineties leaving the bus station, Southern National 771, M242 VYA, is a Wright-bodied Mercedes-Benz 811D wearing the yellow livery with coloured flashes that the company adopted for its minibuses.

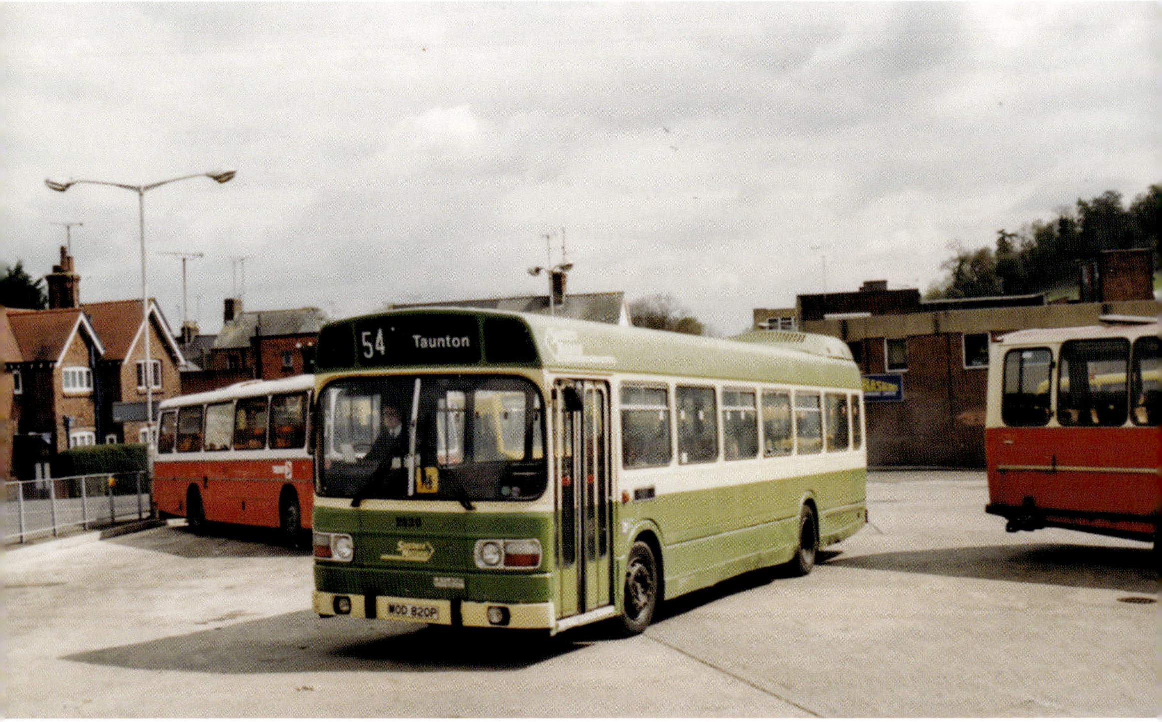

Leaving the bus station on the same day is one of the old guard in the Southern National fleet, Leyland National 2820, MOD 820P, in the original privatisation green and cream livery used prior to joining First Group.

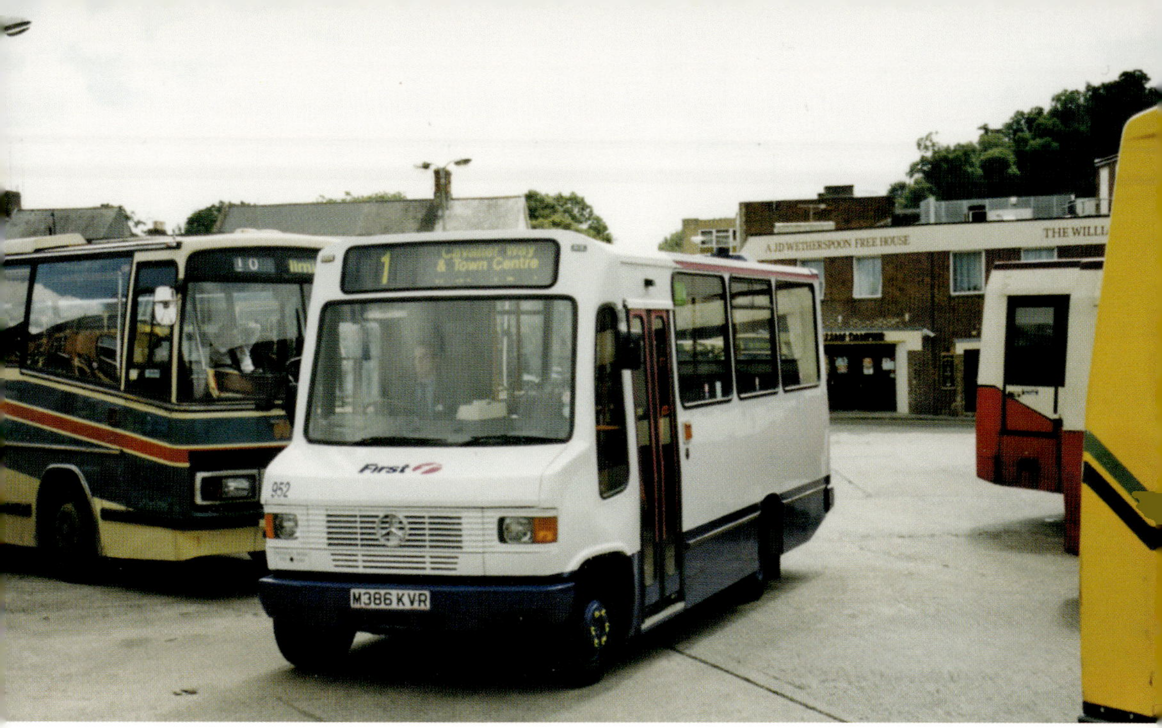

In First Group livery, but minus any fleetnames, this much-travelled Alexander Belfast-bodied Mercedes-Benz 709D, 952 in the First Southern National fleet started life with the TGWU in Chelmsford before moving through various other operators and arriving in Yeovil in 1997. It is seen leaving the bus station on a town service on 8 August 2001.

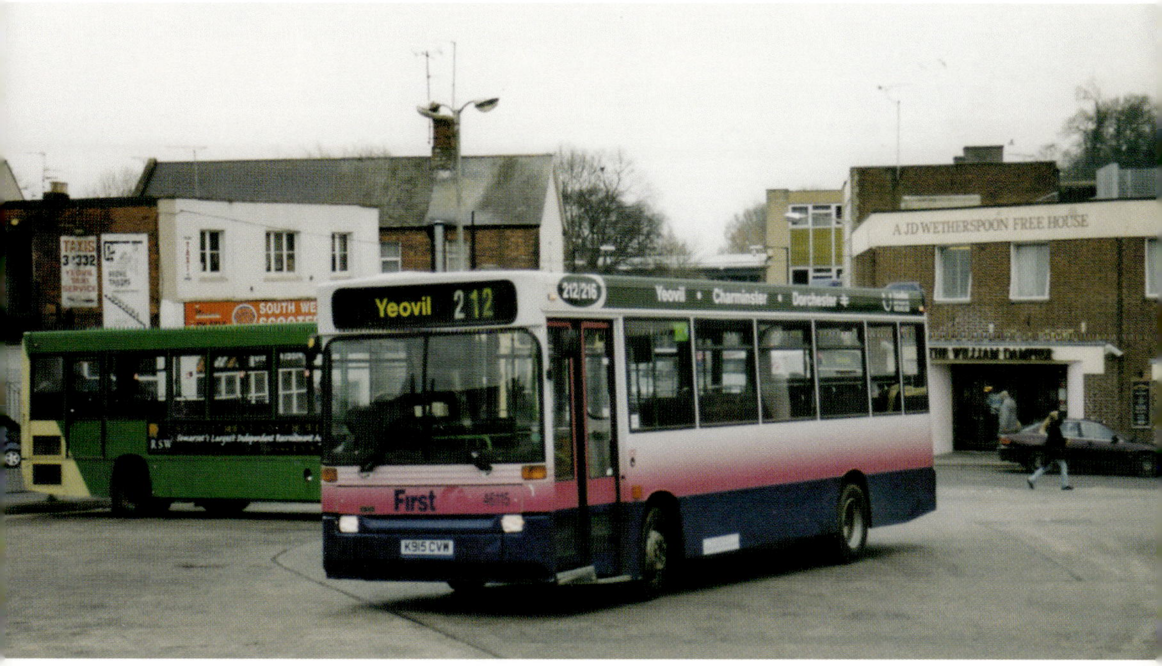

First Southern National merged with First Bristol in 2003 to become First Somerset and Avon. Plaxton Pointer-bodied Dennis Dart 46115, K915 CVW, is seen here on 20 February 2004, arriving at the bus station from Dorchester. This vehicle began life in Essex with Thamesway.

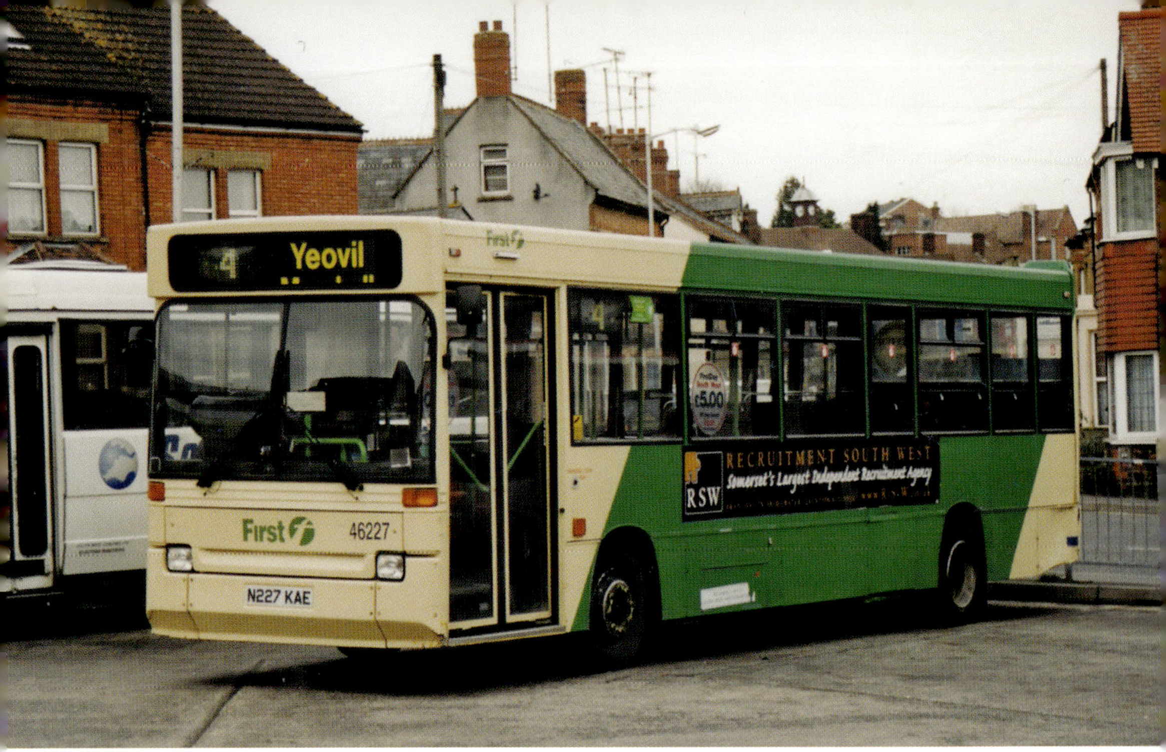

20 February 2004 and Plaxton Pointer-bodied Dennis Dart 46227, N227 KAE, is still carrying Southern National livery, but with First Group logos. New to Badgerline, it arrived with Southern National in 2000.

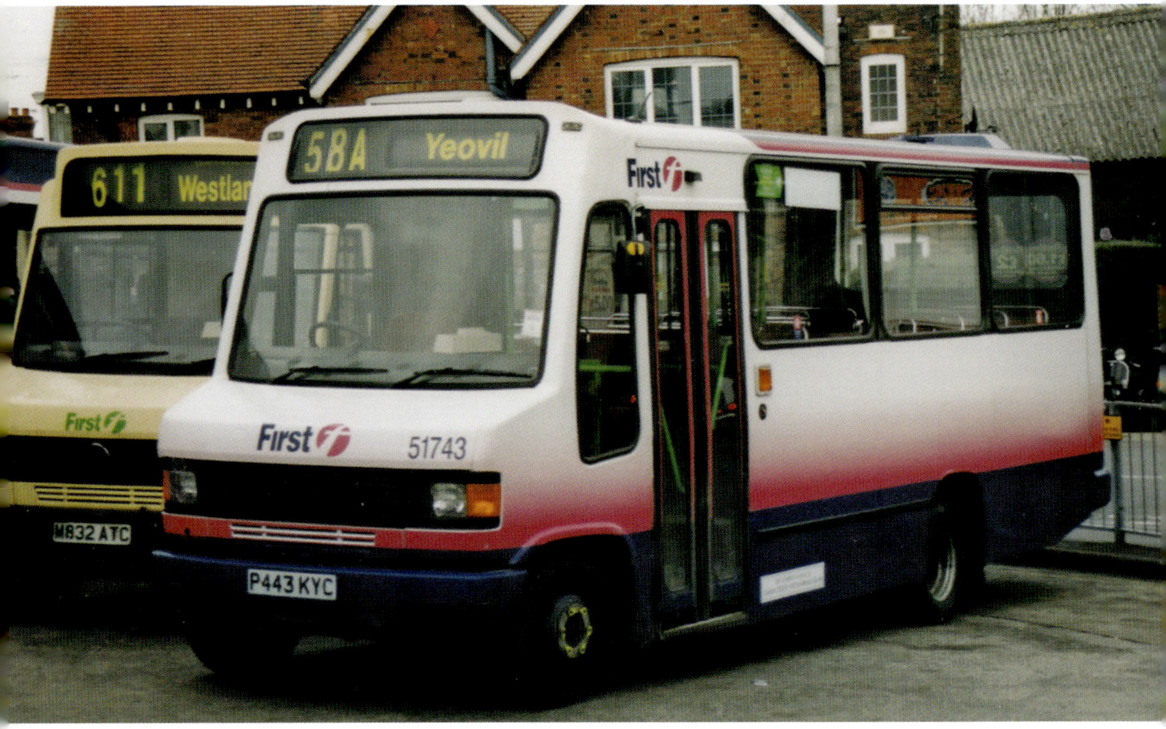

Numbered 51743 in the First Somerset & Avon fleet, Mercedes-Benz 709D P443 KYC was new to Southern National in 1996. Carrying an Alexander Belfast body, it is seen laying over in the bus station on 20 February 2004.

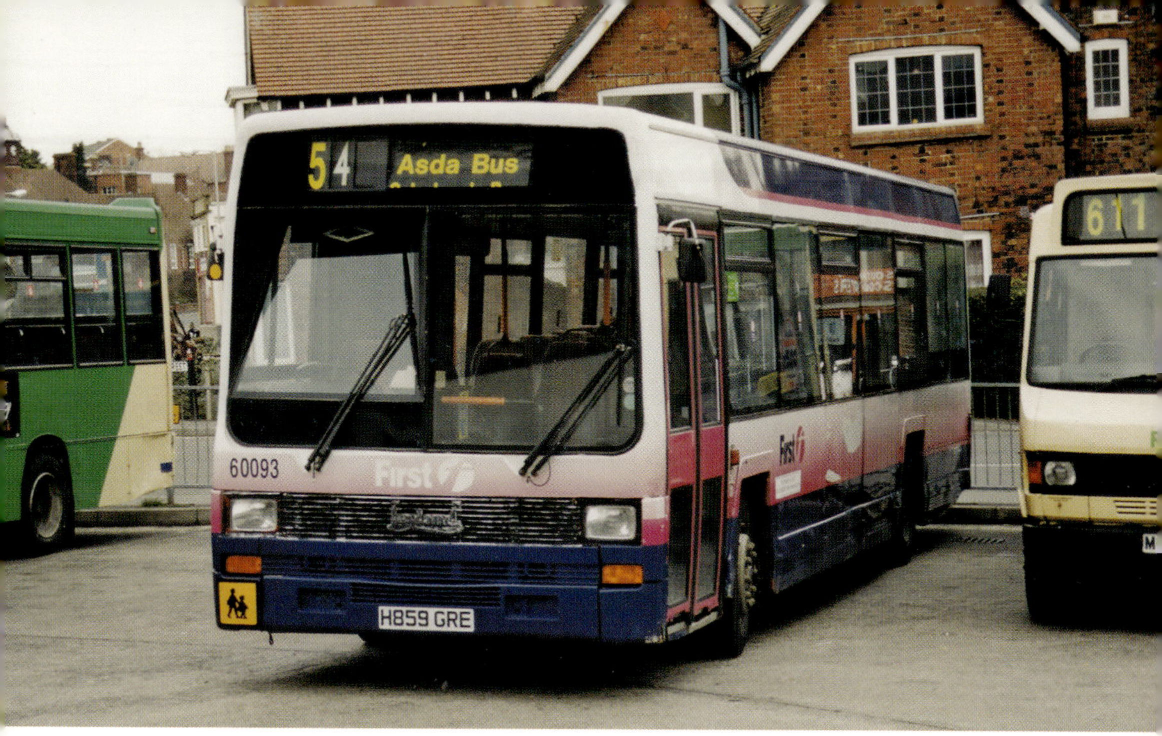

A number of Leyland Lynxes found their way to the south-west's various First Group operations. 60093 came to First Southern National's Weymouth depot from PMT in 2002 before transferring to Yeovil and what was by now First Somerset & Avon. It is seen laying over in the bus station on 20 February 2004 while operating the free service to the local ASDA supermarket.

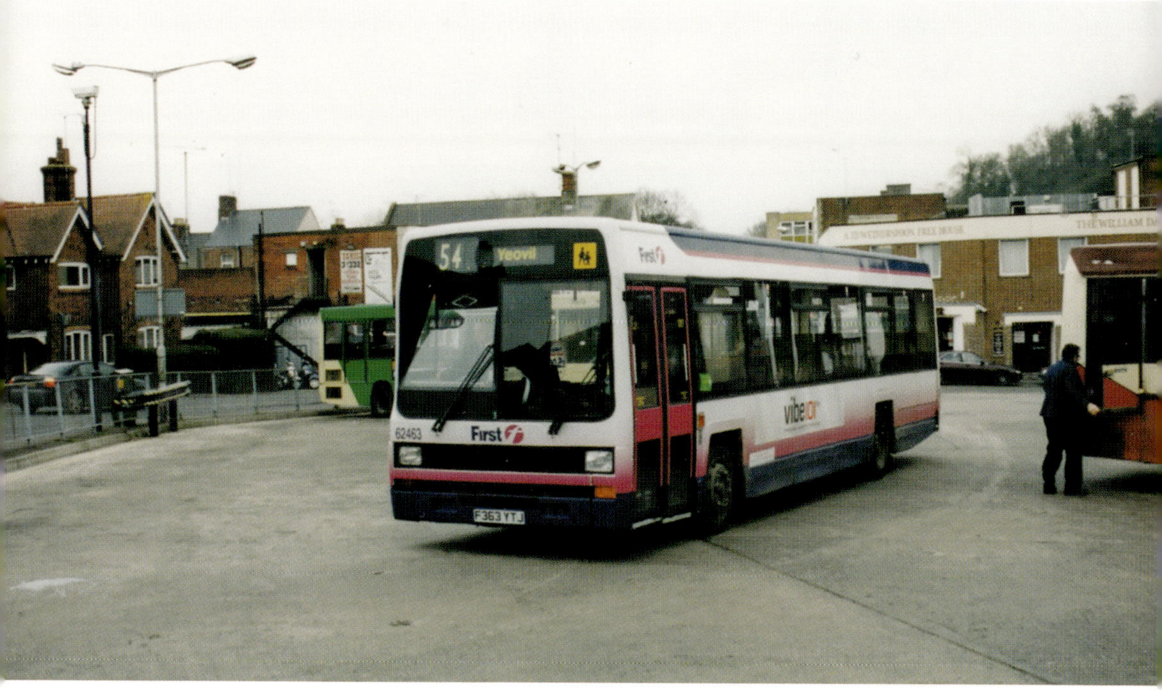

Another Leyland Lynx to find its way to Yeovil from the Potteries was 62463, F363 YTJ, which started life with Topping of Liverpool. On 20 February 2004 it was operating service 54 from Taunton.

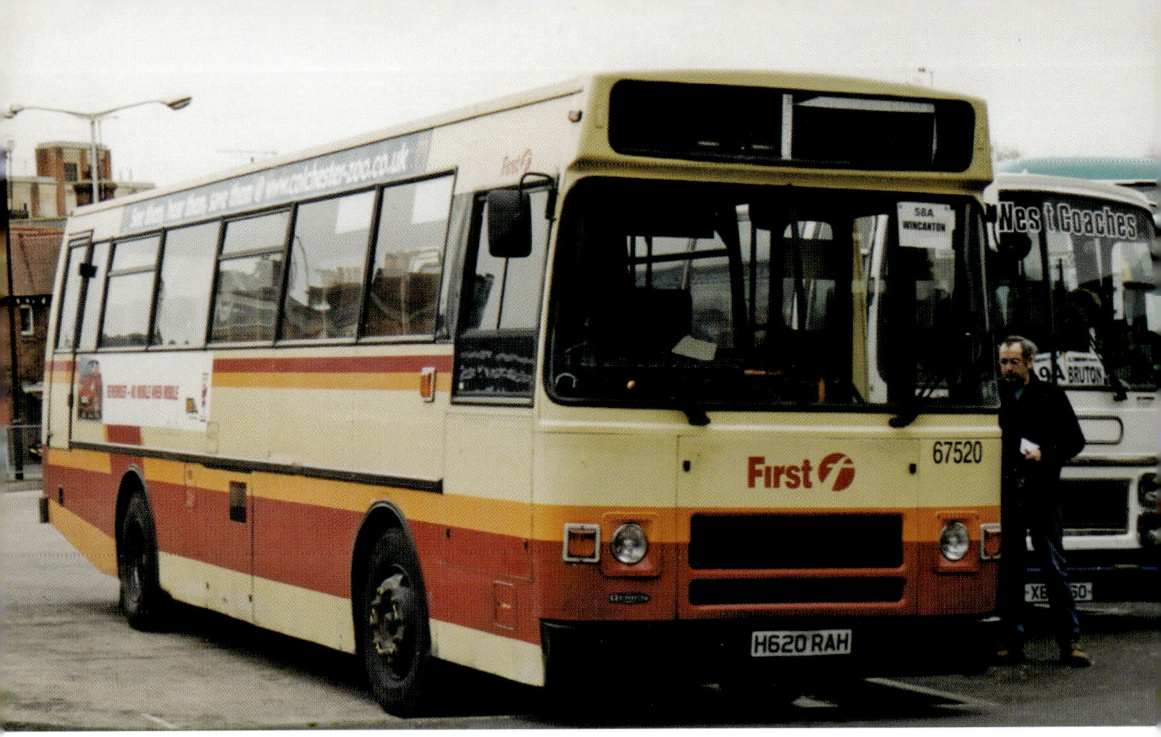

Less usual vehicles to find their way eventually to First Somerset & Avon were three Dennis Javelins with Plaxton Derwent bodies that joined the fleet at Taunton depot from First Eastern Counties in 2003. Lasting until 2006, 67520, H620 RAH, is seen in the bus station, still wearing Eastern Counties livery, and with a paper sticker in the windscreen saying it is on service 58A to Wincanton.

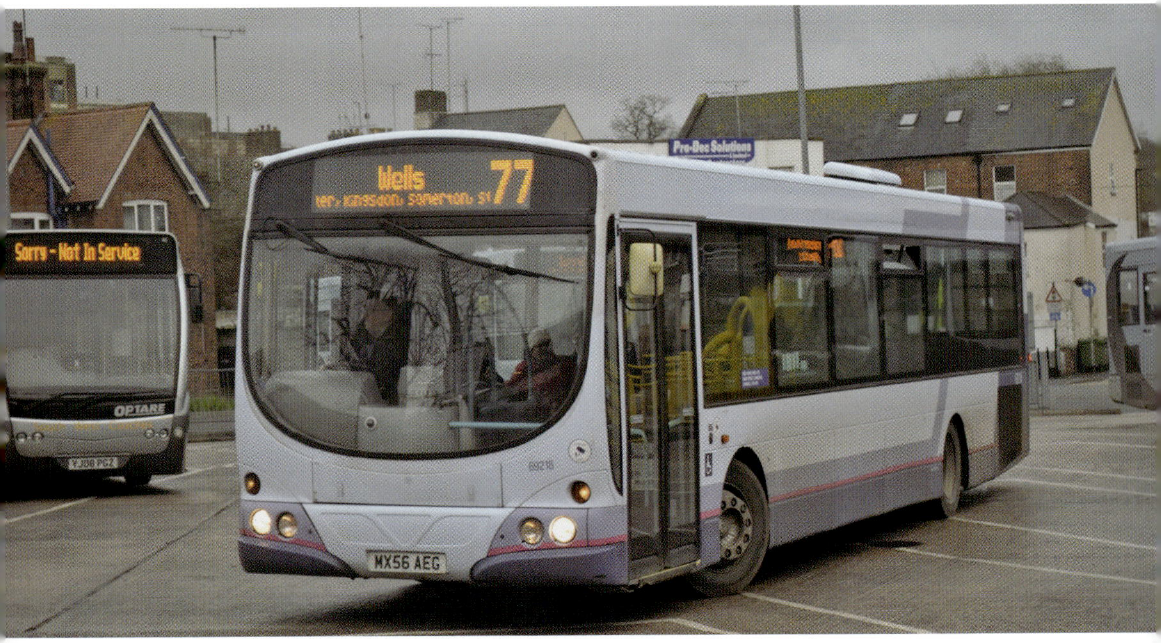

In 2016, operations in Yeovil came under the control of The Buses of Somerset when the former Southern National operations in Weymouth moved to First Hampshire & Dorset. 69218, MX56 AEG, a Volvo B7RLE with Wright Eclipse Urban body was new to First Manchester, moving to the south-west in 2017. It is seen here leaving the bus station for Wells on service 77 on 23 January 2018.

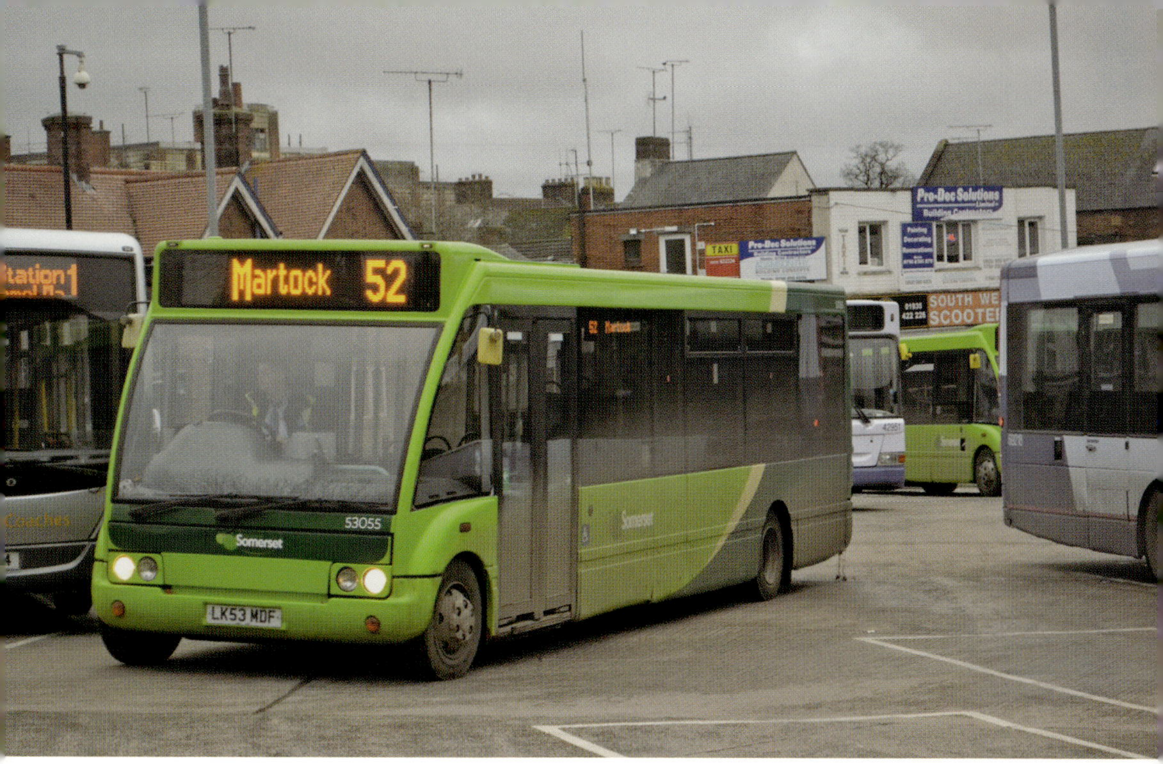

Optare Solo 53055, LK53 MDF, was new to the Slough depot of First Beeline before moving to the Weymouth depot of First Hampshire and Dorset, moving subsequently to Yeovil. In full The Buses of Somerset green it is seen on 23 January 2018 bound for Martock.

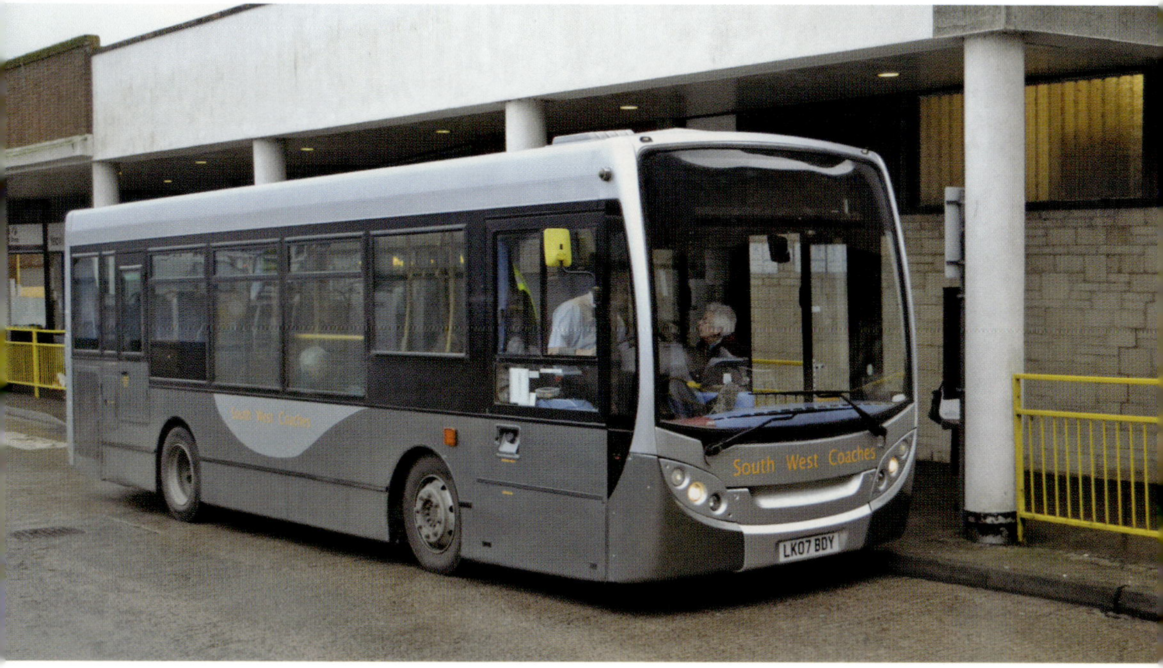

South West Coaches came into being in 1999 when Wake's Services combined with A. G. Hulbert of Yeovil. The firm subsequently took over Safeway of South Petherton in 2008. Former Metroline ADL Enviro200 LK07 BDY is seen in the bus station on 23 January 2018 on the free service to the ASDA supermarket.

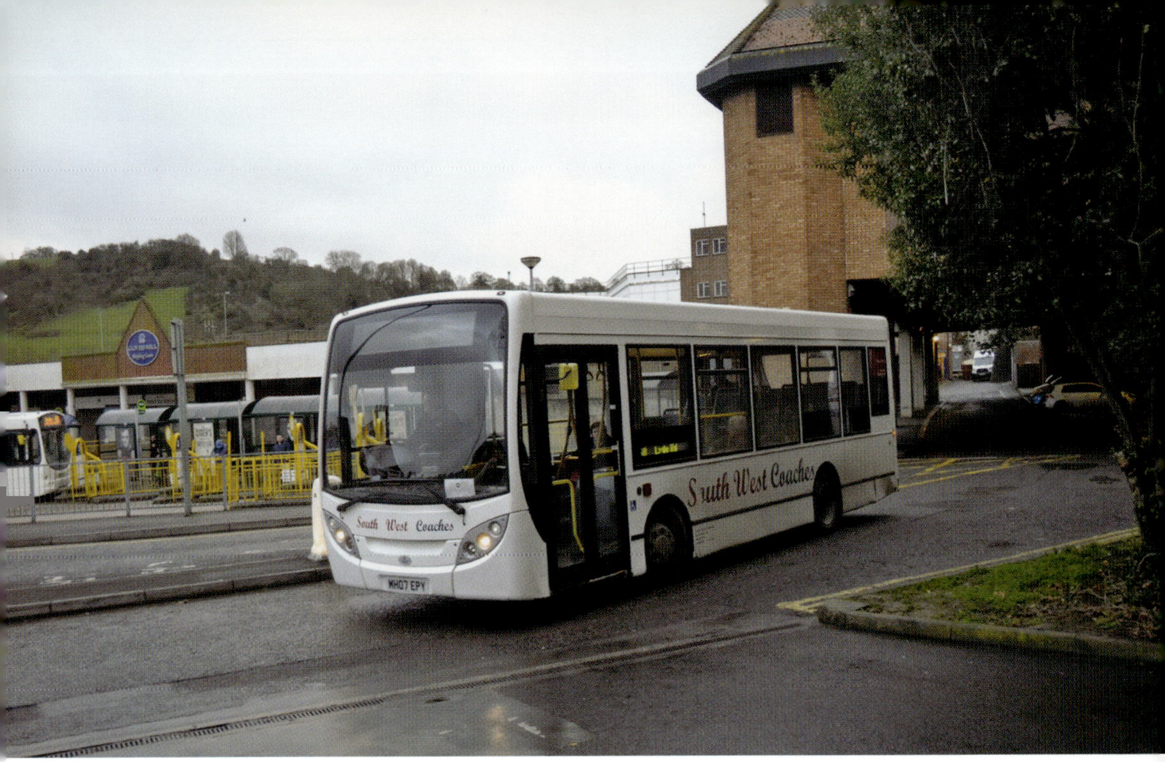

Wearing the second of the two liveries used by buses in the South West Coaches fleet, Enviro200 MH07 EPY, seen here on 23 January 2018 leaving the bus station, started life in the fleet of Jim Stone, Leigh.

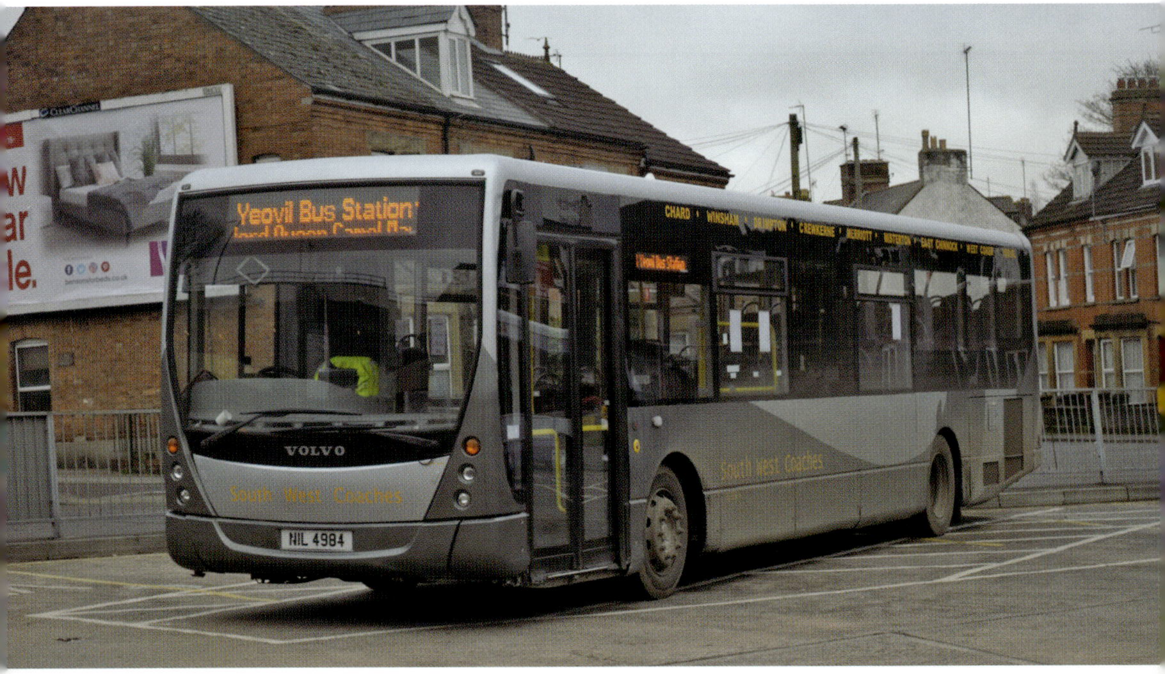

The visit to Yeovil on 23 January 2018 was quite a profitable one as far as photos of South West Coaches are concerned, as the next few images will show. Here, Volvo B7RLE with Plaxton Centro body NIL 4984, is seen laying over in the bus station. New to Dunn Line in 2008, it joined the South West Coaches fleet from Roberts of Hugglescote in 2016. The Plaxton Centro body was phased out by Alexander Dennis and replaced by the Enviro300.

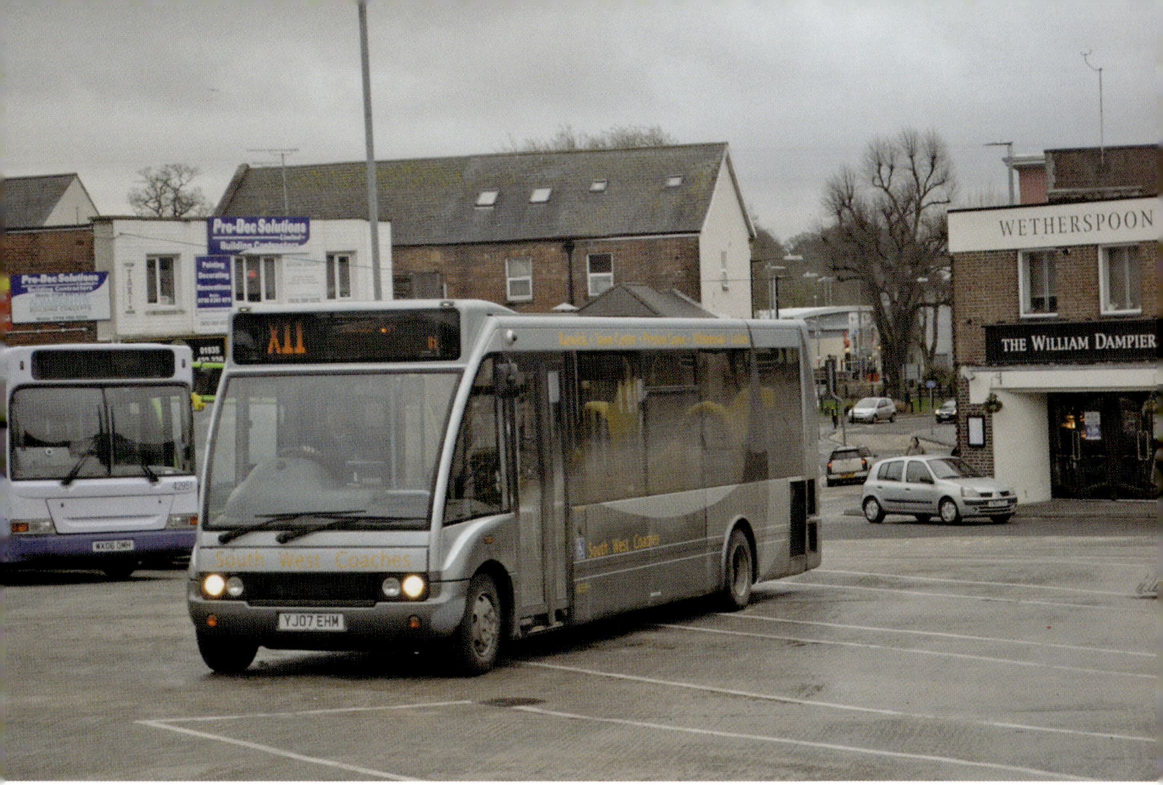

New to South West Coaches in 2007, Optare Solo YJ07 EHM is seen leaving the bus station for Dorchester on service X11.

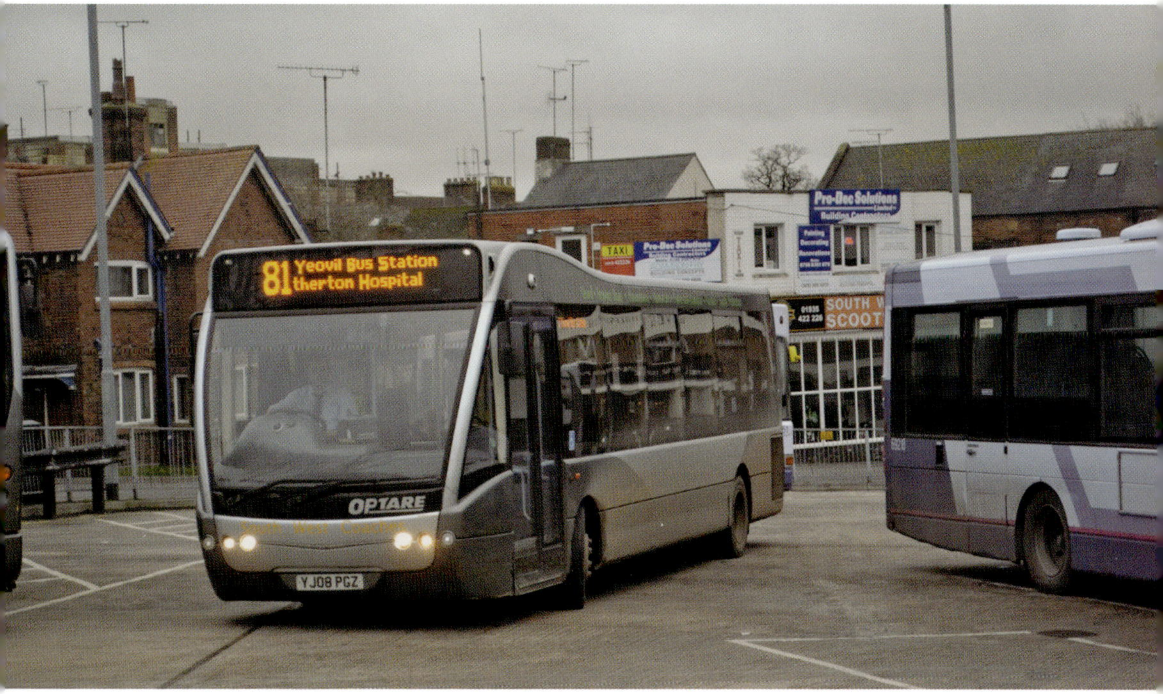

Arriving in the bus station from South Petherton, Optare Versa YJ08 PGZ is named *Miss Vera Gunn* as a tribute to the Gunn family, who ran Safeway of South Petherton for some eighty years.

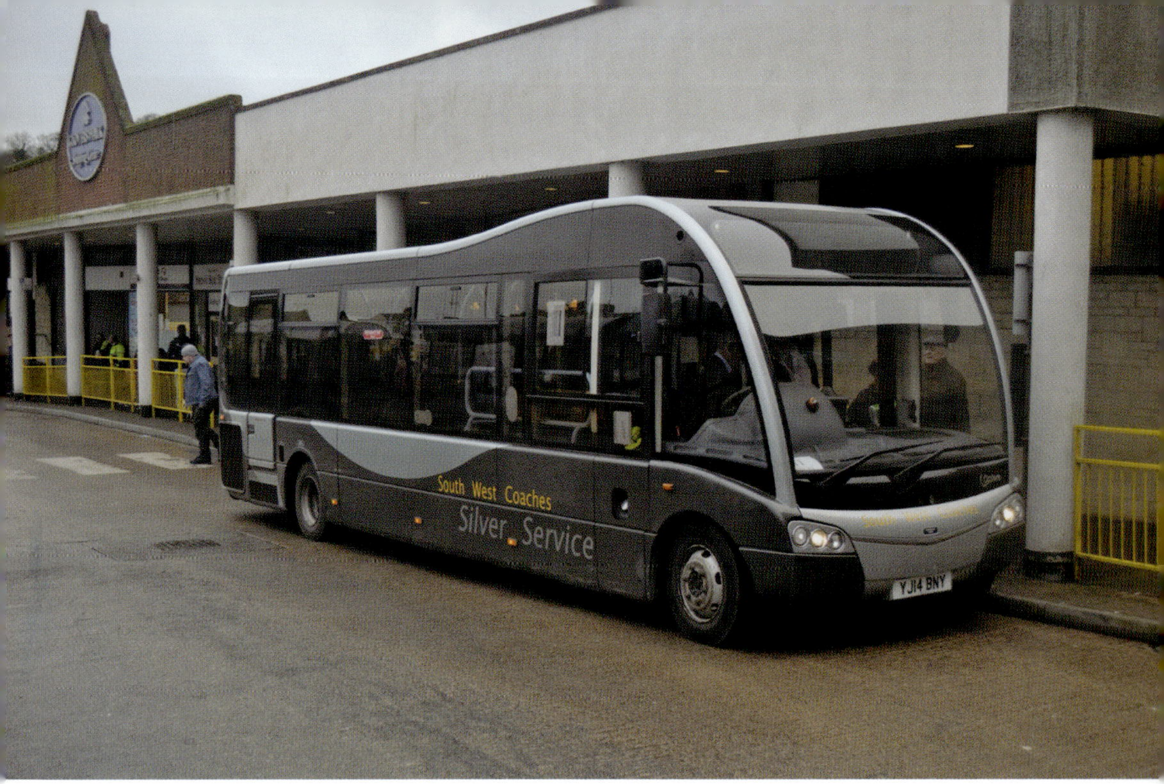

Another vehicle on the ASDA service was Optare Solo SR YJ14 BNY, one of fifteen Solos in the current fleet.

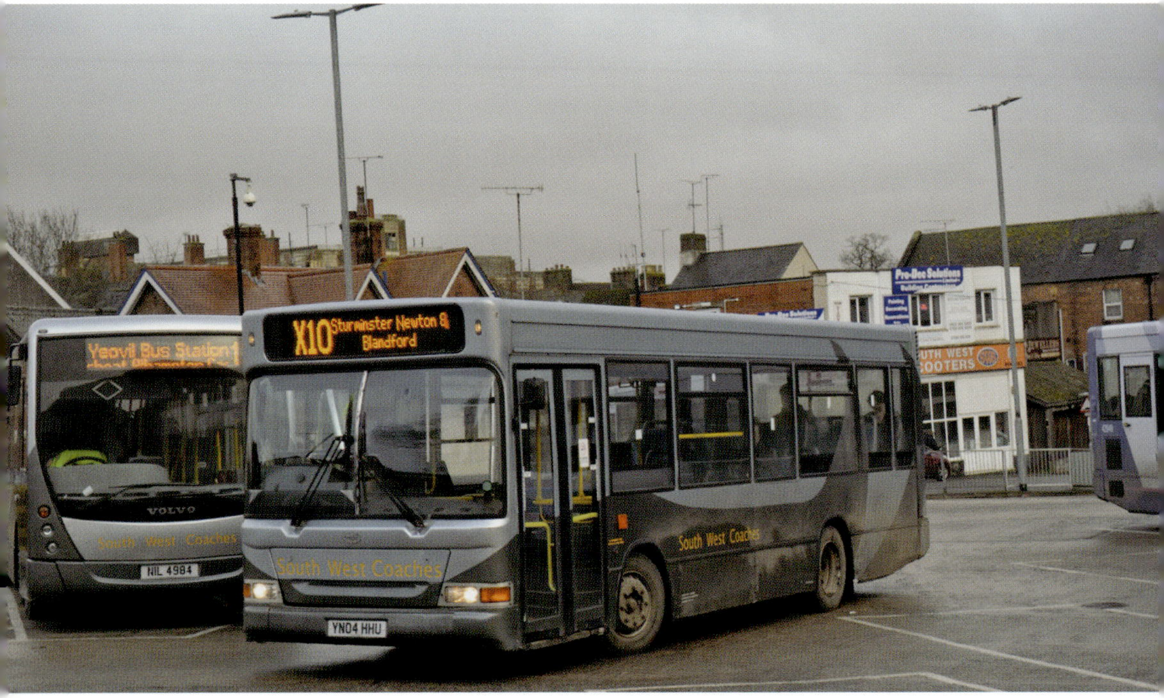

South West Coaches have built up an extensive operation across Somerset and Dorset. Former Huyton Travel Transbus Dart SLF with a Pointer 2 body YN04 HHU is leaving Yeovil for Sturminster Newton and Blandford Forum on service X10.

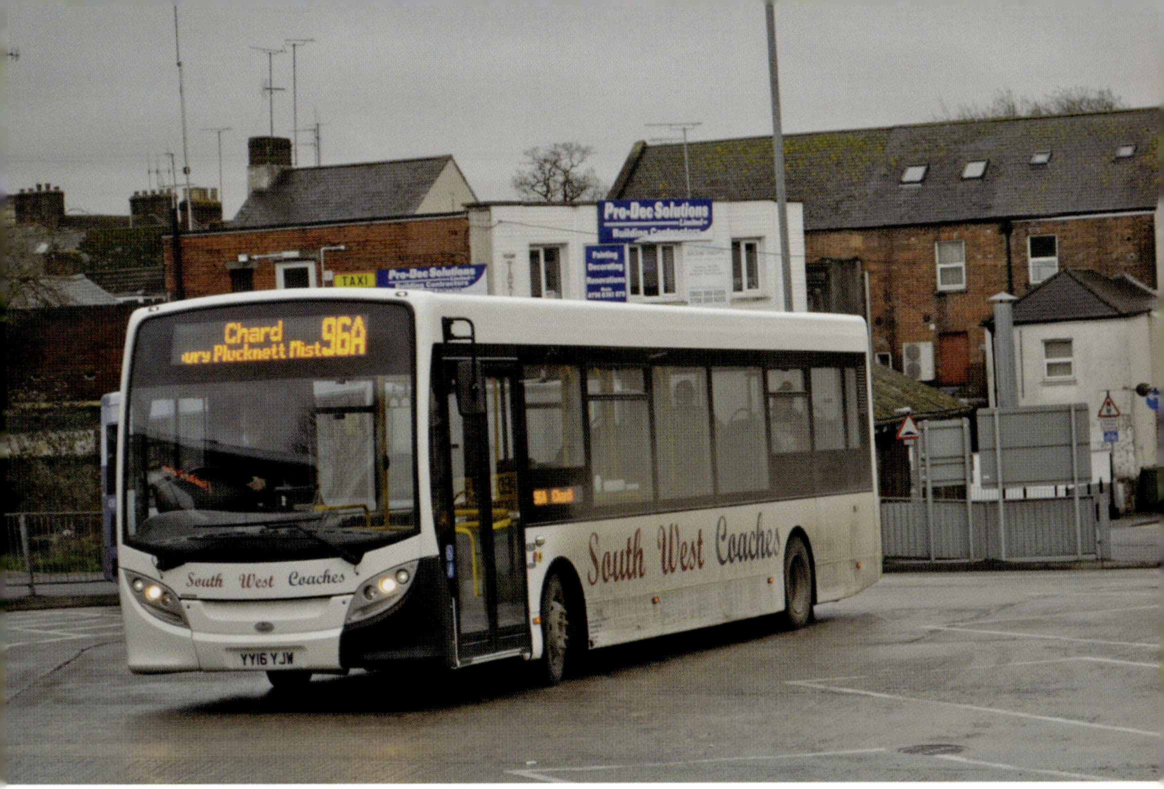

ADL Enviro200 YY16 YJW was new to the fleet of Lloyd, Machynlleth in 2016. Here it is arriving in the bus station to take a 96A service to Chard.

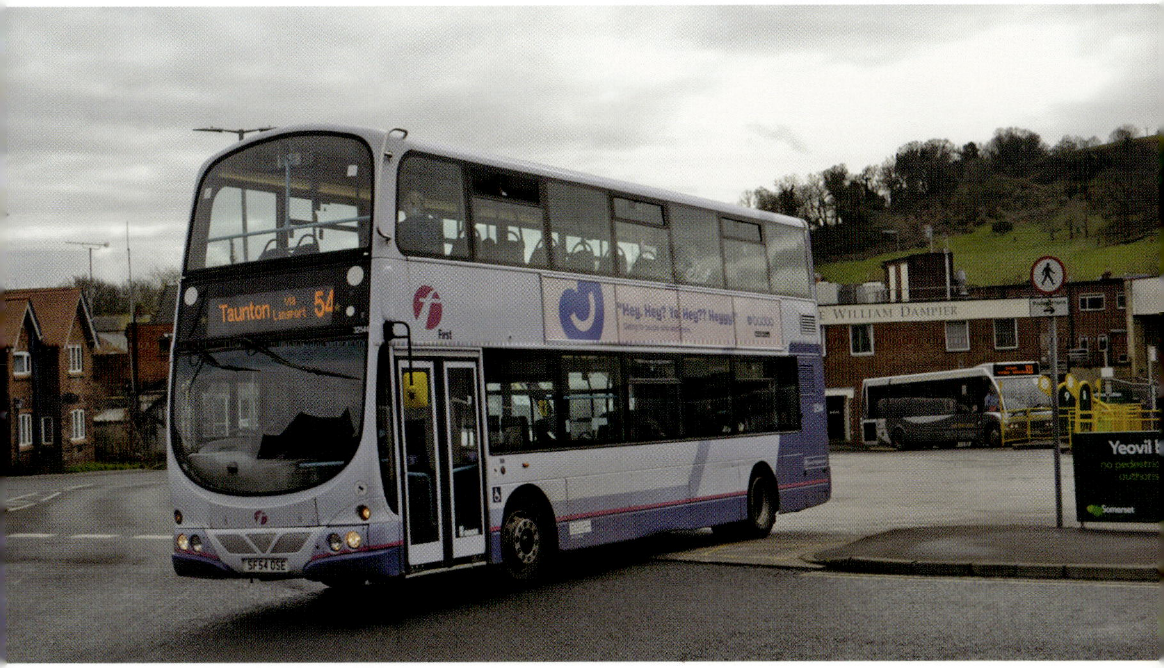

Double-deck operation around Yeovil is really quite limited. Here Buses of Somerset's Taunton-based Wright Eclipse Gemini-bodied Volvo B7TL 32544, SF54 OSE is seen on 23 February 2022 departing the bus station to return to its home town.

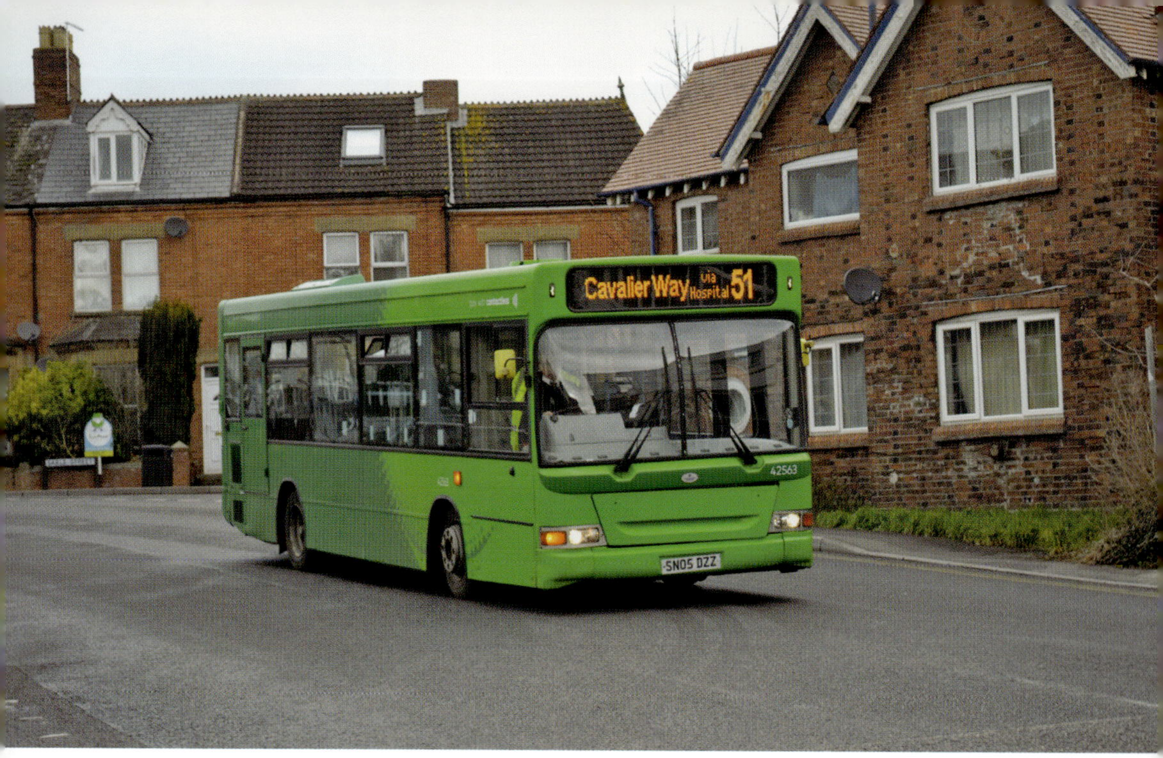

The Buses of Somerset's Alexander-Dennis Pointer 2-bodied Dennis Dart SLF 42563, SN05 DZZ, is seen here on 23 February 2022, turning into the bus station on a town service.

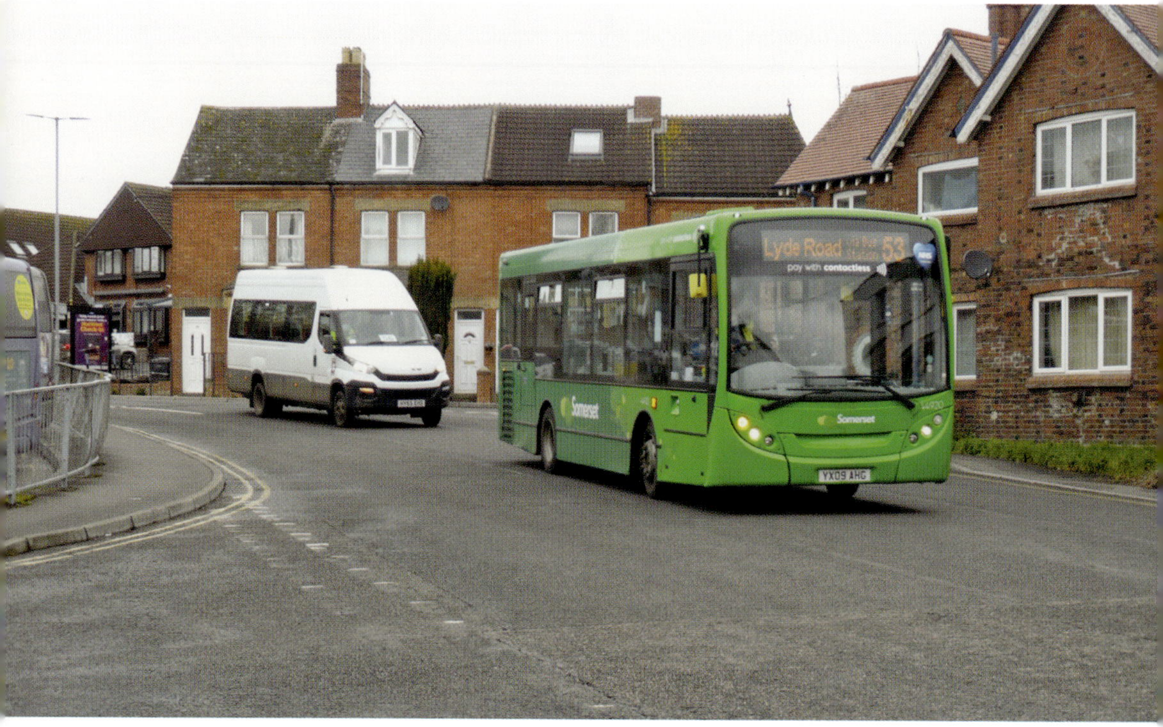

Seen at the same place, on the same day as the previous photo, Buses of Somerset Enviro200 44920, YX09 AHG, is also working a town service.

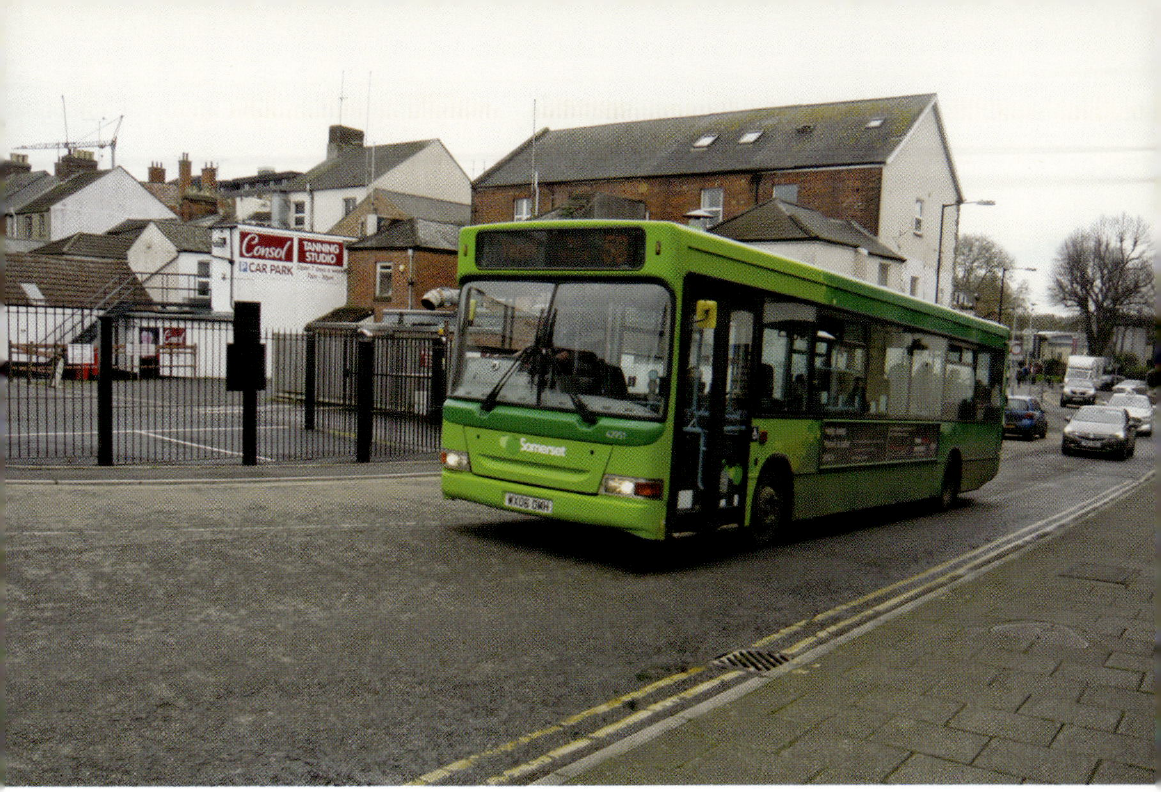

Buses of Somerset Alexander-Dennis SLF Pointer 2 42951, WX06 OMH, is seen here on 23 February 2022. approaching the bus station from the opposite direction on a town service.

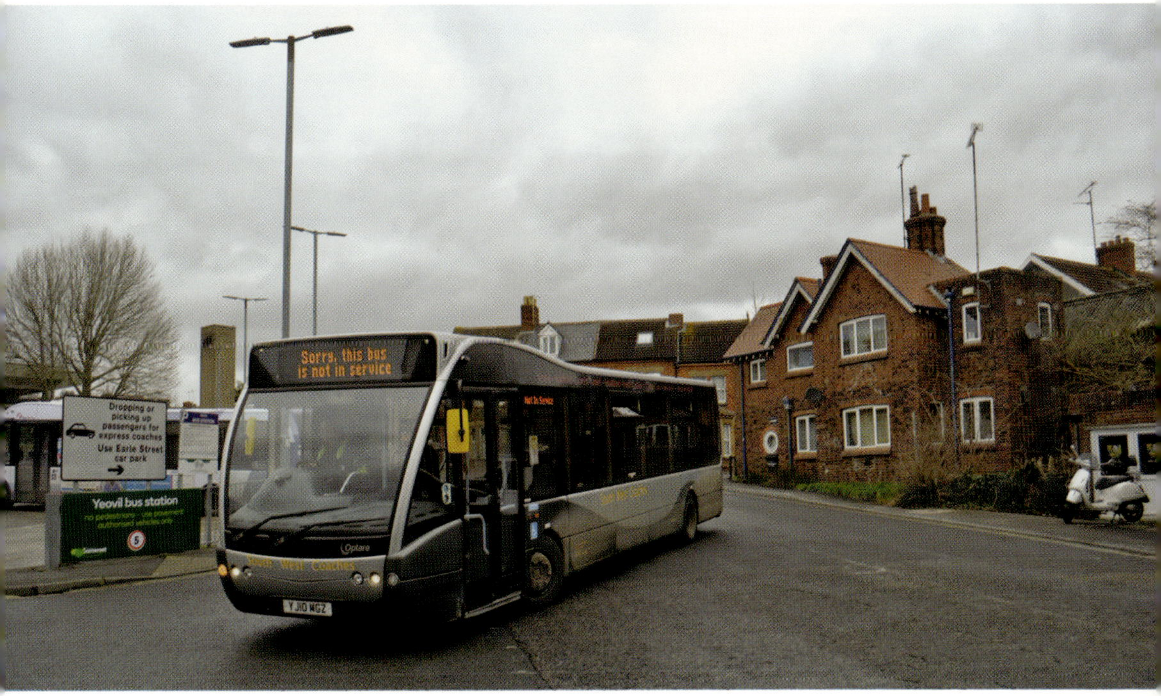

23 February 2022 turned out to be another useful day as far as the South West Coaches fleet was concerned, as these next few shots will show. An apologetic Optare Versa, in the form of YJ10 MGZ, arrives at the bus station.

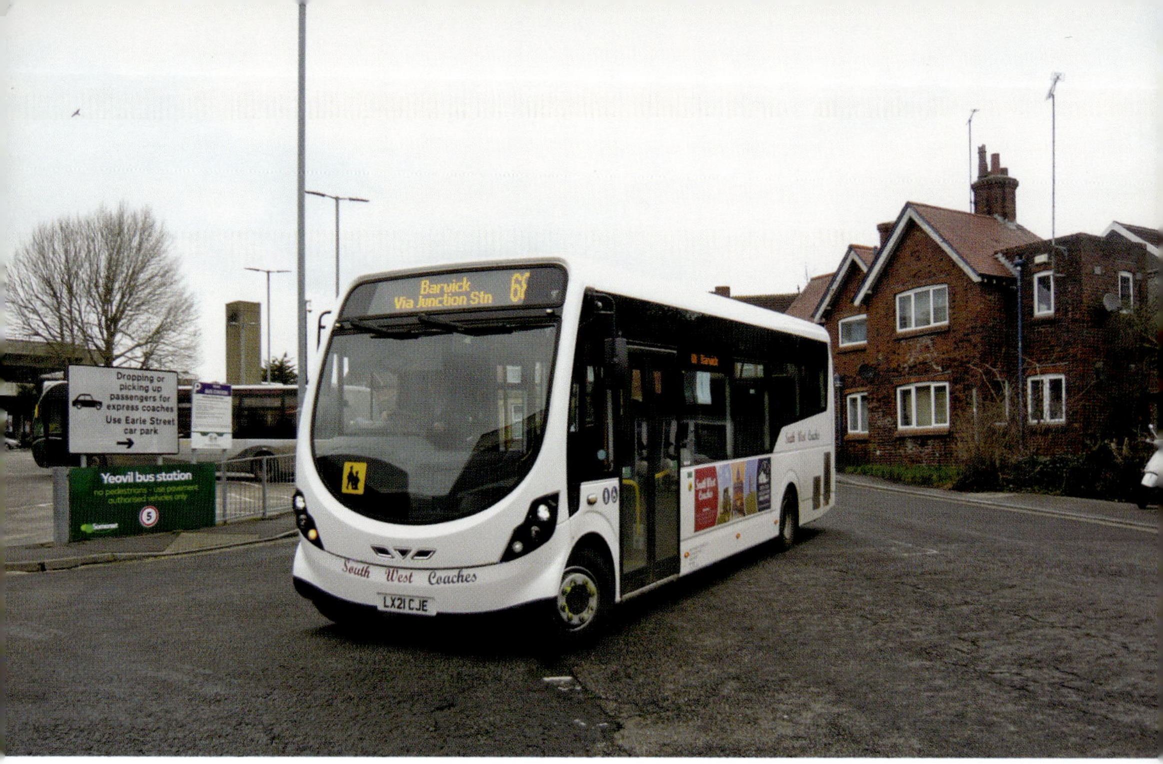

Wright StreetLite WF LX21 CJE is seen here arriving on service 68 from Yeovil Junction. South West Coaches currently have five StreetLites in the fleet, two of the Wheel Forward version and three of the Door Forward version.

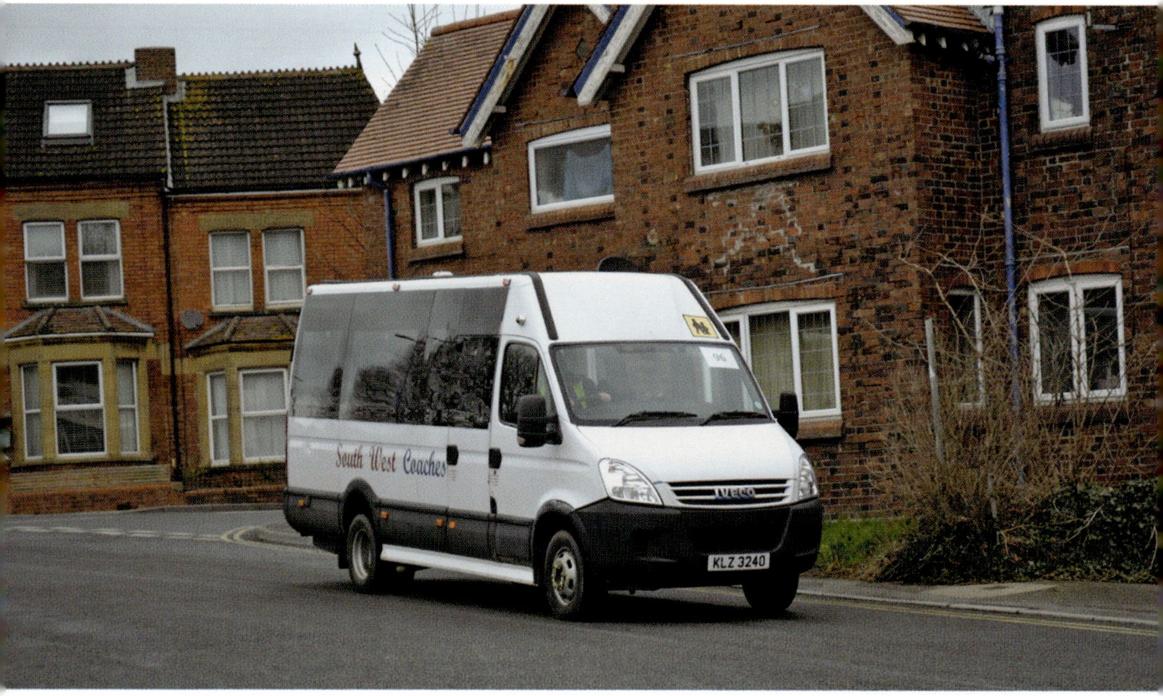

A smaller member of the South West Coaches fleet, KLZ 3240 is an Iveco with body by Elite Conversions. It joined the fleet from Three Star of Luton, and is seen here bound for Chard on service 96.

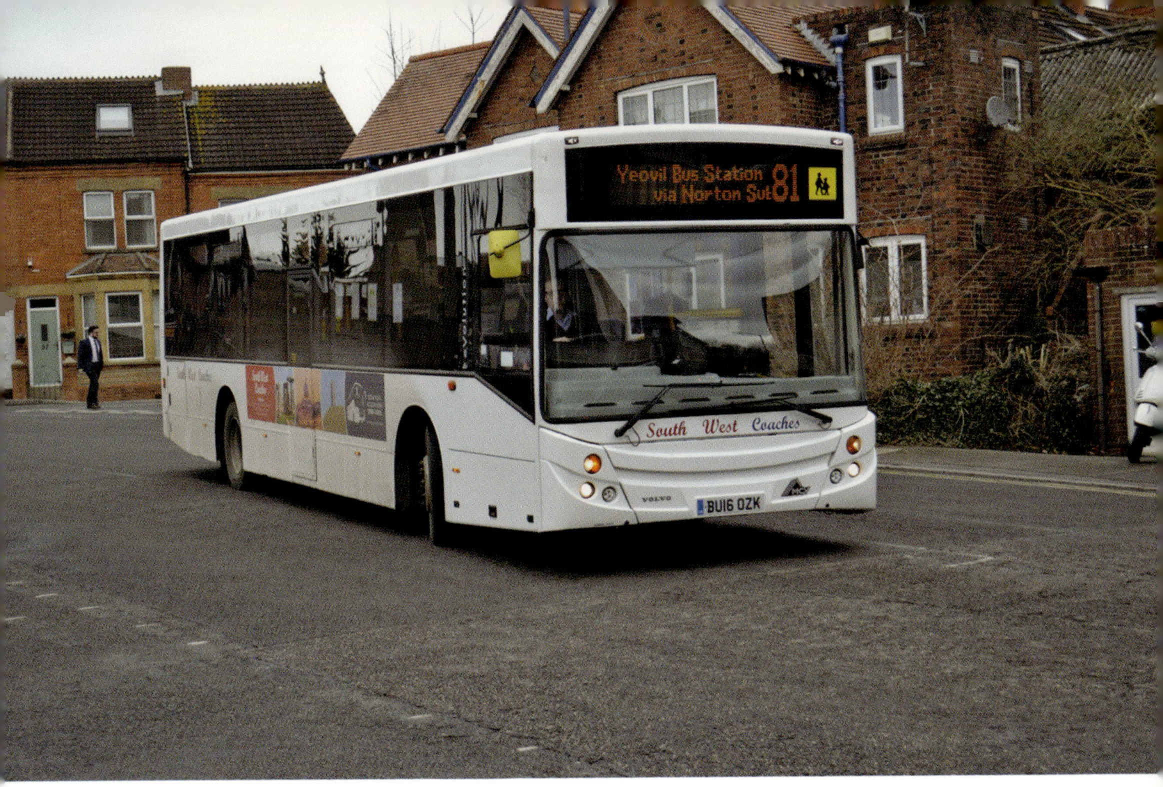

South West Coaches service 81 to Yeovil from South Petherton via Montacute and Stoke-sub-Hamden is a former Safeway service. On 23 February 2022 it was being worked by BU16 OZK, a Volvo B8RLE with MCV body.

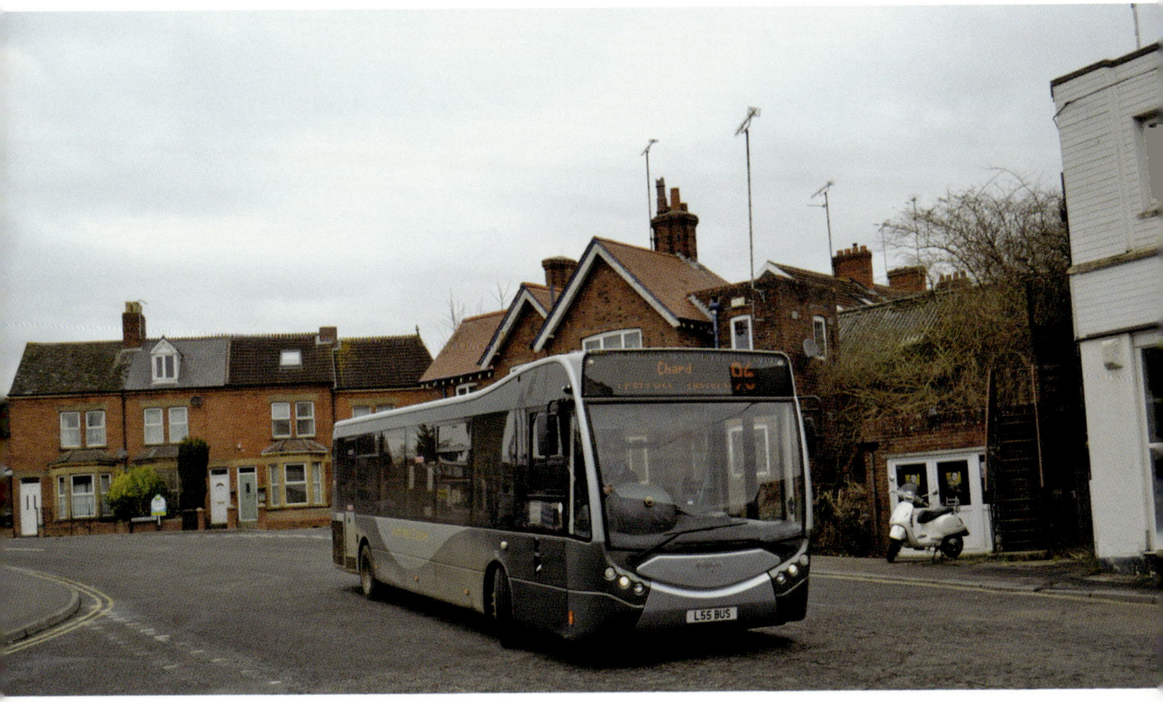

South West Coaches operate this Optare MetroCity, L55 BUS. Delivered as YJ15 AMU, it is seen on 23 February 2022 arriving in Yeovil from Chard on service 96.

Bibliography

Curtis, Martin and Mike Walker, *Bristol Omnibus Services – The Green Years* (Bath, Millstream Books, 2007)

Macfarlane, Allan, *A Pictorial Tribute to the Bristol Omnibus Company and Associated Fleets 1936 – 1983* (Poole, Oxford Publishing Co., 1985)

Morris, Colin, *Southern National Omnibus Company (*Hersham, Ian Allan Publishing Company, 2007)

Morris, Colin, *Western National Omnibus Company* (Hersham, Ian Allan Publishing Ltd, 2008)

Crawley R.J. and F.D. Simpson, *THE YEARS BETWEEN: The Story of Western National and Southern National from 1929* (Exeter, Calton Promotions)

Witton, A.M., *Fleetbook 12: Buses of South West England* (Manchester, A.M. Witton, 1977 – 1980)